Arranging Marriage

Arranging Marriage

Conjugal Agency in the South Asian Diaspora

Marian Aguiar

 University of Minnesota Press
Minneapolis · London

Chapter 5 appeared previously as "Arranged Marriage: Cultural Regeneration in Transnational South Asian Popular Culture," *Cultural Critique* 84 (Spring 2013): 181–214.

Copyright 2018 by the Regents of the University of Minnesota

All rights reserved. No part of this publication may be reproduced, stored in a retrieval system, or transmitted, in any form or by any means, electronic, mechanical, photocopying, recording, or otherwise, without the prior written permission of the publisher.

Published by the University of Minnesota Press
111 Third Avenue South, Suite 290
Minneapolis, MN 55401-2520
http://www.upress.umn.edu

The University of Minnesota is an equal-opportunity educator and employer.

Library of Congress Cataloging-in-Publication Data
Names: Aguiar, Marian, author.
Title: Arranging marriage : conjugal agency in the South Asian diaspora / Marian Aguiar.
Description: Minneapolis : University of Minnesota Press, 2018. |
Includes bibliographical references and index.
Identifiers: LCCN 2016047366 (print) | ISBN 978-0-8166-8947-7 (hc) |
ISBN 978-0-8166-8948-4 (pb)
Subjects: LCSH: Arranged marriage—South Asia. | Arranged marriage—Great Britain. | Arranged marriage—United States. | Arranged marriage—Canada. | South Asians—Great Britain. | South Asians—United States. | South Asians—Canada.
Classification: LCC HQ666.5 .A38 2017 (print) | DDC 392.50954—dc23
LC record available at https://lccn.loc.gov/2016047366

For Roy

Contents

Preface	ix
Introduction: Discursive Contexts	1
1. The Subject of Agency	37
2. "Forced Marriage" and a Culture of Consent	67
3. Britain: The Politics of Belonging	101
4. The United States and Canada: Individual Freedom and Community	139
5. Regenerating Tradition through Transnational Popular Culture	181
Conclusion: A Cultural Studies Approach	215
Acknowledgments	231
Bibliography	235
Index	251

Preface

The ideas and practices of arranged marriage have always been in my life as I grew up in the United States. There are many stories about why my father left Goa, India, permanently in the late 1950s and married my mother, a young German American woman, but one story is that he was trying to escape plans for an arranged marriage by his family in India, who were desperate for him to come home after he completed his graduate education. To his family, an arranged marriage to someone from his caste, religion, region, and even village would have been a way to bind him to home. Even if he did not want to visit or return permanently, his Goan wife would, or so they would have assumed.

It is now a familiar story to me. In college in Montreal and graduate school in Massachusetts, I met a number of international students who were looking at prospective arranged marriages of their own. For some, this was a reason to avoid visits and even phone calls home, as perhaps it had been for my father. For others, arranged marriage just seemed like an easy way to find a mate. For several close friends, arranged marriage beckoned as a way to secure themselves to a home country. Sometimes they or their parents placed a matrimonial ad in a major newspaper. Others had their families find matches in the ancestral villages that their own parents had left to live professional lives in the metropolitan cities of South Asia. This was the case for one close friend, who had been studying in the United States for eight years and was previously in a relationship with an American woman. He told me he wanted to connect himself permanently to his place of origin through an arranged marriage. The decision, such a big one in terms of life consequences, revealed his own anxieties about who he now was, so far from where he began. I have found this openness to arranged marriage in my students as well. When I once asked my class in South Asian literature if any of them would consider having an arranged marriage, four people in a class of twenty put their hands up. Those who self-identified as entertaining the possibility were all second-generation South Asians, including a

Pakistani and a Bangladeshi as well as two Indians. I recognized the impulse. As the child of an immigrant, I understand cultural affiliation.

In that same small town in Connecticut where I grew up, I learned about the more violent side of arranged marriages. There was another Indian family down the street, this one with both parents from Bengal. As a little girl, I played with their daughter while our mothers talked about their marriages. When the wife decided to leave her abusive husband, perhaps influenced by the conversations with my mother, the Bengali wife was remanded by that husband back to India and placed, against her will, in a mental institution. Only recently, more than thirty years later, I witnessed a similar scenario of an unhappy arranged marriage here in Pittsburgh. A new wife, a recent widow, sank into depression after arriving to join her arranged husband. She was asked to return to an uncertain future back in Pakistan, divorced and with the stigma of mental illness. These are the kinds of physical and emotional violence that accompany arranged marriage, in South Asia and in the diaspora.

Among my aunts, uncles, and cousins who have had arranged marriages, some are quite happy with their marriages and family lives. There are others about whom I wonder: what would their lives have been like if they hadn't married, or hadn't been arranged to marry, that particular spouse? I've also seen an alternative model from an early generation. My great aunt, a member of a religious order, lived in Bangalore in a small apartment attached to an enclosed cloister. Over a meal she had prepared for the two of us, I asked her why she became a nun, and she answered that her only other option in the 1920s was an arranged marriage. Ironically, I have witnessed the same pressure on men and women in my own generation, in India and abroad, to get an arranged marriage. Of course, all kinds of families encourage people to get married. However, a social system based on arranged marriage presupposes that marriage is an imperative.

I grew up around the idea of arranged marriage that found fertile ground even in the United States and Canada, but the idea to write this book was actually inspired when I was in the United Kingdom. In fact, it was inspired in a bookshop in London, where I saw one, then two, then three books about arranged marriage on the best-seller and notable shelves at the front of the store. One of these books was Anita Jain's *Marrying Anita*. The promotional materials asked why a cosmopolitan New Yorker would embrace arranged marriage, but I knew the answer all too well. At one moment in my own life, I considered an arranged marriage for reasons very similar to Jain's. I thought that arranged marriage looked appealing after years of noncommittal intimate relationships. Such a marriage, I speculated, might also help me belong to at least one of my inherited cultures and fulfill a growing desire to relocate to India. Perhaps I was romanticizing the practices of a culture different from the dominant one I grew up with, though I've been close enough to those practices to have a sense what living with them would mean. Writing this book, I've learned that I'm not alone in thinking of arranged marriage as a solution. Something powerful is bound up with the fantasy narrative attached to arranged marriage. I was curious enough about my parallel experience to Anita Jain's to read her book, but I was actually more interested in the fact that so many others were becoming interested in the idea of a modern woman embracing arranged marriage. I began to notice books and feature articles everywhere in major venues. Once I started writing this book, I began to have conversations with people, especially non–South Asians, who confessed that they themselves would consider an arranged marriage. I realized that we were in the middle of a cultural moment that needed to be examined.

I've come to recognize the defensive look when I talk about the subject of this book on the faces of people who come from countries or religions where arranged marriage is a common practice. I've had to explain this book to people who have invested personal energy into resisting arranged marriages or political energy into giving other people such a right. Readers of this book will want to know where I stand on arranged marriage. It's a divisive subject. To write on the force and violence associated with arranged marriage is potentially to deny the expression of alternative conjugal forms. To write a book that recognizes what is achieved personally, politically, or socially by arranged marriage is potentially to deny a feminist understanding. I've spent years as an activist and in the classroom teaching young women the importance of recognizing their own agency. I have a young daughter whom I am already teaching that her consent matters. This book has taught me that she needs to recognize her own incipient desires before she can even articulate them and that those desires, and even her expression of them, will come out of what the forces of her world have made her.

So, to answer the question, no, I'm not against arranged marriages, but yes, I recognize that they have historically sometimes led to the denial of personal freedom. As a scholar and as an enthusiast of all art forms, I like to find the complexity of ideas in art and literature that might look too simple in their common understandings; I think such interpretations can be useful interventions to the more pragmatically oriented projects like law or politics. I do not ask whether arranged marriage is good or bad. I don't have that answer. What I offer instead is an interpretation of narrative responses to arranged marriage—responses that are themselves contradictory, nuanced, politically mobilizing, and emotionally affecting. I aim to rethink those narratives that have too simply been seen as expressions of "culture." With this book, I seek to connect these responses to arranged marriage with the forces and fantasies of the world.

Introduction

Discursive Contexts

Arranged marriage has become an object of fascination in a contemporary context of globalization—a point of revulsion, outrage, curiosity, and even envy. Representations of arranged marriage among South Asians appear in the media, in fiction, in film and popular television, in scholarly studies, and even in state discourse produced in the United States, Canada, and Britain, as well as other places around the globe, while works produced in the South Asian subcontinent have continued to make the practice a primary motif. Mira Nair's *Monsoon Wedding* (2001) and Deepa Mehta's *Fire* (1996) examine intimate practices within arranged marriages. The American sitcom *Outsourced* (2010–11) features an arranged marriage plot throughout its first season. American-educated Indian novelist Vikram Seth chose a story about a mother's search for a husband for her daughter to bind together 1,349 pages and multiple plot lines, depicting India in the years after independence in his 1993 novel *A Suitable Boy*. These works have South Asian settings, but other texts focus on arranged marriage in the diaspora. Acclaimed contemporary novels, such as Hanif Kureishi's *The Buddha of Suburbia* (1990), Nadeem Aslam's *Maps for Lost Lovers* (2004), Monica Ali's *Brick Lane* (2003), and Jhumpa Lahiri's *The Namesake* (2003), use the theme of arranged marriage to explore the nature of assimilation. Isabel Coixet's 2014 film *Learning to Drive* features an arranged marriage narrative as part of a Sikh driving instructor's New York life.

A subsection of popular mass-market fiction has also been preoccupied with arranged marriages. South Asian popular women's fiction, sometimes called "ladki-lit" (girl-lit), includes works like Monica Pradhan's *The Hindi-Bindi Club* (2007), Anne Cherian's *A Good Indian Wife* (2008), Kavita Daswani's *The Village Bride of Beverly Hills* (2004), and Shelina Janmohamed's *Love in a Headscarf* (2009). The last example is a work by and about a Muslim woman. A very different popular subgenre about Islamic communities has found a wide audience in Britain, where mass-market memoirs that depict force in arranged marriages gained a wide readership in the 1990s

1

and have continued to find significant audiences. J. Z. Briggs's *Jack and Zena: A True Story of Love and Danger* (1997), Jasvinder Sanghera's *Shame* (2007) and its sequels, and Saira Ahmed and Andrew Crofts's *Disgraced* (2009) represent examples of this popular trend of sensational literature.

Within nonfictional genres, as well, the subject of arranged marriage has garnered considerable interest for sometimes radically diverse reasons. Major newspaper articles with headlines like "First the Marriage, Then the Courtship" (Goodale) describe the continuing practice of arranged marriage in Britain, the United States, and Canada. Arranged marriages are regularly celebrated in human interest stories in the *New York Times,* such as in the weekly Modern Love column's "First Comes Marriage" (Zama), the Weddings section's feature "Modern Lessons from Arranged Marriages" (Lee), and Vows nuptial stories on American-born couples that choose arranged marriage (Henderson, "Rakhi Dhanoa and Ranjeet Purewal"). Anita Jain's memoir *Marrying Anita: A Quest for Love* (2008) begins with the premise that a professional, American-born Indian woman would seek an arranged marriage as an answer to an unsuccessful dating life. Alternately, both major newspapers and tabloids describe "Brides of Doom" (Hall, "22,000") subject to their immigrant husbands' control. Documentary films, including Mira Nair's *So Far from India* (1982), Simon Chambers's *Every Good Marriage Begins with Tears* (2006), and Geeta and Ravi Patel's *Meet the Patels* (2014), look specifically at the everyday lives of various classes involved in transnational arranged marriages. *Meet the Patels* (2014) chronicles Ravi Patel's comedic attempt to arrange a marriage to another American-born Gujrati. Ethnographic work on the South Asian diaspora considers such second-generation relations to arranged marriage as a central aspect of its subject. Sunaina Maira describes how Indian American periodicals and discussion forums coexist with a mainstream media preoccupation with arranged marriages "that attempt to understand how young South Asian Americans can forgo personal will for that of family and tradition in the choice of a lifetime sexual partner" (*Desis in the House,* 153).

In law, legislature, and immigration policy, one also finds a contemporary preoccupation with arranged marriage. British courts participating in ongoing deliberations about force in arranged marriage have taken on increasing numbers of annulment cases since the 1990s, the decisions for which have broadened understandings of coercion. Their judgments reveal how in law, as well, concepts of the individual, family, and community are being negotiated through a discussion of arranged marriage. These considerations are taking place publicly at the national legislative level. Since the 1990s, British state discourses have sought to define arranged marriage and to differentiate it from forced marriage (Ahmed and Uddin, *A Choice by Right*); since 2010, Canadian lawmakers have debated immigration reform in light of a perceived rash of arranged marriages as "bad faith marriages" (O'Neil, "Marriage Fraud").

It is clear that arranged marriage exists in the diaspora, but it is difficult to say whether the number of arranged marriages is increasing or even holding steady in this context. No major empirical studies have been published quantifying conjugal choices in the diaspora, though several have looked at degrees of satisfaction (see Epstein, Pandit, and Thakar, "How Love Emerges"). One major study has even attempted to calculate love within such marriages on the basis of a "Passionate Love Scale" and a "Companionate Love Scale" (Regan, Lakhanpal, and Anguiano, "Relationship Outcomes"). The problem of categories presents a fundamental difficulty to making such a claim: even if a study had tried to measure the predominance of arranged marriage in Western countries, the variable definitions of arranged marriage would make its frequency impossible to quantify objectively, a point to which I will return later. The Regan et al. study, for example, used a sample of self-identified types of marriage.

Although one cannot claim that there has been an increase in the number of arranged marriages, one can safely assert that the discourses concerning the concept and practice of arranged marriage have multiplied and taken on significant roles, and done so globally. First, references to arranged marriage have radically increased in number in Britain, the United States, and Canada within English-language texts. According to a LexisNexis search, the number of major newspaper articles published in the United States that feature "arranged marriage" and "India" as primary search terms jumps from fewer than twenty between 1980 and 1985 to more than three hundred in the last five years of the twentieth century. The same search in Canadian newspapers turns up comparable increases on a smaller scale. In Britain during the years 1980–1985 and 2005–2010, major newspaper references to arranged marriage relating to either "Pakistan" or "Bangladesh" increase from fewer than 5 articles to more than 850.

The prevalence of this set of discourses about arranged marriage conveys the persistence of the idea of arranged marriage in the diaspora and its centrality to public discourse. Some of these textual representations renounce arranged marriage as an oppressive, outdated custom, whereas others reinvigorate the practice in new forms and for new reasons. The latter phenomenon plays against expectations of assimilation—the notion that immigrants will adopt more "Western" cultural practices and that the presence of arranged marriage will simply dissipate over time in new homes. Against this assumption, the representations included in this book suggest that the idea of arranged marriage has traveled from different parts of South Asia to other places. More strikingly, second-generation Indians, Pakistanis, and Bangladeshis born in the United States and Britain are engaged in a dialogue about conjugal forms. They have done so across class lines, creating a point of cultural contact within a diverse group. The most highly educated and mobile upper middle class has conceptually and sometimes practically embraced arranged marriage along with working-class groups, including undocumented workers, albeit in different ways and for different reasons, as this book elaborates.

Discourses are systems of representations by which people elaborate meaning in their worlds. Stuart Hall describes the work of Michel Foucault, who drew attention to the relation between these networks and the production of a historically contextual power. Hall explains, "By 'discourse' Foucault meant a group of statements which provide a language for talking about—a way of representing the knowledge about—a particular topic at a particular historical moment" (*Representation,* 44). Foucault connected this production of knowledge through language to the arena of practice, describing a dialectical relationship in which "all social practices entail meaning and meanings shape and influence what we do" (44). Discourse is both symbolic and performative; thus, although this book is not an ethnography study, its scope crosses between the imaginative and lived experience.

In looking at the discursive production taking place around the idea of arranged marriage, this book has uncovered a closely related set of narratives cohering around the term, each situated in historical conditions mediated by gendered, class-specific narratives of migration within national and global contexts. Read together, this book suggests, the prevalence of this set of transnational arranged marriage discourses shows how conjugal practices have become, first, ciphers for belonging in national contexts that are increasingly permeated by flows of people, practices, labor, capital, and ideas across borders and, second, a means for constructing those global networks. By focusing on the way arranged marriage is reinvented as an emblematic practice within the South Asian diaspora, this book positions arranged marriage as a modern practice emerging from a set of national and transnational conditions. It is part of the book's argument that this set of transnational arranged marriage discourses rewrites the narratives produced about those national and global contexts in both constructivist and disruptive ways. *Arranging Marriage* looks beyond its immediate focus on global South Asian communities to rethink Western social, political, and economic discourses and structures through analyzing a conjugal practice that has been pushed to the margin as exceptional.

Arranging Marriage argues for a closer examination of this set of transnational arranged marriage discourse, a network of representations that includes discussions of what is called "forced marriage." This book is the first critical discourse analysis of South Asian arranged marriage in the twentieth and twenty-first centuries. It is also the first monograph to examine South Asian arranged marriage in a transnational context rather than in India. *Arranging Marriage* charts the increasing importance of discourses about arranged marriage that alternately embrace and refute the practice in a series of interconnected contemporary contexts. This book interprets fictional, filmic, scholarly, and media representations alongside legal and legislative documents that represent arranged marriage in the South Asian diaspora. By identifying and analyzing together a wide range of texts that represent arranged marriage, the book has three goals. First, focusing on select regions within a global diaspora, this book locates representations of arranged marriage within Britain, the United States, and Canada, reading particular narratives within specific diasporic contexts to root them in place. Second, *Arranging Marriage* interprets the discourses produced by and about various South Asian communities as a way to read the construction of a transnational, diasporic space that often disrupts those national spheres.

This project aims beyond identifying and interpreting national and transnational communities that cohere around a set of arranged marriage discourses, however. Thus, third, *Arranging Marriage* reveals how contesting narratives about conjugality have been alternately rethinking and reinforcing Western notions of individual agency that lie at the heart of liberal notions of rights and neoliberal concepts of choice. The transnational arranged marriage discourse presents the displacement of agency from the individual; this is inherent in the imagined subject evoked by the term "arranged" (parents, aunts, uncles, neighbors, or a matchmaker might "arrange," but not the person getting married). The book terms this individualist or collectivist vision "the subject of agency," meaning the subjectivity that marks decision making. This displacement challenges an edifice of identity and rights resting on the ideal of the autonomous, fully vested individual agent and expressed in the deeply symbolic forum of conjugality sanctioned by the state. Such a displacement has been at the heart of debates about arranged marriage, but, on a more pervasive level, it represents a central point of conflict in this period of globalization.

Defining Arranged Marriage

Despite the widespread recognition of arranged marriage as a concept and its common association with South Asian tradition, it is surprisingly difficult to fix a definition. Certain practices are commonly associated with arranged marriage, such as the match being brokered by elder relatives and/or a matchmaker who looks for a spouse from a "good family"; the notion of marrying into an extended family; the significance of region, religion, caste, and even subcaste; dowry; consanguineous marriage to cousins within an extended family (in the case of certain Muslims); and the idea of matching horoscopes. There are also stereotypical scenes associated with arranged marriage. One such scene is the bride viewing, where a "boy's" family comes to "see the girl," who demurely serves tea and then politely answers questions, or the scene of bride and groom first laying eyes on each other on the wedding day. In fact, however, arranged marriage is made up of an amorphous set of practices that are themselves changing. In a study published in 2007 in *India Today*, psychologist Sudhir Kakar describes "a wide variety of marriages that fall under the rubric 'arranged'" and includes a range from the case in which a couple meets during the wedding to instances in which members of a couple validate their love choice to their respective families. Indeed, historically, the "tradition" of arranged marriage has been itself diverse, varying by region, religion, caste, class, family preferences, and individual interpretation. Moreover, many of these practices, such as searching for a spouse from a similar socioeconomic level or seeking family approval, are certainly not confined to arranged marriage.

The identities of fluid categories are often fixed relationally through binary oppositions. It is common in South Asian communities to hear arranged marriage defined in contrast to "love marriage." A mother character in Pradhan's *The Hindi-Bindi Club* advises her daughter:

> "Here, you talk about *love*. There, it's compatibility. Love's fickle. Compatibility endures, sustains marriages," she says. "Here, marriage is about two people on the wedding cake. Couples don't need permission slips from their parents. Families have a lower priority

than the couple. But in India, marriage is the joining of two families, a strategic alliance. The couple's a lower priority than the family as a whole, and permission slips are essential." (183)

Several regular themes in this discourse assert specific characteristics between love marriage and arranged marriage while counterpoising the two. One common narrative is the idea that with "love marriage," one falls in love before the marriage, but with arranged marriage, love comes after. In a Modern Love column in the *New York Times,* Farahad Zama writes of his own experience of an arranged marriage, asserting that, while couples in self-made marriages are under pressure not to change from the people they were when they married, arranged marriage couples start with fewer certainties about personality: "I think that in arranged marriages one starts with lower expectations and realizes the need for compromise that is essential in a successful bond, and that is probably its biggest benefit." Related to this, proponents of arranged marriage describe its accompanying kind of love as different and ultimately more sustainable. For this, they cite the lower rates of divorce for arranged marriage (Lee, "Modern Lessons"), though a recent study comparing couples' assessments of love, relationship satisfaction, and commitment in their relationships between self-identified self-made marriages and arranged marriages found them to be the same (Regan, Lakhanpal, and Anguiano, "Relationship Outcomes"). Another study found that though there were similar degrees of satisfaction, the two models of marriage presented different relations to the idea of love (Myers, Madathil, and Tingle, "Marriage Satisfaction").

Such arguments and such studies are built around challenging "love marriage" as the norm. This book moves away from the logic of love versus arranged marriage by using the term *self-made* (Bredal, "Arranged Marriage"), a term that (along with *autonomous marriage*) has some limited public circulation as an alternative. One reason to change the terminology is to emphasize the more critical difference at stake, which is not love but rather the subject of agency—that locus of decision making. Another reason to alter the language is because the discourses themselves, the very binary of arranged and love, have been deconstructed as textual representations and new practices intermarry previous formations.

Many of today's arranged marriage practices are modified to various degrees to lessen or eradicate historical features like dowries, horoscopes, or not meeting before the wedding and to introduce elements associated with Western love narratives, such as companionate marriage, freedom of choice, sexual desire, and a discourse of intimacy expressed in therapeutic terms like "talking things over." New technologies, like Internet profiles, have changed the practice and increasingly merged more fundamental traditions with ideas and activities associated with "love-matches," such as dating. The changes taking place within the practices and concepts of arranged marriage highlight this modification that has particularly appealed to a professional class. Works of popular film and fiction representing and consumed by a professional middle class encourage new emphases within arranged marriage; these arranged marriage stories borrow from the genre of romance to replace suitability, duty, or marrying two families with personal satisfaction and matrimonial intimacy—a new set of criteria for success. For example, in *Monsoon Wedding*, the narrative trajectory includes conflict that comes after the arrangement and resolution that comes before the wedding, a model that follows the catharsis of romance. One ethnography argues that the modifications in arranged marriage are what make the practice sustainable in the diaspora. In her study of the diasporic youth community in the Silicon Valley, Shankar found that malleability of arranged marriage as a practice, with its introduction of new elements, such as dating, has worked to perpetuate the system (*Desi Land*, 184). Many such young South Asians look to Bollywood, a powerful transnational media space, for a way of mediating the kinds of romantic narratives they see in Western media with narratives of family responsibility. Shankar found that in the models offered by Indian romantic comedies, "heroes and heroines are often able to achieve the impossible balancing act of fulfilling family duty and obligation while participating in the attractive world of consumption, leisure, and young romance" (173). The fantasy of global mobility may play an important role in achieving such individual-based aspirations. In the film *Monsoon Wedding*, the diaspora itself allows for this by separating the young couple from the extended family in India. In the genre of transnational popular women's fiction and popular film, the resolution to marital problems often comes in the form of disengaging arranged marriage from its historically associated social and economic practices, such as the daughter-in-law being a helper in the home. Protagonists in these works get an arranged marriage at some distance from their in-laws, thus solving some of the associated tensions when young women join the extended families of their husbands (chapter 5).

Such optimistic representations are class bound in the sense that they represent a metropolitan subject for whom global mobility does not mean an obligation to send a significant proportion of income back to the extended family's home in the subcontinent (though distant parents might be supported). Nadeem Aslam represents a very different situation for the Pakistani working-class (and unemployed) community in Britain in his novel *Maps for Lost Lovers*. Works like Aslam's or Ali's novel *Brick Lane*, which offer social and political commentary, focus on a different set of reasons for emerging discourses on arranged marriage produced about a different class. These works highlight the experiences of a global underclass that seeks to better its situation through mobility. This is not usually the case in the popular romantic fiction and Bollywood films that build fantasy; the Indian or Pakistani (rarely Bangladeshi) couple is nearly as, if not equally, rich in India as they are when the husband (never the wife) takes a job in a place like Silicon Valley in works like Daswani's *The Village Bride of Beverly Hills*. In these mass-market literary and filmic romances, global mobility through or along with arranged marriage represents a kind of personal satisfaction through independence from the extended family and from its expected familial gender roles (chapter 5).

The middle class of the diaspora is not the only group for whom the ideas and practices of arranged and love marriage do not uphold a strict binary. Jyoti Puri convincingly argues that such a distinction never existed in practice for middle-class women in India. Puri argues that the line between contemporary love and arranged marriage for middle-class women is less definitive than thought but that the distinctions between these discourses shape women's representations of themselves, and in ambiguous ways (*Woman, Body, Desire,* 139). She argues that women themselves blend arranged and love marriage in their discourse about their own marriages, reassigning associated narratives. They romanticize their arranged marriages in terms of companionship, intimacy, equality, and mutuality; conversely, they sometimes bring in the family to legitimate mutual attraction. This discursive slippage reveals how women frame their lives, but the practices historically structured by arranged marriage, which may include sexual activity, a patrilocal practice of moving in with the husband's family, household labor, limited mobility, lack of privacy with the spouse, deference to the parents-in-law, and the joint family, sometimes give lie to this fluidity. Puri sees the women's narration as a way they "negotiate the mandates of wifehood" (136).

While for a diasporic middle class, the intersection of duty and romance might be accompanied by the lightening of responsibilities, for others both in the subcontinent and abroad, it also enables a reinscription of new duties. Simon Chambers's documentary *Every Good Marriage Begins with Tears* (2007) shows how romantic narratives mediate the experience of transnational arrangements among other classes. When a young, working-class Bangladeshi British woman in the documentary sings a love song to herself as she travels to meet her new husband at the airport, she interprets her experience of arranged marriage through the generic formulations of romance. This is a phenomenon Nicole Constable talks about in her study of transnational correspondence relationships, commonly called "mail-order brides." Constable argues that such transactions are accompanied by narratives of romance that need to be understood as reflecting more than false consciousness. She argues against opposing practical and material desires to emotional ones and suggests, "It is also important to consider how and why love, romance, and marriage are linked . . . to money, class, and power, as represented by and embodied in nationality, race, gender, and place at a particular time" (*Romance on a Global Stage,* 118).

A shift in media technologies with matrimonial websites like Shaadi.com and BharatMatrimony.com has brought accompanying changes to the discourse and practice of arranged marriage, some of them surprising. A traditional matchmaker or relatives arranging a match work with known families, demarcating the much-cited quality of a "good family," a measure of reputation. When Ashok comes home from study abroad in *The Namesake* to have initial meetings with young women from the region, Lahiri references a still fairly common practice in which professional young men with visas abroad are matched with women through family networks. However, newspapers like *India Abroad* have had matrimonial advertisements that reach a diasporic readership since the 1970s, with matrimonials containing stated qualities and criteria. Even as early as the 1930s, the use of print media like the *Times of India* and the *Hindu* widened the field for transnational marriage by allowing nonresident as well as resident Indians to post matrimonials. This phenomenon helped build the practice of the young man who returned from abroad to find an Indian bride. One sees this expanding network through print media in fictional representations: at the start of Bharati Mukherjee's novel *Wife* (1975), set in the 1970s, the father searches for a suitable boy by scouring the newspaper ads and sending inquiries. The digital medium of matrimonial websites has expanded the process exponentially—there are now more than fifteen hundred matchmaking websites in India alone (Harris, "Websites"). These websites have the overt goal of connecting people with the purpose of marriage, unlike online dating websites, South Asian–oriented ones, and otherwise. These matrimonial websites still allow parents to post on behalf of their children as well as allowing for individuals to post their profiles. Internet matchmaking changes the speed and scope of these arrangements; more strikingly, the introduction of digital technologies allows for a much clearer search for criteria. Whereas reading a matrimonial ad in a newspaper offers an overall picture at a glance that would allow for a variation to enter consideration (say, a suitably educated prospect from a different region), the digital technologies sort the ads before any such holistic picture and thus preempt randomness. Somewhat surprisingly, given the association of the digital with more democratic impulses, the digital technologies emphasize the endogamous tendencies in arranged marriage practices that might otherwise have begun to erode in the increasingly fluid social structures of a global professional class if they had used print media or even social circles in diasporic cities (chapter 4).

Because of these changes to arranged marriage, it might be argued that its definition is becoming more nebulous, and that is true in some parts of the discourse. There is one discursive arena in which the idea of arranged marriage is being more sharply defined, however. A contemporary political and bureaucratic discourse attempts to draw a more rigid boundary around arranged marriage by separating it from forced marriage in terms of the presence of consent (chapter 2). In this arranged marriage discourse, mostly produced in Britain, mostly representing working-class immigrants, mostly from Muslim countries (but not always), there is an effort to clearly define an arranged marriage. For example, since the mid-1980s, the British legislature, courts, and media have actively taken up the question of what separates arranged marriage and forced marriage. Legal decisions parse out a gray area between arranged and forced marriage while carefully maintaining a multicultural discourse about the importance of marriages, "arranged traditionally which are in no way to be condemned, but rather supported as a conventional concept in many societies" (SK, Re [2004] EWHC 3202 [Fam]). Women's organizations have emphasized the gray area of emotional coercion while continuing to map the discourse definitively in terms of consent (Home Office, "Forced Marriage Consultation," 9). While media articles previously aligned arranged marriage and forced marriage, using the terms interchangeably in a 1986 article on the suicides of Canadian-Indian women (*Toronto Star*, "Indian Wives"), increasingly the media reports echo and reinforce state discourse by distinguishing forced marriage from arranged marriage (Hutchinson, "Our Lost Generation").

The distinction between arranged marriage and forced marriage has been an important component of a multicultural discourse that bounds acceptable from unacceptable difference in a politics of cohesion (Enright, "Choice"). State documents thus reveal a double move in which arranged marriage is both validated and presented as an abomination. In a government report, the British Working Group on Forced Marriage, a governmental committee, asserts that "the tradition of arranged marriage should be respected and valued" but later addresses itself to problematic new migrants with the "innate sense of obligation to maintain our cultures, languages, and traditions," which, it suggests, "overwhelms" the development of the family (Ahmed and Uddin, *A Choice by Right*, 1). Chapter 3 considers the connection between a multicultural discourse and forced marriage legislation. A multicultural discourse depends on a shared set of values, which, in turn, depends on something falling outside those values. Forced marriage presents such an outside. In Britain, state discourse shuttles between official policies of intervention and noninterference in cultural matters, even as it brackets off a separate "cultural" area within the domestic arena, constructed around a multicultural agenda. This is a form of culturalism, Aijaz Ahmad argues, "which treats culture not only as an integral element in social practices but as the determining instance" (*On Communalism*, 95). The area of "culture" appears as a kind of difference that may be validated, and in fact, as Sara Ahmed argues, multiculturalism depends on the presence of this difference: "The others can be different (indeed the nation is invested in their difference *as a sign of its love for difference*), as long as they refuse to keep their difference to themselves, but instead give it back to the nation, through speaking a common language and mixing with others" (*Cultural Politics of Emotion*, 134). The discourse of multiculturalism determines how immigrant communities must be contained in the nation, and from the point of view of the state, the discourse must remain inside the acceptable frame this book calls the individualist subject of agency. The ongoing discussion of forced marriage has constituted a British Muslim South Asian community, especially, in this way, through a discourse about conjugal practices. It is no coincidence that forced marriage, along with honor killing, has emerged as a dominant discourse coincident with rising Islamophobia (see Wilson, "Forced Marriage Debate," 25).

In North America, especially in Canada, state discourse has similarly functioned to define a South Asian community through attempts to both validate and regulate arranged marriage by differentiating it from forced marriage. The use of arranged marriage as a diacritical marker of identity appears in immigration policy that references, to use the preceding example, a "long-established custom." In Canada, one significant ongoing discussion has been about marriage fraud, in which arranged marriage has been represented as a means to commit immigration fraud (Curry, "Fraud Squads"). Here as well, lawmakers and judges carefully navigate separations between what are deemed traditional practices and fraudulent acts, and do so through a discourse of multiculturalism that defines acceptable difference. According to Nancy Caron, a spokesperson for Citizenship and Immigration Canada, visa officers are trained to "take into account the cultures and practices associated with legitimate arranged marriages" as they weigh these elements (quoted in Black, "Ottawa to Take a Closer Look"). As in the United Kingdom, the question of forced marriage has entered the arena of national law with the Zero Tolerance for Barbaric Cultural Practices Act, which has been promoted as a way to "defend Canadian cultural values" (Powers, "Conservatives Pledge Funds"). The act, which prohibits immigration or permanent residency to anyone practicing polygamy and seeks to prevent marriage without consent, including child marriage, categorizes previously existing laws under the rubric of immigration.

This book includes what others term "forced marriage" within the spectrum of arranged marriage. It identifies and interprets a set of conjugal discourses that include a range of practices, and in the process it probes a continuum between consent and coercion, "between which lie degrees of socio-cultural expectation, control, persuasion, pressure, threat and force" (Anitha and Gill, "Coercion," 165). By including a spectrum of force within this conjugal discourse instead of using the presence of consent to distinguish arranged marriage from forced marriage, this book takes a few risks. On one hand, it might seem to reproduce the perspective that sees all arranged marriage as forced. On the other hand, by grouping harmonious and coercive practices within the category of arranged marriage, it might appear to ignore the violence that takes place through the structures of such marriage. Consent is an important legal concept used to measure the validity of a marriage and to punish violent acts, including emotional and physical coercion. Nevertheless, the dependence on this concept in public discourse obscures some important factors that are important to addressing disparities in power. First, legal discourses have had difficulty establishing the binary between arranged marriage and forced marriage on the basis of consent. Second, the issue of consent, though critical, is not comprehensive to understanding the various kinds of physical and psychological violence at work as well as the structural forces that compel decisions. Finally, this nomenclature creates a false binary that separates acceptable forms of coercion from unacceptable types, in practice registering this through a culturally biased perspective that, for example, has historically legitimated parental pressure but not religious authority.

To summarize two of the most prevalent ways in which arranged marriage has been defined by means of an opposition, one opposition sets arranged marriage against romantic love. Such oppositions are erroneously fixed because, both in self-conceptions and in popular narratives, ideas of love and romance have long shaped arranged marriage. Another discourse defines arranged marriage as the opposite of forced marriage and uses the idea of consent as the boundary. This discourse marks a multiculturalist agenda and reflects the construction of the nation around a liberal ideal of freedom. Such an opposition relies on a notion of consent that has been difficult to mark both conceptually and in practice.

Even given the shifting and ambiguous nature of the construct called "arranged marriage," a certain conceptual sedimentation has taken place, enabling one to refer to a concept and set of practices widely known as arranged marriage. To some extent, to define its scope, this book uses nomenclature, the English terms *arranged* and *arranged marriage,* that emerged in nineteenth-century India (Majumdar, *Marriage and Modernity,* 2). It is also informed by other scholarly conceptions. In a book about emerging conjugal practices in the context of colonial Bengal, Rochona Majumdar defines arranged marriage as "virilocal marriages [in which the bride joins the groom's household] negotiated by the families (patrilineal) of men and women with or without the consent of those getting married and celebrated at a wedding in accordance with certain communally sanctioned rules and rituals" (5). Majumdar places emphasis on the form of courtship (negotiation), the agents (families), the ritual nature of the wedding itself that binds people within a community, and the structure of the joint family. U.S. historian Nancy Cott describes arranged marriage among immigrants as that "in which overt economic bargaining and kinship networks beyond the marrying pair played acknowledged parts" (*Public Vows,* 149); her definition emphasizes how the discourse of arranged marriage makes social and economic factors overt, elements that, while present in other kinds of marriage, are often disguised or disavowed. Both of the preceding definitions highlight the definitive role of kin, but they also feature what is arguably the most important difference between arranged marriage and self-made marriage: the subject of agency in decision making. Thus a more productive definition of arranged marriage lies away from the question of love or the parsing of consent: put most simply, arranged marriage is a conjugal practice that gives over decision making to a family or community—allocates it to a degree or entirely. This is the definition of arranged marriage used in this book.

Arranged marriage in the South Asian diaspora is the product of multiple socioeconomic forces articulated as an alternate form of conjugal agency that avows collective identity. An analysis of the contemporary arranged marriage discourse taken as a whole reveals that there is an ongoing debate about who controls agency in the form of decision making in the so-called private realm in the context of globalization—the subject of consent. On one hand, state protectionist campaigns assert the legal rights of an individual as the locus of the institution of marriage. On the other hand, a cultural political movement has made arranged marriage a point of exceptionalism. Around this oppositional identity, cultural nationalists have asserted the family, embedded in a larger ethnic community, as having the rights of decision making. Such a claim gains force in the global context in which the transnational flows of people and capital have posed challenges to the hegemony of the state by creating alternate collectivities based on religious identity, ethnicity, or national origin (individual or familial). While all these rhetorics of traditionalism emerge from the context of globalization, one narrative stands out within this broader set of discourses affirming collectivity for the way it enables neoliberal fantasies of identity. In multiple contexts (including South Asia), the practice of arranged marriage has been transforming to introduce notions like "arranged love marriage" among certain communities. These modifications reconcile the opposition between individualism and collectivity within the practice, showing a recalibration within the concept of arranged marriage that marks a neoliberal moment (chapter 5). Despite the significance of this reconception, the fact that the modifications are made *within* the frame of arranged marriage suggests that a powerful alternative to individual choice continues to be asserted. This book explores the debate over the subject of consent as a definitive conflict of globalization and the neoliberal model as one of its solutions.

National and Transnational Narratives

One of the hidden ideological aspects of modern marriage is the fundamental role of the state, a relationship that shapes contemporary representations of arranged marriage as both an idea that travels between nations and a practice that may be the means to travel between nations. Too often, narratives of marriage falsely create a separation between the private and the public. In her analysis of the relation between marriage and the nation in American history, Nancy Cott notes that "the monumental public character of marriage is generally its least noticed aspect" (*Public Vows*, 1). Marriage has traditionally fallen within the jurisdiction of the state, although, as the British colonial context in India shows, not always within its ideological power. The contemporary state asserts control over the age of conjugal consent, the sex of the person one may marry, and the necessary distance of consanguinity (familial relationship). Marriage is a public institution in other ways. Marriage in the West requires public knowledge (announcements, witnesses, wedding bells) and state sanction (thus the phrase "by the power vested in me") and guarantees a commitment honored by the community at large (Cott, *Public Vows*, 1). Tax structures, legal notions of next of kin, and power of attorney all rest upon the civil legitimacy of intimate bonds. The public nature of this seemingly private institution has become more visible in recent years with debates about legalizing same-sex marriage. The controversy about same-sex marriage has cast into relief the limits of the nation-state in containing the institution of marriage and emphasized the way it articulates its powerful dominion through legislation that reincorporates what was previously seen as deviant.

The national imaginary of Euro-American states rests upon such forms of conjugality. Arranged marriage presents a fundamental problem for these states, for arranged marriage has traditionally challenged the individualist subject of agency that represents its citizenry. Since the nineteenth century in the United States, literary and bureaucratic discourse have presented arranged marriage as the antagonist to the social contract of consent that underpins the modern state (see Sollors, *Beyond Ethnicity*; Haag, *Consent*; Cott, *Public Vows*). Early twentieth-century critics aligned the practice with sexual slavery, both because the freedom of women was in question and because the material concerns imbricated in the practice lay too close to sex work (Haag, *Consent*, 94). From the perspective of the state, "arranged marriage foiled the binary between the realms subject of regulation (economic) and those 'protected' from such interference (noncommercial and nonassociational)" (Haag, *Consent,* 99). Arranged marriage, as an *interested* matrimonial practice, is both intimate and therefore private and represents strategies of economic betterment and sustainability.

British, U.S., and Canadian state discourses have historically looked at arranged marriage as a potential problem in terms of immigration and cultural cohesion. In the heated contemporary debate about marriage and migration, politicians have sometimes advocated for domestic arranged marriage, meaning marriage between two citizens. Such sentiments appear in some diasporic contexts as well, in which parents or brides/grooms suggest the most suitable kind of match might be someone who shares the same geographical upbringing. The desire for domestic arranged marriage reveals the way, for different reasons, the state and minority communities want to sustain the practice, but contain it to citizen participants, within the diaspora. Arranged marriage is a problem for cultural cohesion. While domestic arranged marriage has historically been a seeming resolution to the problem of ideological difference, state and media discourses show how transnational arranged marriage has been perceived as a threatening migration strategy. The transnational tendencies of arranged marriage lead to a mutually defining relation between the practice and institutions like immigration. That phenomenon lies at the heart of how arranged marriage is perceived in xenophobic contexts and why arranged marriage is so closely tied to national immigration politics in diasporic contexts.

The positive and negative ways of looking at arranged marriage in contemporary Western media reports are symptomatic of the aspirations and fears of modern mobility and its relation to the nation-state. In Britain and Canada, especially, arranged marriage has been at the center of public discussions about immigration. In Canada, for example, arranged marriage was the locus for debates about marriage fraud in the early 1990s, when Canadian immigration policy began to demand personal letters and evidence of familiarity to eradicate "marriages of convenience" (chapter 4). The prevalence of forced marriage stories in Britain and Canada reveals fears of transnational mobility in which new cultures might affect the dominant culture or immigration requirements might be weakened. Especially following the terrorist events of 9/11 in New York and 7/7 in London, the Western media has been increasingly preoccupied with the status of women in Muslim communities (Enright, "Choice," 333). Britain and Canada have explicitly sought to fit arranged marriage into a multicultural scheme while maintaining conservative immigration policies. In these discourses, arranged marriage is shown as the more positive counterpart to the violent practice dubbed forced marriage. Chapter 3 discusses the way that multiculturalist discourses distinguish marriage practices as part of a nation-building exercise, and chapter 4 considers this in Canada. The chapters read these conflicts as centered around a subject of agency.

The impact of the politics of belonging upon arranged marriage discourses within the national arena is significant, but these transnational practices and imaginaries may be read within a global context as well. The term *transnational* here is understood as the interconnection of cultures and mobility across space that has intensified during this contemporary period of globalization (Ong, *Flexible Citizenship*). The term seeks to avoid both a unidirectional model of influence from center to periphery in globalization and the separation of the local from the global. As a critical approach, transnational practices seek to expose how "transnational linkages influence every level of social existence" and recognize that "the effect of configurations of practices at those levels are varied and historically specific" (Grewal and Kaplan, *Scattered Hegemonies*, 13). Transnational relations are an important part of contemporary arranged marriage, in which the discourses and practices participate in forms of globalization. Global relations reflect patterns of physical migration and the imaginaries created around such movement. As Arjun Appadurai puts it, "more people than ever before seem to imagine routinely the possibility that they or their children will live and work in places other than where they were born: this is the wellspring of the increased rates of migration at every level of social, national, and global life" (*Modernity at Large*, 6). The global movement of spouses has also meant the transnational mobility of labor, both paid and unpaid, and capital, as people send money back to the home country. Affective bonds connect family and friends, redrawing the geographies of belonging though global circuits of family and support. The transnational lines that cross the globe with arranged marriage are not always dependent on the international migration of the bride or groom, for sometimes it is the practice itself that is understood as connecting a second-generation couple to an ancestral country of origin. In this way, the *concept* of arranged marriage is transnational; it is an idea that travels and resettles. For this reason, arranged marriage discourses should be seen as responding to and producing transnational networks of labor, capital, affiliation, and imagination, as well as being administered by particular states through conjugal and immigration laws as spouses relocate and, in that way, also become transnational.

Arranged marriage has been a material process by which to forge economic as well as social, political, and symbolic ties to the home country through the processes of transnational marriage. As well as the movement of bodies, arranged marriage across national borders has enabled the flow of capital that forges the lines of transnational connections, as people send money back to or maintain property in the home country through community connections. The marriage markets themselves are global social networks sometimes mediated by the exchange of capital. Members of the diaspora locate prospective partners through transnational networks connecting the United States, Canada, and the United Kingdom to South Asia and other parts of the diaspora. These networks might be through family or social relationships, and they might involve monetary exchange in the form of dowry (or an unofficial bride-price for a bride with legal papers). They might also be supported by businesses, for the globalization of marriage markets has also meant their commercialization through "intermediaries of one type or another—including newspaper advertisements, introduction agencies and matchmaking services, purpose-specific tour companies, as well as, nowadays, Internet dating sites" (Palriwala and Uberoi, *Marriage*, 35). The matrimonial website industry is expected to grow to $15 billion by 2017 (*India Today*, "Online Marriage Business").

Transnational arranged marriages secure economic and familial lines of connection between the diaspora and the country of origin but also imaginative links, making arranged marriage, both domestic and international, part of a transnational imaginary. Arjun Appadurai argues that people in the diaspora become interconnected in global relations, "deeply perspectival constructs, inflected by the historical, linguistic, and political situatedness of different sorts of actors" (*Modernity at Large*, 33). Contemporary representations of arranged marriage have shown how the idea of arranged marriage is a means to imagine and structure a global subjectivity. The transnational flows do not simply follow the lines of migration out from a homeland and then return back with nostalgic recollection; rather, these interconnections produce a kind of network that has social, political, and economic relations and affective and ideological movement back and forth and across different parts of the diaspora.

The global networks created by the discourses and practices of arranged marriage are mediated by gender and class. Marriage itself fosters mobility;

along with wage labor, it has historically been a primary means for people to move. That is especially true for women, and especially for those who come from societies with patrilocal practices in which the wife joins the husband and the husband's family. Representations of arranged marriage feature two important aspects of this gendered form of migration. First, they show how transnational marriage creates a mobile, global labor pool for often unpaid domestic work. Mukherjee's *Wife*, Ali's *Brick Lane*, Chitra Banerjee Divakaruni's short story "Clothes" in the collection *Arranged Marriage* (1995), and Lahiri's *The Namesake*, among other works, represent brides who travel transnationally to care for a household that sometimes includes elderly parents (Divakaruni) or future children (Ali; Lahiri). South Asian diasporic women's writing has historically been an arena for explicating the domestic space and the intimate practices within it; such visions as these literary works provide a corrective to images of migration that focus on the—often male—paid laborer and obscure the material labor of "dependents." Rajni Palriwala and Patricia Uberoi assert the need for studies to recognize the particularity of women's marriage migration and critique the dominant trend in earlier migration studies in which "women's marriage migration was seen as a social institution determined merely by kinship and custom and to this extent outside the realm of political economy and the operation of modern market forces" (*Marriage,* 25). In Ali's novel *Brick Lane,* the character Nazneen walks through a Bengali section of London and reflects on exactly this kind of labor: "But now the waiters were at home asleep, or awake being waited on themselves by wives who only served and were not served in return except with board and lodging and the provision of children whom they also, naturally, waited upon" (38). This book interprets Ali's novel to show the parallel between men's labor migration, which is seen as the paradigm of global mobility, and the less-studied women's unpaid labor migration that is in part a by-product of arranged marriage.

As Ali shows when Nazneen first ventures outside into London, such marriages reinforce the hierarchies in traditional gender roles and often increase the disempowerment of a woman who may lack language as well as other skills that would allow her to integrate into her new environment. While Ali represents this as a breakthrough in consciousness, Mukherjee highlights the experience as a kind of psychic rupture, such that her protagonist Dimple in *Wife* has lost her mind by the end of the novel. Even Lahiri's relatively satisfied immigrant bride Ashima in *The Namesake* finds herself facing abject depression before and after the birth of her child. What these works present, then, is the alienation of the female marriage migrant, for whom the gender role that appears to provide continuity—the role of wife and mother—is the source of increased alienation in the immigrant context as it is severed from the social conditions that give it meaning. Such alienation is presented as cutting across class.

The line between the transnational traffic of unpaid "wife labor" and global sex traffic is very fine and even sometimes porous, because some of the unpaid labor is sex work. Many feminist works, from the North American bildungsroman discussed in chapter 4 to the "forced marriage" narratives in chapter 3, feature the arranged marriage wedding night as a scene of rape. The sexual exploitation of women through conjugal arrangements has taken center stage in British contemporary forced marriage narratives (chapter 3), while the very same aspects of compulsory sex with a relative stranger are consistently glossed over or even celebrated in the fantasies of the popular and commercial. For example, an image from a Punjabi graphics company quips, "Arranged Marriage: Exciting in More Ways Than One" (Punjabi Graphics). In critiquing the institution of arranged marriage as one that promotes sex traffic, the critical discourse has centered on the introduction of the material, to gauge registers of exploitation based on commercial aspects. In other words, the economic elements of dowry or even the idea of a "suitable" spouse as a financially viable one, elements that are more readily visible in arranged marriage than in self-made marriage, become important to equating arrangement with sex trafficking.

This is very tricky ground, and it is worth thinking through how ideals of autonomy and normative concepts of marriage are mobilized to equate arranged marriage and sex traffic. Here the representation of fraud is introduced as a way to differentiate between situations either seemingly invested in individual agency (entering an abusive marriage of one's own volition) or appearing to be characterized by a lack of agency (being "sold" into such a situation). Palriwala and Uberoi point out that "much of the academic and activist interrogation of transnational marriages has been predicated on the assumption that the introduction of material calculations or commercial operations into the process of spouse-selection self-evidently impugns the authenticity of the marital relationship" (*Marriage*, 34–35). That discourse has a long history in North America, where nineteenth-century arranged marriages among Asians were equated with prostitution in a public discourse that elevated self-made marriage as more free (chapter 4). The problem with this discourse is not that it calls attention to the very compelling plight of exploitation in arranged marriages of all kinds, including rape, but that it reduces the cause of such oppression to the overt materiality of such marriages rather than the violence in both bartered and freely given marriages. Ali challenges this opposition in *Brick Lane* by juxtaposing the story of a sister in a "love" relationship who is sex trafficked with another in a transnational arranged marriage. Moreover, the ubiquitous emphasis on the bride glosses over how men's sexual bodies are being exchanged on this global marriage market and assumes an ever-readiness for any sexual opportunity on a man's part.

Media reports, law, immigration policy, cultural representation, and self-representations feature arranged marriage as the transnational flow of culture. Women's transnational marriage migration in particular carries symbolic overtones because of women's role as representative of such culture. Lahiri's novel *The Namesake* gives perhaps the fullest exploration of the symbolic desires that center on transnational marriage with its treatment of Ashok and Ashima's marriage (chapter 4). These desires include the stereotype of the South Asian girl as more "traditional," an amalgamation that can (sometimes mistakenly) signify sexual inexperience, domestic skills, and limited assertiveness vis-à-vis the husband's wishes. South Asian American fiction references these stereotypical constructions in which native brides of highly educated professional men are viewed as purer and more culturally appropriate than European American girlfriends. Describing his bride, Nazneen, in Ali's *Brick Lane,* the husband, Chanu, explains his rationale: "As I say, a girl from the village: totally unspoilt" (11). While Ali's representation appears critical of Chanu's mind-set, since his unfaithful bride turns out to be less pliable than he assumed, some of the popular fiction reinforces the idea of the appropriate South Asian bride by negatively depicting the European girlfriend as promiscuous and unsuitable for the long term. Bapsi Sidhwa's novel *The Pakistani Bride* (2008), for example, portrays an extremely unsympathetic Euro-American wife, and Lahiri's short story "Sexy" portrays the Euro-American mistress outside the inner sanctum of her Indian lover's family life. The cultural symbol of the South Asian bride is a powerful one in arranged marriage discourses; it is an identity that is bartered on a global marriage market. While this book tracks the traffic of symbolic capital, it also challenges the reduction of arranged marriage as only a cultural process by connecting arranged marriage to political and economic processes. It also identifies how both state and feminist discourses reinforce the emphasis on the symbol of the South Asian woman.

It is important to recognize that women who participate in arranged marriages are not only "trafficked" or turned into symbols. Palriwala and Uberoi point out that the same sociological literature that overlooks the political economy of women's marriage migration has also undervalued the agency of such brides in their own mobility. Literary and filmic works introduce the idea of a female desiring subject in this global process. When Lahiri represents in *The Namesake* the phenomenon of the U.S.-educated groom returning during his break to select a wife, she also shows how the would-be wife, Ashima, chooses him precisely because he represents new possibilities outside the scope of her world (chapter 4). In Divakaruni's short story "Clothes," marriage opens possibilities; a bride looked at California on a metal globe and "felt the excitement leap all the way up my arm like an electric shock" (18). Mah Jabin travels in the opposite direction in Aslam's *Maps for Lost Lovers*, seeking to escape a failed romantic relationship in Britain by moving to a village in Pakistan. When the mother in Divakaruni's story "Clothes" frames this in terms of a gender role, asking, "Wasn't it every woman's destiny... to leave the known for the unknown?" (18), she is articulating both the problem of such compulsory roles and the imaginative power of such passages for women. This book retrieves these representations of female desire that are inside the arranged marriage process.

Despite that the discourses on arranged marriage focus predominantly on women, it is not only women who relocate for marriage or are sought for their reproductive capacities or symbolic significance. While the transnational bride is frequently presented as the victim of global exchanges, the transnational groom is often portrayed as the fraudulent agent of such processes. A political debate in Britain has centered on the phenomenon of working-class grooms from the subcontinent marrying British women from within their ethnic communities who sponsor their visas (chapter 3). Such marriages have rarely been imagined sympathetically from the perspective of the groom, though Kureishi's novel *The Buddha of Suburbia* and Chambers's documentary *Every Good Marriage Begins with Tears* are exceptions in different ways. In *The Buddha of Suburbia*, Jamila's father seeks a groom for his daughter from his community in India to help him work in his shop; the father-in-law imagines the match as a means to purchase inexpensive labor, but instead the new unassuming groom becomes lazy, lying around while his wife and brother in India support him. Kureishi turns the stereotype of the fraudulent (and therefore agential) transnational groom by having the wife maintain control.

Transnational arranged marriage can shift patriarchal gender dynamics when the woman is the British citizen. Chambers represents this phenomenon in his film *Every Good Marriage Begins with Tears* in a scene in the car on the way back from the airport. After British-born Shahanera teases her new husband, Mamun from Bangladesh, about a picture of her he carried in his pocket, the subject turns to her weight. Shahanera swears in English at her husband when he says, in Bengali, that he prayed she would lose weight. He rebukes her in English, saying, "Language." She tells him, in English, that she will knock him when they get home, discursively asserting her own power, to his discomfort. She compounds this unease with a display of affection, as she grabs him in an embrace and squeezes his head affectionately to her chest. Mamun is clearly as uncomfortable with the public physical affection as with the half-joking threat, and both reflect a power reversal from the traditional gender role of the husband that he most likely grew up with in rural Bangladesh. Her power derives first from her citizenship, since she holds the power to determine his residency and legal work eligibility in Britain. It also derives from her comfort in the cultural context, linguistic and otherwise. Of course, when he says "language," he means that she should not swear, but in this case the word also reflects the power of linguistic belonging, which the fluent Shahanera has over her husband. In different ways and through the different modes of a humorous ironic reversal and documentary verisimilitude, both Kureishi's and Chambers's representations show how the British-born or British-raised woman may gain relative power through familiarity with the local context and language and by being the one with the official status of valid citizenship. *Arranging Marriage* offers a close reading of these texts to overturn the assumptions of the state discourse on male migration as simply carrying over patriarchal cultural tendencies, instead showing it as a dynamic form both changing gender formations and reinstating them.

The shift in gender relations that takes place with the transnational groom can also lead to difficulties and even violence inside the marriage. In the memoir *Jack and Zena,* Zena muses on the violence of male immigrants from Pakistan sponsored for visas through marriage: "Was it because they felt insecure over here, we wondered, that they had to assert themselves in this way?" (Briggs, 25). This is a phenomenon the field of migration studies has examined; Palriwala and Uberoi cite the problem of "asymmetrical 'adjustment'" for Pakistani grooms who join their in-laws' families and take on a matrilocal role mocked in their own society at the same time as they cannot take a provider role because of the undervaluing of their skill sets in an immigrant context. In such cases, "reassertions of masculinity may be at the cost of male migrants' wives, their children and their marriages" (*Marriage*, 43). Although in public discourses, this gets reduced to Muslim identity, it should be read in the context of global migration.

It is clear, then, that the transnational mobility of both women and men through arranged marriage impacts gender roles in ways that are closely associated with class and citizenship. Sometimes the migration reinforces gender roles. This might be by investing those roles with symbolic overtones, as in the global labor exchanges of transnational brides, in which the domestic roles of femininity are functioning as signifiers of culture as well as gender, or by rearticulating patriarchal forces. What is less obvious is the ways such mobility may foster agency, either because that woman now gains an important role in the brokering of future transnational marriages (Palriwala and Uberoi, *Marriage*) or because she herself has gained a global mobility that might have otherwise been out of reach. Transnational marriage migration for men might upend traditional male gender roles in the diasporic context at the same time as it reinforces it globally, as the man gains an ability to support his family abroad.

Beyond the Binary: The Method of Literary and Cultural Analysis

Having laid out a rationale for the national and transnational scope of the project and explained some of the intersecting discourses that infuse those arenas, this introduction now returns to some methodological choices. To assess what is at stake in the transnational arranged marriage discourse taken as a whole, this analysis moves through the opposition of individuality and collectivity mobilized by the different representations to gain insight into why such a binary is constructed. This book does this by reading representations both symptomatically, to understand a kind of cultural imaginary reproduced there, and critically, to interpret forms themselves overtly engaged in articulation, intervention, and reinvention. *Arranging Marriage* offers a new perspective on South Asian conjugal practices through the disciplinary lens of literary and cultural studies. Projects in anthropology, history, and sociology have dominated the scholarly discussion of South Asian marriage, arranged and not. A literary and cultural study emphasizes the construction of meaning through narrative. A representational analysis is a fundamental way to approach diaspora, because the diverse histories are wound together as "a confluence of narratives [that] is lived and re-lived, produced, reproduced and transformed through individual as well as collective memory and re-memory" (Brah, *Cartographies*, 183). This disciplinary approach draws attention to how representation mediates lived experience. It also challenges culturalist interpretations of arranged marriage, meaning notions of arranged marriage that are based in essentialized as opposed to dynamic definitions of culture.

Whereas culturalist discourses construct a binary between the desires of the individual and duty to the collectivity, the critical interpretation of literary and filmic works helps undermine this opposition. The study of literature and film shows the active constitution of meaning for arranged marriage in ways that reproduce long-standing narratives of the practice, but sometimes bring challenges to this. Thus, for example, when Lahiri begins her novel *The Namesake* with an arranged marriage, she represents how this practice marks a form of cultural affiliation for the young Bengali couple. She also displaces stereotypes of arranged marriage by describing the prospective bride's nascent desire as she steps into the "still warm" (8) shoes of the prospective groom, an excitement fueled by the possibilities of the unknown and the potential intimacy with a stranger. Kureishi, in *The Buddha of Suburbia*, delineates the forces of racism and capitalism that shape the urban community of South London and give rise to transnational interconnections through arranged marriage. In the film *East Is East* (2000), Damien O'Donnell shows arranged marriage as a heteronormative cultural practice employed by members of an older generation to preserve an identity under erasure in working-class Britain, even when they themselves have departed from those practices. Ali brings complexity to the stereotype of the oppressed arranged marriage bride by humanizing the husband and showing the woman's transformation through desire in her novel *Brick Lane*. By analyzing these texts, this book identifies and interprets contradictions of these discourses and the production of transnational subjectivities within them.

Such complex articulations that challenge a culturalist notion of arranged marriage may be found in other modes of cultural discourse—in the state discourse and media representations described earlier or in the ethnographies referenced throughout this book—but they are harder to retrieve in these discursive modes that promote coherency. *Arranging Marriage* sets up literary and cultural analysis as an entry point to locate these complexities that sometimes lie more hidden in other kinds of texts.

Literary and visual culture opens up to the contradiction and nuance that other kinds of textual forms promoting coherency or applied relevance—for example, legal or bureaucratic discourse—attempt to foreclose. For example, take the reference to the "strict and long-established customs of your or your fiancé(e)'s foreign culture or social practice," referenced in U.S. immigration documentation as a way to exempt participants of arranged marriages from the burden of proving legitimacy through intimacy (U.S. Department of Homeland Security, "Fiancé(e) Visas"). That document works to characterize practices in ways that would allow for policies of immigration law to provide exceptions from the norms of love marriages. Such kinds of legal and bureaucratic discourses reveal, upon closer inspection, ambivalences and conflicting ideals; for example, the policy concerning forced marriage that seeks to curtail the scope of familial power repeatedly reaffirms the centrality of that institution to British society (chapter 3). However, the bureaucratic genre of policy attempts to minimize contradictions, but does so with the effect of creating fixed notions of culture. A literary work like Kureishi's *The Buddha of Suburbia* revels in precisely the multiplicity, contradiction, and nuance foreclosed by the more praxis-oriented genres. When Jamila pursues an arranged marriage in this novel, she does so not simply as a form of cultural belonging, though that is there, but because she loves her father, the family needs the extra worker, she lacks a viable alternative as a young female alone within her local and national communities, she occupies a disenfranchised position as a South Asian in London in the late 1970s, and she simply figures she will work the decision to her benefit.

Writers and filmmakers, in particular, reveal how forces like racism, nationalism, and global capital are shaping factors in the production of competing constructions of agency; their works often challenge these structures by exposing their inscription within culturalist rhetorics. By closely reading these creative works by and about South Asians, this book uncovers the hidden national and global socioeconomic forces that lie within references to tradition. For example, chapter 3 interprets Aslam's novel *Maps for Lost Lovers*, arguing that Aslam ultimately shows the concept of honor invoked in conjugal practices in the Pakistani diaspora as a rhetoric obscuring the alienating conditions of a place the inhabitants dub "The Wilderness of Solitude." As a group of men and women react to these conditions, which include racism, anti-Muslim sentiment, conditions of immigration, and unemployment, patriarchy becomes expressed in violent form in the name of culture. In interpreting literary works like Aslam's, this book exposes how culturalism disguises the socioeconomic factors at work in assertions of collectivity through arranged marriage produced in the context of contemporary globalization.

Literature and film are not the only genres that shape their subjects through representation, even if they are made more flexible by their freedom from practical application. This book examines representations of South Asian arranged marriage found in immigration policy, legal cases, and journalistic articles as well as in texts like literature and film. In doing so, this book brings two important threads about arranged marriage—bureaucratic and cultural texts—into extended conversation for the first time to show the production of a social imaginary with discursive effects in a wide range of forums. *Arranging Marriage* analyzes an interdisciplinary set of texts with an eye toward interpreting the *dynamics* of arranged marriage as a fraught nodal point. Within this point, relations between generations and sexes are worked out within communities constituted around the practice; at the same time, different kinds of national and global relations are forged through the practice.

The fact that this work is done around the subject of marriage is not coincidental, for the texts represent the intersection of public and private that is conjugality. Marriage narratives are a dynamic site to read the processes of inscription or reinterpretation of agency, because these stories reveal commitments on the part of individuals, communities, and states. Marital fictions exist in a range of texts, from the literary texts that represent a "marriage plot," in which marriage acts as a form of closure, to the ritualistic words "I do." Describing "marital fictions" as a "set of reconstructive processes," Kellie Holzer argues that they may be "scrutinized in order to denaturalize marriage, to show the institutions' limits, failures, elasticities, and possibilities" ("Tying the Knot," 2). These fictions affectively generate affiliations to forms of power, processes that are formalized through genre. This is why this book often approaches representations through genre, including romance, bildungsroman, documentary, social realism fiction, comedy, and autobiography.

This book groups together a set of representations about South Asians that are by South Asians and those that are produced in the more heterogeneous national public spheres, but not necessarily by South Asians. The portrayals represent a disparate South Asian diaspora from the outside (with representations of South Asians) and from the inside (as a cultural practice claimed, modified, or refused). *Arranging Marriage* reads these etic and emic, or outside and inside, portrayals together, first as a way to avoid positing an authentic position for representing a group's experience. While such identity politics can be valuable as a way to construct a community and foster dialogues within it, these communities are ultimately heterogeneous and fluid, with well-populated borderlands comprising minorities of various sorts. More importantly, the privileging of representations by an ethnic group can also be mobilized in dangerous ways, as in the sensationalistic forced marriage memoirs that purport to represent the "true story" of Pakistani girls in Britain (chapter 3). Politically invested discourses assign credibility to certain identities over others in a way that shifts; in other words, "authentic" representations are contestable and politicized in problematic ways.

Second, this book includes both discourses by South Asians and discourses in which that group is in some way represented as "other," because the two sets of representations shape each other in important ways. For example, states have embraced multicultural projects, categorizing and identifying groups in terms of ethnic difference and cultural identity. They have looked to community leaders to articulate the values of such collectivities (Mohammad-Arif, "Religion," 169). Though the state might play a primary role in naming such communities (as in the case of "British Muslims"), such identities have later been claimed and celebrated by South Asians as a point of exceptionalism. By collapsing the binary between the locations of "inside" and "outside" in works about South Asians, this book positions arranged marriage discourses within national and global sites of production, in which representations of culture are both generative and reactive.

As well as moving across the separation constructed between insider and outsider accounts of South Asians engaged in arranged marriage practices, this book groups together positive and negative representations of arranged marriage. The chapters of this book show depictions that advocate sustaining the practice intact or with modifications, ones that oppose arranged marriage outright, and ones that wish to parse consensual from nonconsensual practices as a way to create a concept of arranged marriage based on consent. Although strategies of representation promote different pragmatic outcomes, proponents of and opponents to arranged marriage share assumptions and emphases. Across these divisions consistent themes emerge, including culturalist understandings of arranged marriage that articulate community, an emphasis on women and especially girls within the practice as the locus for individual freedom, the articulation of the state through discourses of multiculturalism and immigration, the construction of an opposition between public and private, and the focus on the subject of agency.

The South Asian Diaspora as a Critical Fiction

The South Asian diaspora is heterogeneous, made up of different languages, religions, customs, classes, races, and histories. Different communities originate from vastly different parts of the subcontinent, only some of which are dealt with in this book, and these enter diverse national and local contexts. Their passages are structured by various economies, from slavery to the feudalism of indentured labor to mercantilism to the finance capitalism and service economies of the present day (Koshy, "Introduction," 3). Some groups have reinvented themselves as new communities, such as when Punjabi farmers intermarried with Mexican women in Southern California in the nineteenth century, while others have held closely to the idea of their original identities, such as the Guajarati motel owners described in Pawan Dhingra's book *Life behind the Lobby* (2012). As Susan Koshy puts it in her introduction to *Transnational South Asians: The Making of a Neo-Diaspora*, "the rubric South Asian diaspora uses a regional political identity to organize a multitude of diasporic formations that have seldom imagined themselves in those regional terms" (9). This book recognizes that multiplicity by specifying national, linguistic, regional, and religious identities when those categories are featured in the discourse or history. At other times, it uses the generalized term *South Asian* as a way to mark collective experiences, especially around the shared significance of arranged marriage, even if the particularities of those meanings are diverse. In this way, the term *South Asian* operates here as a critical fiction.

In this book, diaspora is not looked at as the common practices of people of South Asian origin around the world; rather, it is explored as a "concept and a set of social formations" (Shukla, *India Abroad*, 4) that emerge in uneven, disparate ways from a history of global migration, reinvention, and the forging of transnational bonds. In approaching this vast arena of diaspora, this project takes a genealogical approach by selecting specific national contexts and movements to organize the chapters. The study focuses on the British and North American contexts to follow the path of two large twentieth-century trajectories of the South Asian diaspora, one to post–World War II Britain and a later one in the 1960s to North America. To confine the scope, *Arranging Marriage* focuses on Britain and North America as sites of textual production rather than on other important locations of the South Asian diaspora, such as Australia, Europe, the Middle East, East Asia, the Caribbean, East and South Africa, and Mauritius. Similarly, the project focuses on only one part of the South Asian diaspora. Although arranged marriage is a defining aspect in many South Asian regions, this book concentrates on texts by or about Indians, Pakistanis, and Bangladeshis. This is not because arranged marriage is not important in Sri Lanka, Nepal, or other parts of South Asia, of course; rather, it is a way to specify and explicate some key narratives in the meeting point between South Asian and Euro-American cultural discourses that center on exemplary national, class, or religious identities. The hope here is to inform future projects that take up other narratives in the set of global arranged marriage discourses.

In this way, this book might be thought of in terms of a collection of global narratives that interrelate. Each arranged marriage narrative is located, in the sense that it has its own historically specific context. For example, chapter 3 reads Sikh and Muslim working-class memoirs of "forced marriage" alongside state legal reforms around conjugal practices; it looks at these as producing a discourse in which state sovereignty is reinforced and British national identity is affectively mobilized through the language of family displaced from arranged marriage onto the state. Chapter 5 follows a transnational professional class of mostly Hindu Indian Americans around whom a set of fantasies about arranged marriage is constructed. Each story in this collection illuminates others, even though they might be about different classes, religious national origins, or diasporic contexts. The broader constituency being referenced might be South Asian identity built around a perceived shared ethnicity and set of cultural practices, but at other times, more specific national, religious, or class identities emerge. It is part of the argumentative logic of this book that arranged marriage as a discourse binds together an otherwise heterogeneous South Asian diaspora into a cluster of discourses that might be interpreted.

Chapter Summaries

Chapter 1 provides a theoretical frame for the discussion of the subject of agency. It argues that we need to understand the subject of arranged marriage constituted through the discourses of individualism and communitarianism rather than as an autonomous agent that chooses those affiliations. The chapter locates this constituted subject within national and transnational contexts, retrieving the embedded power relations that produce those discourses. Chapter 1 offers a genealogy for the contemporary modern discourses of arranged marriage that form around a public–private split. It does this by tracing debates about conjugality that begin in colonial India, develop through the discourses of nationalism, and continue into the postcolonial period. By offering this genealogy, chapter 1 explores narratives of family and community that have surrounded arranged marriage since the colonial period in South Asia, narratives that articulate the political agendas of the state as well as resistances to those agendas. Returning to the contemporary period, chapter 1 looks specifically at the narratives of endogamy, focusing on the notions of religion, caste, sexuality, and gender. However, rather than read these as a list of a community's rules, chapter 1 interprets these intersecting discourses as constituting community's national and transnational arenas. Chapter 1 lays the theoretical and historical groundwork for the case studies developed in each chapter, which together show how the subject of agency has become the borderline between acceptable and unacceptable forms of difference within a period of contemporary globalization.

Chapters 2 and 3 examine the discourse generated around the question of force in arranged marriage in the contemporary context of Britain. Chapter 2 focuses on the subject of consent as it is alternately represented in court cases dealing with the annulment of arranged marriages and in literature and film about arranged marriage. This chapter identifies and investigates the contemporary discourse that centers on consent as the primary means to distinguish arranged and forced marriages. It describes the ways that legal cases have increasingly liberalized notions of coercion as a way to extend the range of force to include more kinds of interpersonal pressure. Building on feminist legal theories about subjectivity, this chapter argues that the primary focus on consent falls short of interpreting the forces and processes that surround the agent in arranged marriage. As a way to supplement the discourse, the chapter turns to literature and films that elaborate those social, economic, and political forces. Ayub Khan-Din's play *East Is East* uses the figure of the father, George, and his sons to show how arranged marriage is mobilized as a masculinizing discourse by which the immigrant man expresses his national identity. Ali's novel *Brick Lane* represents the ways that a young Bangladeshi woman enters what the state sees as the decision-making moments of arranged marriage. Chapter 2 interprets Ali's novel, along with Chambers's documentary *Every Good*

Marriage Begins with Tears, to elaborate the problem of looking to consent (or lack of consent), a moment of decision that may never be fully articulated within those structures and forces.

Chapter 3 also focuses on Britain since the 1990s, but it looks specifically at the ways policy proposals, the mainstream media, and forced marriage memoirs together create a rhetoric of honor crime and forced marriage. The chapter interprets both the official discourse and sensationalist memoirs in the context of a state-sponsored multicultural discourse. Documents like the report by the Working Group on Forced Marriage, titled *A Choice by Right* (Ahmed and Uddin), advance the notion that a just guardianship allows for choice and that the state provides such a parent. In looking at a body of literary texts that feature sensational stories of escape from forced marriage, this chapter highlights the way national assimilation is imagined through the intercaste, intercommunal, or interethnic love story. These memoirs, it argues, that are part of a broader discourse on honor crimes that advocate the assimilation of the South Asian girl through images of romantic integration outside the community. In doing so, they become part of the "exit strategy" that sees the resolution to forced marriage to be exit from the community. While such tactics are necessary in individual cases of violence, as a political stance, such a strategy positions the state over the community. Chapter 3 offers alternatives to these narratives in two forms that seek to maintain a progressive, feminist valence. First, using critique, the chapter rereads arranged marriage back into its highly politicized context of immigration and neoliberal commitments to multiculturalism. It exposes the other kinds of investments made by the discourse on honor crime and on forced marriage in particular. Second, employing literary interpretation, Chapter 3 finds, in Aslam's *Maps for Lost Lovers,* a critical vision of community from within an ambivalent, resistant position. Chapter 3 reads Aslam's work as engaged in the difficult task of recasting the values of a community from within. Aslam locates such values, including the two most often mobilized in political discourse, shame and honor, as emerging from the economic exigencies of transnational labor and global economies. In this way, he challenges both the rationales of communalism that see violence as an expression of the pure culture of the homeland and the way the state discourse elides such materialist structures in its representation of forced marriage as a problem of culture.

Chapter 4 shifts the discussion across the Atlantic, considering the South Asian diaspora in the United States and Canada. This chapter reads the arranged marriage discourse as the product of a post-1965 generation in the United States and post-1967 in Canada. Looking back to early histories of immigration, the chapter places this late-twentieth and early-twenty-first-century discourse in broader historical national contexts. Through the early text of Dhan Gopal Mukherji, the chapter considers how the ideas of consent positioned as the antagonist to arranged marriage modeled a national identity.

Looking at the post-1965/1967 generation, chapter 4 identifies two major strands that represent arranged marriage: a community-based one that celebrates arranged marriage as a way to "be" Indian, or Pakistani, or Bangladeshi, and a feminist one that features the notion of arranged marriage as antagonistic to women's agency. The first narrative has led to conservative expressions of communalism, whereas the second narrative is fully vested in liberal values of freedom that increasingly give way to the neoliberal affirmations of choice using arranged marriage as an antagonist. Chapter 4 looks at the construction of diasporic community identification through an interpretation of the matrimonial website Shaadi.com.

While the discourses of arranged marriage in the United States and Canada continue to promote the subject of agency articulated as community, an alternate set of texts has presented the individual as the primary site for agency. Chapter 4 looks at the ways literary representations support these narratives of individual, especially female, freedom, while sometimes offering unexpected ways of conceptualizing arranged marriage. Mukherjee's, Divakaruni's, and Lahiri's works feature the role of marriage as a means for women's mobility, exploring the kinds of freedoms and constraints attached to this movement. Chapter 4 considers the idea that a second generation moves against arranged marriage. Interpreting Lahiri's novel *The Namesake* in light of some ethnographic work on second-generation South Asian Americans, chapter 4 suggests that a second generation is working within, rather than refusing narratives of arranged marriage as cultural identity, in sometimes successful and sometimes unsuccessful ways.

Whereas chapter 4 presents the discourses of community and individual agency as antagonistic, chapter 5 considers their synthesis in modified forms within neoliberal, postfeminist popular culture. This chapter looks at how arranged marriage narratives are merged with romance narratives more commonly associated with self-made marriages in a way that views arranged marriage as a choice. This chapter treats a transnational set of texts, in the sense that some are produced in India and some in the United

States, but also in the sense that they are circulating to a global English-language reading public. In Bollywood film and popular women's fiction, popular works are increasingly refuting the notion that arranged marriage love is duty-bound love. They retrieve a kind of romantic love that articulates personal satisfaction, therapeutic discourse, and choice, values associated with neoliberalism. Chapter 5 uses the idea of the intimate public as a way to conceptualize how people read themselves into these narratives, even if they don't necessarily get arranged marriages. The works affectively mobilize them toward certain kinds of community affiliations while allowing them to invest in individual agency.

1

The Subject of Agency

The question of agency, or the capacity to act, is a crucial one in the discussion of arranged marriage. The subject of such agency differentiates arranged marriage, in which decision making is given over in whole or in part to others, usually members of an extended family, and self-made marriage, in which the individual makes all decisions regarding courtship and commitment. Liberal conceptions of the fully volitional subject invest in the notion of autonomy a value expressed in the capacity to consent, but also in other areas, such as the will to remain in a marriage or even the freedom to fall in love. A rhetoric of modernity that separates the modern from tradition makes this individuated subject its cornerstone, in the process portraying arranged marriage as anachronistic. The processes of globalization have disseminated the liberal rhetoric of individualism, but the same conditions have also given rise to communitarian notions of agency. The arranged marriage practice empowers agents, usually elder members of a family representing the interests of a larger social group, to make some or all conjugal decisions; in this way, the communitarian discourse that circumscribes this conjugal form centers on a collectivist rather than individualist agency. Discourses of community constitute arranged marriage subjects in ways that are inflected by narratives of gender, caste, and religion as well as by regional and national identities.

This book in its entirety explores the globalization of concepts of conjugality and agency through analyzing arranged marriage as a discursive locus. It does not arbitrate the rightness or wrongness of arranged marriage. Instead, this book considers the representational work that discourses about South Asian arranged marriage do in contemporary transnational and national diasporic contexts of the United Kingdom, the United States, and Canada. Through critical discourse analysis, the book argues that the positions of individualism and communitarianism should not be seen as absolute truths but rather as situated discourses emerging with national and transnational contexts and reflecting political, economic, and affective forces within globalization. What is being debated has implications far beyond conjugal practices. On a global scale, competing narratives about arranged marriage, meaning both those that denounce and those that support arranged marriage, have been alternately reinforcing, refusing, and rethinking Western notions of individual agency that lie at the heart of a liberal conception of rights and a neoliberal ideal of choice. This displacement of decision making that is a fundamental part of arranged marriage challenges an edifice of identity and rights resting on the ideal of the autonomous, fully vested individual agent. This book as a whole identifies and interprets a set of responses to that challenge, while this chapter provides some of the theoretical and historical grounds for those readings.

The project of liberalism has been focused on individual freedom, and for this reason it has been important to feminism and central to critiques of the more communitarian practice of arranged marriage. Philosopher John Gray characterized one of the common elements of the liberal tradition as individualist "in that it asserts the moral primacy of the person against the claims of any social collectivity" (*Liberalism*, x). The liberal tradition aligns notions of "will" and "freedom" with the ideal of self-realization, casting certain forms of collectivism as a kind of antiquity against the modernity of individualism. Although many contemporary feminists have complicated feminism's relationship to individual autonomy in ways discussed later, a significant part of the political project of feminism as developed in the West has been to promote the rights of the individual to self-determination. It is not surprising, then, that liberal feminists and liberal states associate arranged marriage with oppression, given that the idea and practice elevate collectively held agency.

Nancy Cott argues that the ideology of the democratic sovereign state makes self-made marriage a natural sign of Western democracy (*Public Vows*, 3). For the modern state, to preserve individual decision making in the area of matrimony is to maintain personal rights. Legal and state discourses often frame this claim to rights in terms of individual consent. Human rights law considers legitimate marriage to be based, as the United Nations Convention on Consent to Marriage puts it, in the "free and full consent of the intending spouses," and national laws like the British Marriage Act of 1949 reinforce the notion of the individual as primary agent in matrimonial decision making. John Kleinig schematizes the idea of consent as between two parties, A and B, in which A must be at a certain level of maturity. He argues that consent requires that a proposition in some form be in place: there must be something to which A might consent. Finally, he suggests that the contractual nature of consent must involve communication: "consent requires signification—not in the sense that a state of mind is reported but in the sense that a right or entitlement is created or permission given or obligation assumed" ("Nature of Consent," 11). A state discourse of rights has made consent a primary means for promoting individual agency, a point this book takes up as problematic in the way legal decisions based primarily on consent have overlooked affective, sociopolitical, and economic elements in decision making (chapter 2).

Romantic love forms both the means and the rationale for the expression of individual will. Love mediates the border between the individual and the social worlds as a "code of communication, according to the rules of which one can express, form and simulate feelings, deny them, impute them to others, and be prepared to face up to all the consequences which enacting such a communication may bring with it" (Luhmann, *Love as Passion*, 20). The narration of individual agency often appears as the unstoppable love story that overcomes opposition from family members. William Shakespeare's play *Romeo and Juliet* is probably the most famous example of a literary work that sets arranged marriage against the desires of the individual. By the eighteenth century in Britain, marriage plots regularly depicted individuals who challenged the wishes of extended families; Jane Austen's novels represent self-made marriage based on love as the foundation for a companionate marriage that offers a "new recognition of the need for personal autonomy, and a new respect for the individual pursuit of happiness" (Stone, *Family*, 273). These critical representations of love stories interfering with arranged marriage plans have a long and prominent history in Western literature and film. Within this convention, many contemporary South Asian diasporic works correlate the experiences of cultural and personal reinvention with the experience of love. For example, in Gurinder Chanda's films *Bhaji on the Beach* (1995) and *Bend It Like Beckham* (2003), the heroines' decisions to pursue self-made romance resonate beyond the interpersonal to suggest the remaking of an immigrant self. These portrayals work to elevate love as an idealized expression of individual freedom against prohibitions articulated by family elders that define conduct in terms of community belonging.

Scholars have connected the discourses of love, individualism, and freedom. Interpreting the history of love, Giddens argues that "ideals of romantic love ... inserted themselves directly into the emergent ties between freedom and self-realization" (*Transformation*, 40). While works like Austen's appear simply to feature romance as a site for the expression of self, Giddens argues that it is the romantic love narrative that "introduced the idea of a narrative into an individual's life—a formula which radically extended the reflexivity of sublime love" (39). In other words, the discourse of love produces as well as validates the narrative of individual agency. Simon May argues that this process works on an ontological level such that the rapture of love "inspire(s) in us the hope of an indestructible grounding for our life" (*Love*, 6). He describes "the lover, who becomes authentic through love. In love he becomes not selfless but a self" (12). May closely ties love to the production of subjectivity, "man as a free and self-transforming creator" (137). The loving subject, for both Giddens and May, appears as a free subject, with the love standing in as both a metaphor and a means to freedom—in fact, to being itself.

Modern discourses present sexuality as well as love as a primary site of this individualism and the constitution of self, and negative representations of arranged marriage contribute to this construction. The notion of free choice of a spouse, along with the close association between marriage and sexual intimacy, leads to the common assumption in these portrayals that self-made marriage expresses self-made sexuality, which in turn expresses freedom. A set of literary texts represent arranged marriage, in which a man or woman is expected to have sex with someone "arranged" for him or her after the marriage, as the antithesis of this sexual autonomy. Saira Ahmed's memoir *Disgraced* (coauthored by Andrew Crofts) exemplifies this perspective vividly by detailing the husband's awkward attempts to consummate the marriage that take place over several nights after the wedding, a process that turns increasingly violent until it results in a series of rapes. Memoirs in which the protagonist escapes before the marriage, such as Sanghera's *Shame*, align the young woman's freedom with sexual freedom by narrating how her family attempts to stifle her burgeoning sexual development through arranged marriage. These protagonists find their sexual expression extramaritally, and the works invest such sexuality with the quality of freedom. This is also the view in Ayub Khan-Din's play *East Is East*, in which premarital heterosexual activity is illicit for both Pakistani British men and women and homosexual identity (much less activity) means exclusion from the community, a point discussed more fully later. The discourse of autonomy presents sexuality as an emotionally and physically intimate site for the constitution of the subject.

The question of agency has been an important one in feminist studies, a scholarly and political tradition that has included both the assertion of women's rights through the idea of individual agency and the rethinking of classical Western philosophical notions of agency in ways that are relevant to this study. While liberal perspectives have promoted the ideal of individual agency, and feminist writing has played an important part in this, other works of feminist and poststructuralist theory have challenged the idea of an autonomous agent invested with free will that has become a cornerstone of Western philosophical understandings of moral truth, rationality, and economy. Their work helps illuminate a very different meaning of agent, "a person or organization acting on behalf of another" *(OED)*, that is relevant to this study. Marilyn Friedman has argued for the redefinition of autonomy to involve social relationships ("Autonomy," 36). Some of these writers link this interconnection to the idea of intersectionality, which theorizes crossing discursive vectors like race, gender, class, nationality, and sexuality in the constitution of the individual subject (Crenshaw, "Mapping the Margins," 1244). As well as asserting a kind of interconnectedness, and thus troubling the notion of the individual as an essential locus of free will, these feminist thinkers have rethought the value of dependency that is offered as the oppositional counterpart to agency, shifting attention to a positive view of such entanglements with family or community.

Coming from a different philosophical tradition, Michel Foucault deconstructed the idea of individual autonomy with his theories of the mediated subject. For Foucault, the discourses and practices of power constitute the subject in multiple and contradictory ways. The idea of subjectivity shifts away from the reified notion of the individual to a "complex but nonetheless unified locus of the constitution of the phenomenal world," in "dialectic with that world as either its product or its source, or both" (Smith, *Discerning the Subject*, xxvii). Foucault challenges the idea that this subject precedes the expression of will with his idea that power relations produce individuated consciousness. Saba Mahmood has used Foucault's work to recast agency as a power effect embedded in discourse rather than an expression of individual will, finding agency "within semantic and institutional networks that define and make possible particular ways of relating to people, things, and oneself" (*Politics of Piety*, 34). British legal scholars Anitha and Gill develop this critique in terms of the law, challenging the way the courts in the United Kingdom "have continued to apply a similar standard of individual rationality and volition, which presumes that the individual in question is a pre-social, ahistorical, self-constituting subject who does not belong to an identity-conferring community, nor values relational aspects of personhood" ("Coercion," 177).

For Mackenzie and Stoljar, who elaborate an idea called relational autonomy, the displacement from this ideal of the individual self toward a mediated subject does not preclude agency but rather enriches our understanding of such subjectivity and the "rich and complex social and historical contexts in which agents are embedded... agents who are emotional, embodied, desiring, creative and feeling, as well as rational, creatures" ("Introduction," 21), and they highlight the ways in which agents are both psychically internally differentiated and socially differentiated from others. In other words, this agency expresses itself in other modalities, such as memory, creation, and affective bonds like affiliation. Simone de Beauvoir gives an example of this in her description of marriage as the site of oppression, in which a woman "chooses to desire her enslavement so ardently that it will seem to her the expression of her liberty" (*Second Sex*, 643). For de Beauvoir, love in the context of marriage (even self-made marriage) is not a means to freedom but an affective means to structure a woman's oppression.

Foucault's theory of the mediated subject and Mackenzie and Stoljar's conception of the multifaceted nature of agency present an opportunity to conceptualize the arranged marriage subject as constituted *through* the discourses of individualism and communitarianism rather than as an agent that must decide between them. Whereas Mackenzie and Stoljar's point is to enable political activism from a collective agent, and Mahmood's is to recognize the potential normativity of such agency in the service of tradition, this book attempts to elaborate this more complex vision of a constituted subject by using a critical reading of representations as a way to challenge national and transnational discourses of culture and belonging that obscure the power relations constituting this subject. It does this by situating the narratives within their historically specific discursive moments, read within national and transnational contexts as articulated in a series of generic forms—law, policy, fiction, memoir, feature and documentary film, and digital and print media. The goal of deconstructing the consenting subject is not to suggest that agency doesn't matter but to show how discursive structures and performances produce a subject in which such decision making is already precluded, enabled, or constituted within a set of ideological structures.

Genealogies from South Asia

As a way of situating the contemporary South Asian diasporic discourse within its longer histories, this section turns to the British colonial context before returning to the twenty- and twenty-first-century representations that are the subject of this book. Contextualizing the diaspora in terms of the subcontinent runs some risks in a book that seeks to upset the story of arranged marriage as an unchanging custom rooted in a historic homeland. As Rajeswari Sunder Rajan cautions on relating the "native" and diasporic, "while sharing a common identity, [they] do not inhabit the same historic space: questions of politics and method therefore impinge upon and compel 'same' identities in significantly different ways" (*Real*, 9). Heeding this caution, this chapter does not look back to the subcontinent as the origin of an unchanged tradition. Instead, it seeks to tell the story of earlier arranged marriage narratives as they were shaped by a colonial discourse on South Asian marriage and continue to change in a later postcolonial period in different sites. By reading this intimate history through the scholarship on colonial and postcolonial conjugal reform, this chapter offers a genealogy, "a conceptual mapping which defies the search for originary absolutes, or genuine and authentic manifestations of a stable, pregiven, unchanging identity; for pristine pure customs and traditions or unsullied glorious pasts" (Brah, *Cartographies*, 196). What may be understood from this genealogy is how discourses of modernity produced both individualist and communitarian subjects of agency in the construction of a private realm subject to the state. What may also be gleaned is how women become the object of these narratives in a way that has continued in contemporary global narratives of arranged marriage.

In the eighteenth and nineteenth centuries, British colonial discourses in India, as well as an important nationalist discourse that opposed such rule, made the religious community, the joint family, and the native woman (or girl) important components in their political programs. The colonial state intervened in conjugal practices as a means for establishing the basis of its sovereignty, pitting itself against earlier versions of the joint family in a discourse framed in terms of modernity (Sreenivas, *Wives*, 53). Women and girls became the primary object of reform, though conjugal practices included both males and females (Hall, "Of Gender," 52). Cultural, religious, and state discourses constructed a private, domestic sphere under the name of religious community, seemingly separate from but also fully subject to the state (Majumdar, *Marriage*, 7). The colonial discourse perpetuated an opposition between free will and community even as it ostensibly afforded religion primacy in conjugal matters. Marriage ultimately acted as a point of contestation, developing its significance as a marker of culture for both the colonial state and within the nationalist imaginaries that opposed colonial rule.

In a study of the conjugal family ideal in colonial India, Mytheli Sreenivas argues that eighteenth-century changes, as a new state emerged under the influence of the East India Company, represented the incursion of the colonial state on the powerful conceptual site of the domestic arena that organized economy and society in ways that gave rise to contemporary notions of the joint family (*Wives,* 12). Through new laws on property ownership, the concerns of joint families were set against the professional and mercantile interests that "invoked a national 'modernity' rooted in individual ownership, capitalist development, and the conjugal relationship" (53). Ironically, this shift reinvigorated the centrality of the family as an object of state regulation. Indeed, the joint family, which came over the next century to rise as the central point of arranged marriage, may be seen to emerge during this time in a now recognizable form:

> The de-politicization of the family, the disavowal of non-blood related kin as household members, the shifting power and authority of propertied families within agrarian society, the transformation of gendered power dynamics within families, and the development of novel colonial discourses on domestic life all formed the basis upon which the "family" became the target of state regulation under colonial rule. (28)

The notion of a joint family that developed seized a primary ideological position representing tradition that continues to this day. This overdetermined notion of the family was the product of transformations associated with colonial rule accompanied by a rhetoric of modernity that emphasized civic belonging. These transformations sought to shift power away from the extended family toward the state, filling in the empty space with a legal and cultural entity resting on a primary conjugal relationship—husband and wife—a relationship sanctioned by the state. The site for collective agency, in other words, was both transformed and circumscribed. This process was never fully successful, and the legacies of the conflict over the power of the joint family have continued into the postcolonial period. During the colonial period, the idea of arranged marriage entered its modern form in India. Rochona Majumdar argues that a diversity of practices congealed into an idealized notion during the colonial period in India, formulating what is commonly understood as arranged marriage (*Marriage*, 2). One of the more surprising aspects of colonial modernity was its invigoration of elements associated with "tradition" rather than their simple repudiation. South Asian scholars have interrogated the object of modernity, challenging the way it rhetorically constructs binaries of tradition and modernity. This process reinvents in the conjugal arena "a discourse about tradition which was entirely modern" (Mody, *Intimate State,* 77–78). The joint family became emblematic of tradition and the locus of community expressed in terms of culture rather than, for example, politics or economy. By the nineteenth century, laws that ostensibly circumscribed the limits of the state, or "personal laws," helped constitute the modern family and create what appeared as a distinct conceptual space grounded in community and religion (Majumdar, *Marriage*, 7). The sovereignty of that "cultural" space would continually come into debate into the postcolonial period throughout South Asia and its diaspora as a powerful expression of cultural nationalism.

Even as changes effected on joint families eroded the real political power of women (Sreenivas, *Wives,* 25), their symbolic status as wives gained currency. "Once colonial rule was firmly established in India," Majumdar observes, "native marriages began to be treated by foreign observers as a shibboleth of Indian tradition" (Majumdar, *Marriage,* 7). Literary works sometimes even elevated the Indian wife above the European one as "patriarchy's feminine ideal" (Sunder Rajan, *Real,* 47). However, missionary and state discourses represented the Indian wife more negatively, in the sense that they sought to change her position in Indian society. Women—wives, in particular—were the object of colonial domestic reform. The discourse of modernity played a role in this as well. Catherine Hall suggests, "The idea that the British were saving Indian women from the barbarities of their archaic world, and that this was a necessary precondition for modernizing India, became a critical tool in the legitimation, whether amongst colonial officials, missionaries, or social reformers, whether utilitarian or evangelical, of their country's right to rule" ("Of Gender," 52). As the treatment of Indian women became a hallmark for the measure of Indian "civilization," the conjugal relationship was considered a key register of their treatment, a place where ideas on women's health, education, and civic rights were articulated through a colonial discourse about marriage.

The British colonial state's project in relation to conjugality was not simply to abolish or reform certain practices; colonial conjugal discourses were a way of reading Indian society and creating a dominant relationship to that society that functioned through this interpretation. The issue of sati, or the immolation of the widow on the funeral pyre, was a focal point for conjugal reform in the nineteenth century, as was the legalization of widow remarriage and the regulation of child marriage (see chapter 2 for a discussion of the colonial and national reforms around age of consent). These campaigns on conjugality made women their object of reform and a cause for state intervention. Both colonial and nationalist discourses shifted agency from the women themselves to the communities empowered with their representation and, in doing so, constructed narratives of religious community around the symbolic locus of Woman (Mani, *Contentious Traditions*, 79).

The colonial discourse on sati was one of the most active objects of reform in the colonial context. Sati was also one of the earliest objects of colonial reform, with the issue coming up during the 1813 parliamentary debate on the East Indian Co. charter renewal. One of the insights scholars have gleaned from the sati debate has been the notion that in public discussions about the social roles of women, women themselves are made primary symbolic objects but silenced in practice. That silence might refer to the lack of their writing in the official documents or a lack of power to represent themselves in the legal sphere. Their silence might also extend more broadly to how their position as subjects may be elided by the different modes of representation that speak on their behalf, as Gayatri Spivak describes in her essay "Can the Subaltern Speak?" (306). Lata Mani focuses on what fills in that empty space left by women's lack of voice within this forum. She describes a dialogue between representatives of the colonial state and a "Bhadralok" comprising elite Bengali men that appears in the colonial archive of debates about sati. Mani tracks how the colonial officials sought to understand Indian society as based in religion, and that religion as based in textual scriptures. For the Bhadralok, an emerging discourse on modernity used the question of women to position itself vis-à-vis the colonial government and the rest of the indigenous society. For both groups, women were the "ground" rather than agents or even real objects of these debates (*Contentious Traditions*, 79).

The mid-nineteenth century reflected a change in the governance of the Indian state, as control was consolidated in the colonial state known as the Raj. Widow remarriage and age of consent were prominent questions debated during this period in colonial state discourse like legislative debates and judicial decisions and in the colonial and metropolitan public sphere through the media and literary works. Deliberations about marriage reform in India reflected a tension between intervention and nonintervention in what were deemed cultural matters. Catherine Hall suggests, "The official British position on matters of religious practice amongst their subject people in India was one of toleration. In reality, however, the ascendance of liberal reforming perspectives towards India from the late 1820s meant there was intervention in matters that were seen as particularly undermining to British notions of civilization" ("Of Gender," 53). Conjugal law was not simply imposed on an Indian public—indeed, the colonial lawmakers rested their authority partially in this separation and ostensible noninterference in native matters concerning family. In the mid-nineteenth century, British administrators in India centralized, unified, and codified laws in the interest of efficient colonial rule by splitting law into two spheres. They replaced local criminal justice systems by British law and applied Hindu and Islamic law as "personal" law in matters relating to marriage, divorce, inheritance, succession, custody, and guardianship of children (Sunder Rajan, *Scandal,* 46). This had several effects. First, it unified formerly diverse legal practices. For example, Muslim legal practices that existed in colonial India were subsumed under a uniform and consistent code of Islamic law, and this universal set of rules was applied to every person who identified with Islam (Jamal, "Gender," 292). Second, under colonial rule, religion was granted authority as a guide for family law, including marriage (Carroll, "Law," 2).

As the discourse on sati shows, the colonial state promoted versions of culture not simply as a kind of respect for other cultures but as a means for ruling through selectively empowered groups. Colonial regulations and discourse surrounding conjugal reform worked with certain aspects of Indian society, selectively empowering those elements while disempowering others. As Tanika Sarkar argues, "it is apparent that colonial structures of power compromised with—and indeed learnt much from—indigenous patriarchy and upper-caste norms and practices which, in certain areas of life, retained considerable hegemony" (*Hindu Wife,* 194). These reforms emerged in dialogue with an elite educated class in India, primarily in Bengal, and thus conjugal reform was determined by the few for the many.

For example, the 1856 Hindu Widows' Remarriage Act was enacted in response to social reform agitation organized by Pandit Vidyasagar to allow women to legally remarry. Yet, members of lower castes (Sudra, Dalit), which represented approximately 80 percent of Hindus, did not practice child marriage, nor did they prohibit widow remarriage (Carroll, "Law," 2). Thus, as the colonial discourse responded to the issues in the colonial space, it also framed those issues. Colonial lawmakers interpreted authoritative religion in terms of their own values and priorities, even as they presented these interpretations as authentic cultural traditions. They ascribed a cultural authority to Brahminism, modeling their version of religion on the hierarchical structures of European religion. They focused on the textual aspects of Hinduism as a religious guide when that had not been the previous model (Carroll, "Law," 2). To transform a practicing, dynamic, interpretive religion into reified form, certain texts were validated as seminal. Furthermore, certain Brahmin pundits, or spiritual leaders, were authorized to interpret these texts (Carroll, "Law," 2). After 1857, the colonial state increasingly sought to limit intervening in family matters and deferred to local Hindu authorities and regional differences (Sarkar, *Hindu Wife*, 199). These authorities included, by the end of the nineteenth century, a body of Hindu lawyers and judges, despite the fact that Brahminic practices were not hegemonic and the laws concerning that caste did not always extend to other castes (Sarkar, *Hindu Wife*, 209). Thus, even as colonial law entrenched Brahminic understandings and codes as an authoritative marker of custom, and colonial reformers selectively debated the civility of those customs, they foreclosed alternate practices.

Given the way conjugality became an articulating point for the nation, it is not surprising that conjugal practices attracted the attention of nationalist reformers like Mohandas Gandhi in the early twentieth century. For Gandhi, a primary point of contact between nationalism and conjugality was in the promotion of exogamy in the form of intercaste marriage. After first supporting prohibitions in 1920, Gandhi, influenced by B. R. Ambedkar, revised his opinion to advocate lifting taboos, arguing that "restriction on inter-dining and intercaste marriage is no part of Hindu religion" (Gandhi, *My Soul's Agony*, 5). He argued, moreover, that such prohibitions were weakening Hindu society. Moving more militantly toward advocating intercaste marriage, by 1946, he advocated upper-caste intermarriage with the Harijan, or Dalit, caste, thought of as "untouchable." Gandhi's changing position on one of the primary structures of arranged marriage should be read as a political strategy as well as moral conviction. He was advocating superseding the caste system as a way to strengthen the nation. Gandhi well understood the multiple endogamous structures encoded by conjugal practices and sought not so much to eradicate arranged marriage as to use its powerful discourse toward nationalist political ends.

Public discourse has focused on conjugal practices as a disciplinary site for constituting notions of modernity in postcolonial India. Prime Minister Nehru also recognized the centrality of conjugal relationships to a modern national imaginary as he made marriage reform a priority for the newly independent nation. In the first decade after independence, India saw the passage of two important laws, the Special Marriage Act in 1954, which defined civil marriage, and the Hindu Marriage Act of 1955, which was part of the Hindu Code bill that formalized Hindu personal law aimed at equalizing social laws, such as those of marital inheritance. By pushing forward these two bills, Nehru made an effort to nationalize the arena of marriage in keeping with other modernization campaigns of this postcolonial period (Majumdar, *Marriage*, 208).

The tension between state and community continued to be played out through conjugal discourse in India's postcolonial period. That community was concerned with "the domestication of female sexuality through primary marriage, the role of the marriage in forging appropriate affinal and kinship relations, and the appropriate expansion of the social group through the birth of children, in particular, males" (Mody, *Intimate State*, 192). These reforms were not so much about affording new powers to women, though the rhetoric of uplift was certainly there, as they were about an attempt to shift power from community to state. The nature of marriage—at what age men or women may get married or who may sanction a marriage, for example—became central to this power struggle. At stake was not just the question of marriage or jurisdiction but the very heart of legal subjectivity, as the Special Marriage Act sought to shift the object of rights from the village, caste, or ethnoreligious community to the individual, who was a constituent of the state (Mody, *Intimate State*, 240).

Despite Nehru's efforts, the Indian state's secular vision did not fully enclose the arena of practice. Reformers were not able to displace the powerful role of community at the heart of marriage that functions through ritual and is symbolized by the joint family. Conjugal reform became a place to see this disjunction between law and the practices of local communities. Majumder notes that even after the Hindu Code bill, "Indian marriage and divorce laws manifest a peculiar combination of emphasis on ritual performance and liberal rhetoric at the same time" (*Marriage*, 225). Sunder Rajan describes how the subsequent compromise between the state and these community-bound rituals affected women disproportionately, as the state sought to protect religion, only to undermine the equal rights of women. Thus, despite the sovereignty of the state in this early postcolonial period, communities continued to mediate the relationship between the state and individuals (Mody, *Intimate State*, 241, 253). The powerful borderline was occupied by the joint family, a symbolic, legal, and economic entity that was central to the constitution of religious, class, caste, linguistic, and regional communities.

For Muslims under colonial rule, as well, a parallel set of two, sometimes conflicting public and personal laws continued into the twentieth century, first under colonial rule, then within the independent nations of Pakistan and Bangladesh. The Shariat Application of 1937, a personal law that regulated marriage-related issues like divorce, property, succession, and remarriage, was later incorporated into Pakistani and then Bangladeshi law, becoming foundational to those new nations (Esposito and DeLong-Bas, *Women*). After 1947, the new Pakistani nation, which comprised at the time West Pakistan and East Pakistan, reflected a dynamic relationship between these different components of civil and Islamic law. An integrated concept of an Islamic republic took shape around questions of conjugality, representing political, social, and economic changes. After the civil war, Pakistan's 1973 constitution guaranteed a series of fundamental rights for women and men but mediated these within Islam to determine constitutional validity. The regime of General Zia-ul Haq from 1977 to 1988 intensified a program of Islamization that has shaped the present-day relationships between women, the state, their communities, and their families, with the emphases on issues of honor and disciplining extramarital sexuality. Thus the Pakistani state enacted a distinctive reconfiguration of the private and the public, in which areas typically designated private, such as sexuality, personal relationships and liaisons, and modes of dress, are deemed to be matters of public interest, while other issues typically designated as public have been subsumed under the private rights of families and communities (Jamal, "Gender," 300).

Since Bangladesh gained independence in 1971, the nation has moved from more secularly oriented governance in the period of its formation with the Awami League to more overt Islamicization, reflecting the increasing importance of the Jama'at-i-Islami (Feldman, "[Re]presenting," 48). Feldman argues that political Islam, or the expression of politics in terms of Islam, formed in the breach created in Bangladesh between "an outward-looking entrepreneurial elite, and a consequent loss of various economic and political benefits for a segment of urban elite and rural petty bourgeois and agricultural interests" (35). Islamist parties have carved out a place in this breach by reclaiming social practices (36). These social practices include forms of arranged marriage that draw on a discourse of Islam. Bangladesh continues to be shaped by the separation of personal laws that guide family and marriage, which are based in a version of Shari'a for that predominantly Muslim country, and secular state law. As Dina Siddiqi notes in her analysis of forced marriage in Bangladesh, while marriage lies within the seemingly private realm, as a public institution, marriage is the political face of a religious community. Thus, she argues, a community might "absorb a certain amount of transgressive behaviour" that remains in the private realm, but "marriages that are potentially disruptive to kinship and political alliances, community, caste, and class boundaries frequently provoke opposition. The situation becomes especially volatile when existing power relations are disrupted through larger economic and political processes" ("Of Consent," 295). The contemporary perspective on forced marriage views the strictures placed on Islamic women as the product of a cultural identity that places a censorious emphasis on values like honor and shame, but Siddiqi interprets the important place of marriage as spanning the private and public such that an arranged marriage becomes a key public performance emerging from the political and economic *interests* of a community rather than an expression of tradition.

In summary, colonial and nationalist discourses in South Asia initiated certain tendencies within the arranged marriage discourse that have helped shape its form in the diaspora. In constituting a version of modernity, these conjugal discourses carved out a space of tradition identified with religion that was seemingly separate from the state but ultimately subject to its construction. This separation simultaneously displaced the family as an economic and legal locus, while investing it with symbolic force. Women became the "ground" (Mani, *Contentious Traditions,* 79) for this discourse, the object of reform, yet themselves without agency. These colonial and nationalist discourses located religious tradition in the realm of the private, constituting an alternative realm structured by the powerful discourse of conjugality. As in the colonial and postcolonial contexts, in the contemporary diaspora, that arena has become a powerful locus for the articulation of a nationalist resistant identity, and the relative power of that communitarian collectivity is once again in debate.

Arranged Marriage and the Construction of Community

In the contemporary period, a set of conjugal discourses that push to the fore a notion of community inscribes the concept of arranged marriage and its accompanying social formations through the idea of culture. Intersecting discourses of religion, caste, gender, and sexuality, among others, invigorate this arranged marriage subject, beneath the "scattered hegemonies" (Grewal and Kaplan, *Scattered Hegemonies*) of transnational contexts. As Inderpal Grewal advises, "if feminist practices are to address the multiply constituted and linked hegemonic formations (not only of class or capital) that operate upon women's lives, then these practices must emerge from understanding the transnational localisms that constitute sites of struggle" ("Women's Rights," 348). By using a discursive analysis to analyze the production of these localized communitarian subjects, this section proposes to do several things. First, it attempts to upend the way that culture (cultural practice, cultural values) is too often conceptualized as a set of predetermined, long-standing rules and instead conceptualizes culture as a dynamic, albeit historically situated, practice. Thus, second, it reads how arranged marriage in the South Asian diaspora has become a means to articulate an oppositional identity and a politics of affiliation in a global context marked by the histories of colonialism, neocolonialism, and immigrant experiences of differentiation. Third, this section provides an intersectional approach to the idea of community that reads the concept of collectivity as constituted *through* the discourses of sexuality, gender, caste, and religion rather than as providing a script for those identities. In that way, it follows the genealogy of the last section out of the colonial and postcolonial periods to show how South Asian marriage in the diaspora continues to be the site for the articulation of cultural nationalism in ways that are deeply politicized. Following that process to one of its extremes, the end of this section interprets how political projects of communalism have mobilized narratives of community constituted by arranged marriage discourses and practices.

Globally, a range of communities have turned to arranged marriage as an oppositional symbol that coheres the collective against the global force of Westernization. Speaking of contemporary India, Perveez Mody describes how "the pleasures of the 'joint family' lifestyle and of being 'respected and respectful members of society'... derive inexorably from the critical point of departure—the arranged marriage—such that the way one marries continues to define the moral essence of one's personhood and provides the strata on which one builds all relationships, including that with the modern nation and globalised world" (*Intimate State*, 45). Just as narratives of love provide an "indestructible grounding for our life" (May, *Love*, 6) in an individualist narrative, the collective of the joint family becomes foundational. Mody argues in the context of India that "arranged marriages must be valourised because they indicate a resistance to the moral values depicted by the wealth and bodily-bedazzling images of the Western world that both tantalise and bewilder Indians" (*Intimate State*, 45). Across South Asia, arranged marriage, already the most prevalent practice by far, has been ideologically reinvigorated, especially for middle-class subjects.

This transnationally circulating narrative of anti-Westernization is threaded through the articulations of arranged marriage as a diasporic practice resistant to assimilation. In representations both by and about South Asians, arranged marriage comes to function as a diacritical marker of national or ethnic origin—a way to "be" Indian, Pakistani, or Bangladeshi, to belong to a particular religion or caste, and to identify with "South Asian" more generally. While these discourses have historical roots in the way nationalist movements turned to marriage practices as a means to cohere and express their identities, they have also been shaped by the processes of migration and integration. Arranged marriage promotes the reproduction of social relations within the diasporic community to assert ethnic or religious belonging in a way that is contrary to dominant notions of assimilation. For example, South Asian parents in the diaspora see religion as an "efficient means for curbing the effects of acculturation" (Mohammad-Arif, "Religion," 167). These marriages might be transnational marriages, or they might be between members of the diaspora, but in either case, they function to materially and symbolically connect a diasporic community to an imagined homeland, even as they build the strength of the South Asian community in, say, Leicester, England; Edison, New Jersey; or Toronto, Ontario.

There is a common idea that a second generation resists such affiliation. Many representations of arranged marriage, especially those in the mainstream media, show a second generation rebelling against what are seen as the antiquated customs of their parents by choosing intercultural intimate relationships. As the young Gogol puts it in Jhumpa Lahiri's novel *The*

Namesake, arranged marriage is "something at once unthinkable and unremarkable" (138). The idea of a second generation resisting a first generation's conjugal practices forms one of the most familiar tropes of arranged marriage in ethnographic research and public policy, as much as in fiction. Karen Leonard, for example, asserts that the "generational clash is strongest on the issue of marriage" (*South Asian Americans,* 159). A *Toronto Star* article suggests that "Western culture looks like freedom" to young people who resist arranged marriage ("Indian Wives").

Recent scholars have questioned this assumption of intergenerational conflict. Lisa Lowe argues that such a singular way of understanding the experiences of displacement obscures differences within class, gender, and national diversities. These differences cut across the horizontal lines that separate generations such that each layer can no longer be considered a homogeneous set and connections may be seen between two or three generations along the line of certain discourses and practices (Lowe, *Immigrant Acts,* 63). These heterogeneous histories mobilize the continuing importance of arranged marriage. In her ethnography of second-generation South Asians, Bandana Purkayastha describes both Indian American and Pakistani American children of immigrants who embrace the practice as a grounding point for the expression of their ethnic identity and national culture *(Negotiating).* In Shalini Shankar's study of South Asian youths in Silicon Valley, young people reproduce social structures with an eye toward investing in the future communities to which they aspire to belong; she finds that the ways these youths are brought up emphasizes endogamous practices that advocate relationships within the community, though the construction of that community may be caste, religion, or even a vaguely ethnically identified desi identity (*Desi Land,* 171). Arranged marriage in particular, which teens witness among their older cousins and siblings, becomes a defining marker of belonging, and the teens "value it as a means of remaining in their communities" (183). Sunaina Maira identifies the importance of authenticity to the second generation:

> For many of the youth I spoke to, the notion of being "truly" or "really" Indian involved possession of certain knowledge or participation in certain activities, and these criteria differentiated those who were more essentially ethnic from those who were not. (*Desis in the House,* 88)

Dating and courtship practices are key signifiers in these processes of seemingly authentic identification.

These imagined communities are not necessarily geographically proximate. Avtar Brah describes a diaspora space, rather than diaspora, that "includes the entanglement of the genealogies of dispersion with those of 'staying put'" (*Cartographies,* 181). Transnational communities live their lives in geographically separate but intertwined spaces in which social relationships are not necessarily experienced more intensely in the bounded geographical territory (Rouse, "Mexican Migration," 10). Fictional works represent such networked sets of communities that span the globe in affective as well as social and material relations. The actions of characters in Jhumpa Lahiri's *The Namesake* reverberate in the extended family in Bengal as well as in the professional Bengali community living in the Boston area. In Simon Chambers's documentary *Every Good Marriage Begins with Tears,* the father worries that his daughter's actions with her newly arranged husband will ruin their reputation, not in Britain, where they live, but in his ancestral village in Bangladesh, where he sends much of his money to build property to establish and maintain his symbolic presence.

The processes of community affiliation are also not necessarily pleasurable ones, as Chambers's and many other works make clear. Shankar finds that South Asian teens in California are held by the fear of censure within closely knit communities if they deviate from scripted conduct (*Desi Land,* 177). This pressure of community reputation is one highlighted in many of the forced marriage memoirs discussed in chapter 3 that depict how gossip about social behavior patrols the line between a "good family" and one censured by the community. In looking at this phenomenon, one might be tempted to separate volitional community members from those who are coerced, or people who want to follow the script from those who resist, but even these critical memoirs challenge such definitive lines in community belonging by showing how emotionally and logistically difficult it is for people to fully exit a community.

A better approach, then, is to look at the production of both good and bad (not fully interpellated) subjects through communitarian discourses that are themselves changing. Such an approach also serves to undo reified notions of culture. The discourses of sexuality, gender, caste, and religion are critical in constituting an arranged marriage subject in collective terms within an intimate arena. Such discourses function affectively as well as ideologically, producing embedded mediated subjects that are "emotional, embodied, desiring, creative and feeling, as well as rational, creatures" (Mackenzie and Stoljar, "Introduction," 21).

Arranged marriage has historically defined South Asian communities through heteronormativity, meaning that the ideas and practices associated with arranged marriage have constructed heterosexuality as normal, and social relations are dependent on that model. Ayub Khan-Din's play *East Is East* begins with the scene of an arranged marriage wedding, in which the oldest son of a conservative Pakistani immigrant stops the ceremony, presumably because the son is gay. As this play shows, given the important emblematic status of arranged marriage in the South Asian community as a marker of community, the placement of same-sex unions outside the bounds of the practice functions as a disciplinary force as to who may legitimately belong to those communities. In other words, if arranged marriage is a way to "be" Indian, or Pakistani, or Bangladeshi, or Hindu, Sikh, Muslim, Jain, or Christian, for example, that symbolic performance is only possible in a heterosexual union, and, more specifically, in a marriage. In South Asia, where most marriages are arranged, the normativity of arranged marriage forces the discussion about sexual identity into the framework of conjugality: as Sandip Roy puts it, "coming out in India is really about marriage" (Roy, "What It's Like"). Roy goes on to say that the classic coming-out line for Indians is "Mom, Dad, I don't think I'm going to get married." Anyone who steps outside such unions has not generally had access to the representational status of arranged marriage. Because arranged marriage as a practice has disempowered lesbian, gay, bisexual, and transgender (LGBT) people by excluding them from community belonging, representations of same-sex arranged marriage have almost always advanced an individualist rather than collective subject that is based in notions of sexual freedom rather than duty.

In a small but growing arena, that is changing. A new website, *Arranged Gay Marriage*, caters to South Asian Americans and promotes arranged marriages among same-sex couples. A widely reproduced newspaper matrimonial ad placed by a mother for a husband for her gay rights activist son appeared in 2015 (Pandey, "Harrish Iyer"). The ad made headlines internationally with its intention to liberalize arranged marriage to include same-sex marriage but received some criticism for stating that, though caste was no bar, an Iyer caste was preferred in the prospective groom (Jaiswal, "Old Custom"). The recalibration of same-sex marriage within communitarian discourses is not limited to the website and ad but also includes other speculative forms (for what is a matrimonial ad if not speculative), such as conjecturing or ironic humor, that suggest the primacy of nation, religion, or caste. In a piece about his friends' same-sex marriage, media commentator Sandip Roy imagines such a possible future and offers the anecdote about a Chinese friend whose family would prefer that he be gay with a Chinese partner and children rather than single in his forties. This anecdote and the matrimonial ad suggest that endogamy might be more important than sexual preference, at least in the hypothetical realm. The British comedy show *Goodness Gracious Me* spoofs this cultural nationalism in a skit in which a son brings home his male lover. Upending the viewers' expectations that South Asian British parents will find an insurmountable problem in their son's sexual orientation, the skit's punch line comes when the mother and father wonder why their son couldn't have found a nice Indian boy (Sardana et al., "Gay Son"), a joke built on the power of Indian nationalism. In fact, the prospective groom in the earlier mentioned matrimonial ad has suggested in an interview that his mother listed caste preference as a similar inside joke (Jaiswal, "Old Custom"). Although the queering of the arranged marriage discourse suggests new possibilities for the future, the practice is so strongly dependent on heteronormative gender roles within the family that such roles would have to alter to produce new communitarian narratives based in same-sex marriage—something many secularist LGBT activists do not want (Jaiswal, "Old Custom").

Another discourse of sexuality that coheres notions of diasporic community through arranged marriage is that of sexual purity idealized in the virginity of the unmarried and the faithfulness of the married. Some more cosmopolitan groups, both in the subcontinent and in the diaspora, view sexual experience as a common and "private" matter for both women and men. A short video on arranged marriage in India represents the young woman rebuffing her suitor's questions as to whether she considers herself sexual with the line "that's a very private question" (Krishnamachari, *Arranged Marriage*). However, the narrative of sexual purity, especially but not exclusively for women, is far more pervasive and crosses national, religious, caste, and class lines. Though chastity has long been tied to arranged marriage both in the subcontinent and in the diaspora, arguably, and ironically, one sees an increased emphasis on this in popular representations circulating transnationally since the 1990s. For example, Sanjay Leela Bhansali's widely disseminated 2002 version of *Devdas* explicitly establishes the character Paro's sexual chastity at the time of her marriage, as she comments that nothing happened in her unchaperoned evening alone with Devdas. Neither Sarat Chandra Chattopadhyay's original 1917 novel nor Bimal Roy's 1955 film version unequivocally makes that point. One might argue that Bhansali's later version deals with the introduction of that possibility proscribed in the earlier versions—in other words, the 1917 reader or the 1955 viewer would never imagine that Paro was unchaste by the time of her wedding. However, the more contemporary film also makes Paro's fidelity a far more contentious issue in her marriage. In the earlier versions, the arranged marriage between Paro and a widower appears more as a socioeconomic arrangement than the narrative of sexual possession that appears in the 2002 film. Bhansali represents the articulation of female chastity in the context of arranged marriage as an expression of idealized womanhood in a period of liberalization. The expression of this chastity constitutes narratives of traditionalism focused on what Sunder Rajan calls the "New Indian woman," which use the image of the chaste wife, identified with Hinduism, to inflect versions of modernity with idealized versions of India's past (*Real,* 129).

This interpretation of the shifting representations of sexuality in film suggests that the discourses of arranged marriage construct and reinforce gender roles as well as those of sexuality as a means for constituting forms of community. As a heteronormative practice, arranged marriage would appear to equally affect men and women. However, as in the colonial and nationalist periods in South Asia, women have become the grounds for a contemporary transnational arranged marriage discourse, meaning most of the discussions about arranged marriage, positive and negative, are about brides. Being a bride in an arranged marriage becomes a way to be an Indian (or Pakistani, or Bangladeshi, or South Asian) woman. Just as a masculinist discourse has cast arranged marriage as filial duty, belonging here takes the form of making the same decisions as one's female ancestors. In Vikram Seth's novel *A Suitable Boy,* Lata's mother asks, "What on earth had got into the girl? What was good enough for her mother and her mother's mother and her mother's mother should be enough for her" (22). Such a perspective dislocates the practice from historical and personal specificity and connects women through their shared practices over generations. The arranged marriage practice in India (and elsewhere) relies on several well-rehearsed concepts of what constitutes suitable, terms that are repeated throughout Seth's novel and include "good family" (418), "educated" (418), "wife material" (597), and "sober" (940). Suitable means appropriate, but also embedded in the values of the family and community; a suitable love is based in commitment to the collective. Lata, the heroine of the novel, comes to accept the framework of suitability in her considerations of love and individual satisfaction and chooses a suitable boy with her mother's approval. Seth, writing from his temporary home in California, presents the search for a suitable future in the context of both a U.S. diaspora and an economically liberalizing India that project the values of family and community, and normatively affirming arranged marriage through a marriage plot becomes the way to do that.

Transnational arranged marriage becomes a locus for articulations of masculinity as well as femininity. Several diasporic works, including Ayub Khan-Din's play *East Is East* (as well as Damien O'Donnell's film) and Bali Rai's 2001 novel *(Un)Arranged Marriage,* represent the disavowal of arranged marriage as a defining moment for a man whose adulthood is produced through cultural conflict. Conversely, arranged marriage may be seen as bringing a man into his responsibilities to the family. In O'Donnell's film version of Khan-Din's play, the father, George, says, "Pakistani believe that if father ask son marry, son follow instruction." In Rai's story of a young British Sikh man, a father who has manipulated his son into an arranged marriage tells his son, "You are one of us. Ours. I know things have been wrong between us, I know. But haven't I made you a real man? Haven't I?" (251). "Ours" in this context means Punjabi. The discourse ties ethnic nationalism to masculinity through the ideal of arranged marriage. Both these works present arranged marriage critically, turning arranged marriage into the issue of conflict in an intergenerational struggle.

As well as sexuality and gender, another important aspect of community articulated through arranged marriage is caste, a category used in the subcontinent and diaspora by Hindus as well as Sikhs, Muslims, Christians, and members of other religions. Although some argue that caste, and especially subcaste, is becoming less important for many South Asians in the diaspora (Indo-Canadian Women's Association, *International Arranged Marriages,* 27), it is still relevant, and arranged marriage remains a locus for its expression. In an ethnographic study, Shankar found that caste, which is an "otherwise invisible topic" within diasporic communities, reappears prominently in arranged marriage (Shankar, *Desi Land,* 184). The reasons for this might be the positioning of a community in relation to a mainstream. In her study of suburban South Asian Americans, Purkayastha found that one subject felt he had to uphold caste traditions in the United States precisely because they are increasingly ignored there (Purkayastha, *Negotiating*, 102). Matrimonial advertisements on transnational websites like Shaadi.com, BharatMatrimony.com, or Muslima.com form an active site for the construction of caste communities, as advertisements that specify for caste as well as religion perpetuate those groups by limiting the dating pool. One sees these structures in the search mechanisms: on Shaadi.com, the selection of the Hindu religion category includes more than three hundred types of communities, including caste. The fact that these categories are still relevant is apparent in the number of profiles that do not check "caste no bar." Even some of the advertisements that state "caste no bar" still list the caste of the profiled.

The bounds of a community do not remain the same; changes in marriage practices mark the (re)articulation of a community's identity in a dynamic context of diaspora. This might mean the liberalization of a community though more exogamous practices, but changes do not always represent increased flexibility. In thinking about globalization, theorists have posited the notion that increased mobility has produced more distinct rather than more fluid notions of identity. In no place is this more visible and contested than in the production of religious community.

Communities function as more than identity categories; they are also loci of power in the diaspora. Some of these discourses temper or outright reject the autonomous subject of agency in support of the communal one, expressing communalism, which idealizes a transhistorical political community that finds expression as a religious collectivity (Ahmad, *On Communalism*, xii). Although all expression of belonging may be understood as inherently political, communalism is distinct within the broader category this book has been calling communitarianism in the way communalism engages overtly and systematically in politics (Chandra, *Communalism*, 38). Arranged marriage becomes an important intimate site for the expression of these ideologies and strategies. This is true for different religions, but communalist Hinduism may provide a case in point. As Christophe Jaffrelot and Ingrid Therwath argue, "far from being a product of nostalgia, Hindu nationalism in the West is a carefully crafted graft first developed in the motherland then methodically spread around the world to serve ideological and strategic purposes" ("Western Hindutva," 44). Arranged marriage has an important role in communalism as both a signifier of tradition and a means for reproducing religions through endogamy. A website on global Hinduism that Jaffrelot and Therwath cite as articulating a Hindutva agenda suggests, "While not all marriages must be arranged, there is wisdom in arranged marriages, which have always been an important part of Hindu culture" (HinduNet, "Marriage"). The website connects arranged marriage and the sustenance of Hinduism. Another piece on the same site asks, "Must we marry within our religion?" and answers its own question with a resounding yes, warning, "When we marry outside our religion, we create disharmony and conflict for ourselves and our children." While these admonitions do not directly incite violence, and might initially appear simply to validate religious practices, as Internet texts on a website that also contains extensive anti-Muslim discourse, they enter into a global context in which intercommunal marriage has been met with violence, for example, the 2014 "Love Jihad" controversy centered on the Bharatiya Janata Party and its affiliate groups Rashtriya Swayamsevak Sangh and Vishwa Hindu Parishad (or World Hindu Council), which accused Muslim boys of forcing Hindu girls to marry them and convert to Islam (Verma, "ABVP"). In this discourse, the idea of endogamous marriage was held to denote an ideological identification based on fundamental Hindu values. This contemporary discourse in both the subcontinent and the diaspora sustains colonial and nationalist narratives of marriage as the locus for a highly politicized private sphere cohering around certain versions of religion. Although decolonization is no longer the object of such cultural nationalism, what is at stake is a resistant anti-Western communal identity within a globalizing context. Nadeem Aslam's *Maps for Lost Lovers*, discussed in chapter 2, represents how concepts of justice within that private sphere become an articulation point for Islamic communalism in a novel in which arranged and self-made relationships are counterpoised.

Choice, Culturalism, and the Conjugal Subject

Contemporary multiculturalist discourses that parse acceptable from unacceptable difference have made the conjugal subject of agency a kind of border. As Máiréad Enright puts it, "the boundary of belonging is drawn between acceptable cultural diversity and unacceptable cultural difficulty" ("Choice," 337), a boundary this book argues divides visions of agency. Communalism lies on the side of unacceptable cultural difficulty, but that does not mean that all visions of collectivity, or of arranged marriage, lie on that side. On the contrary, multicultural discourses have gone far to affirm forms of acceptable cultural diversity in the form of arranged marriage as choice. A contemporary diasporic discourse of community retains the ideal of the individual subject while affiliating through the concept of culture. This book identifies this discourse as expressed in a range of popular texts and describes it as a neoliberal one (chapter 5). Unlike communal discourses, these discourses of cultural belonging continue to embrace the ideal of individual will; moreover, their subjects are not constituted by the affective strategies of duty and responsibility but rather by the ideals of choice, personal satisfaction, and belonging. Within both communalist discourses and forced marriage rhetoric, choice is frequently presented as incompatible with tradition. However, in this discourse circulating globally among the elite in metropolitan centers, the ideas of choice and culture have been yoked together.

In the individualist narrative of arranged marriage, people decide to adhere to endogamous marriage practices through the discourse of choice. Diane Crespo and Stefan C. Schaefer's film *Arranged* (2007) offers this point in its positive representation of two women living in New York City who bond over their shared path of pursuing an arranged marriage. Although the film does not show South Asian women—one woman is an Orthodox Jew and the other a Syrian Muslim—the depiction presents many of the same validations that may be found in South Asian discourse. The women in the film find themselves in a culture seemingly oversaturated with sexual titillation, bodily familiarity between near-strangers, and casual romantic relationships in which the woman must coerce the man to become serious about marriage. Their own decisions are contested by well-meaning liberal feminists who want to save them from their families. At one point, Rachel, the Orthodox Jew, finally responds to her boss, a principal, who has been lecturing her on her oppression, by shouting that arranged marriage is her choice. An earlier discourse might use the language of duty instead—or not find it necessary to validate itself at all, because it is a given practice. For these members of a diaspora, arranged marriage is a choice that performs a cultural resistance, a way of being at odds with the dominant society that nonetheless reproduces its fundamental values of choice.

A similar kind of discourse emerges in the transnational South Asian popular culture novels that affirm arranged marriage. These novels show young Western women (mostly Indian American) choosing to pursue arranged marriage as a way both to connect to their identities and to escape what are presented as superficial relationships. The narrator of Monica Pradhan's *The Hindi-Bindi Club* presents this rationale as one character muses on how it goes against the commonplace narrative of assimilation that an American-born Indian would, as the heroine of one popular novel puts it, "contemplate something [she] always deemed impossible, dismissed as cold, archaic, backward. The mate-seeking process that served [her] parents, most of their Indian-immigrant friends, and generations of ancestors for centuries. An arranged marriage" (7). The character validates arranged marriage for its functionality, citing the practice as one that has "served," but she also connects that service to parents, Indian friends, and ancestors—in other words, community.

In the neoliberal context of a global professional workforce, this discourse of arranged marriage in the diaspora idealizes, but also sometimes modifies, a notion of culture in a process Smitha Radhakrishnan calls "cultural streamlining." In a study of a set of diasporic communities, Radhakrishnan identifies a version of Indian culture that is reproduced in simplified form among a transnational class of Indian information technology workers. These forms of culture both feature and rewrite the narratives of home and family such that they are compatible with the economic and geographic mobility of a global economy (*Appropriately Indian,* 4–5). Cultural streamlining functions in a transnational context of mobile subjects, producing a form of identification in which the formulation of community is limited to culture. The ideal of individualism is maintained in the neoliberal rhetoric of choosing to express cultural identity. This then is a neoliberal variant of "the fantasy of the liberal subject, the perspicacious and choosing 'I'" (Butler, "Judith Butler"): the fully formed subject chooses a selective version of community.

The mediation of arranged marriage discourses through the construction of an individual subject of agency has produced new narratives of sexuality. Some contemporary works attempt to negotiate the disjuncture between a liberated sexuality dependent on freedom and commitments to collectivity by narrating individual volition within the sexual practices of arranged marriage. Recent Bollywood films that circulate widely in a transnational context seek to bring arranged marriage into alignment with sexual autonomy. The husband in Sanjay Leela Bhansali's *Hum Dil De Chuke Sanam* (1999) waits for his wife to love him before he attempts to consummate the marriage. In Aditya Chopra's *Rab Ne Bana Di Jodi* (2008), the husband and wife are joined by the bride's father's wishes before he dies, but sexual intimacy is deferred until the wife is interested. In both these films, the decision to wait is put in the hands of the man, but in Vipul Amrutlal

Shah's *Namastey London* (2007), it is the woman who mandates a delay until she feels desire. In social media, one may find a striking polarization in the discourse about individual agency in sexual matters within arranged marriage. On the website Quora.com, the question "how does it feel to have sex with your spouse on your wedding night when he/she is a stranger?" draws about fifty answers, which range from "I was almost raped on my wedding night" to "he was gentle with me," to one that says he let his wife "set the pace for the sexual relationship," to one that says, "we didn't have sex on the wedding night because the whole thing felt awkward." Many heartfelt responses on the website advocate openly discussing sexual matters with one's spouse or even one's fiancé, if possible. The responses do more than report or imagine individual experiences (and given the nature of anonymous posts on the Internet, the veracity of any of them is uncertain); they show how the question of individual sexual agency affectively mobilizes the polarized debate about arranged marriage.

In this neoliberal form found in multiculturalist discourses, culture is not excised but rather featured, even as it appears as something added on after. The study of diasporic South Asian American youths has identified how communitarian practices among the second generation have been reinvigorated by transnational romantic narratives and the performance of culture. These visions also use idealized notions of culture reimagined through a discourse of consumption. Maira describes a "third place" as an emerging set of disparate, sometimes contradictory experiences and narratives *(Desis in the House)*. A keen desire to maintain identification with the subcontinent, along with an inability to assimilate to parents' versions of practices, motivates the construction of this third place. Other recent ethnographies have also been attuned to the nuanced ways in which a younger generation might express affiliation and reinvention, as well as refusal, of some of the practices that "circumscribe the locus of tradition" (88). Shankar finds that Bollywood films synthesize romantic narratives and stories of filial duty expressed through arranged marriage, creating an affective fantasy of arranged marriage, because, "especially in romantic comedies, a favorite genre among Desi teens, film heroes and heroines are often able to achieve the impossible balancing act of fulfilling family duty and obligation while participating in the attractive world of consumption, leisure, and young romance" *(Desi Land,* 173). Bakirathi Mani uses the concept of locality to "capture the affective experience of creating transnational communities across differences of generation, national origin, religion, and language" (*Aspiring to Home*, 3). Looking at South Asian beauty pageants, she interprets the ways that identity is mediated by location as second-generation immigrants create new forms of ethnic and national affiliation. Such performances require that the young women balance "the contentious relationship between preserving and perverting culture at this public event"; they do so through locality, "the means through which first- and second-generation immigrants, of varying regional, religious, and linguistic backgrounds, come to experience what it means to belong" (3). Such a performance finds its counterpart, with much higher stakes, in the affirmation, refusal, or reinterpretation of the practice of arranged marriage. Even the discursive engagement with arranged marriage constitutes such a performance in the sense that it continues to invest arranged marriage with a highly symbolic function.

In contemporary multicultural contexts, arranged marriage appears repeatedly as ancient culture. In an episode from the American television show *Outsourced,* the protagonist Todd, who is about to lose his Indian love interest to an arranged marriage, bemoans that he has to compete against "ten thousand years of tradition" (Borden, "Truly, Madly"). There is a powerful narrative about South Asia that presents arranged marriage as a tradition that has been passed down intact from antiquity. When Kiran finally stands in front of the sacred fire with her arranged husband in the popular Indian American novel *The Hindi-Bindi Club,* she imagines "brides and grooms who came before, over thousands of years, who stood as we are" (Pradhan, 395). Such notions are visible not only in cinema and literature; they also appear in legal documents. In the 2002 Scottish court case *Sohrab v. Khan,* addressing the annulment of an arranged marriage, justice Lord McEwan contextualized the case in terms of an eroding culture: "Eastern established cultural and religious ethics clash with the spirit of twenty first century children of a new generation and Western ideas, language and what these days passes for culture." The U.S. immigration forms on sponsoring a spouse's visa refer to "strict and long-established customs of the beneficiary's foreign culture or social practice, as where marriages are traditionally arranged" (U.S. Department of Homeland Security, "Fiancé[e] Visas"). Less liberal-mindedly, the Canadian forced marriage law is called the Zero Tolerance for Barbaric Cultural Practices Act, a name that locates the problem of violence within cultural inheritances.

A neoliberal discourse of multiculturalism divorces such culture from its economic or political entailments (Duggan, *Twilight,* xiv). At its core, the "arranged marriage as choice" discourse also relies on culturalist interpretations of arranged marriage, meaning notions of arranged marriage that are based in essential as opposed to dynamic notions of culture. Such culturalism has in the context of globalization become an ideology "which treats culture not only as an integral element in social practices but as the determining instance" (Ahmad, *On Communalism*, 95). Culturalism is the collapsing of social and material processes into a concept of culture that is naturalized, "as an unalterable and ahistorical fact of life" (Parekh, *Rethinking Multiculturalism*, 11). These reductions result in the "aestheticizing commodification" of difference along with a denial of "immigrant histories of material exclusion and differentiation" (Lowe, *Immigrant Acts*, 63). Culturalism has become a "determining instance" of the social practices of contemporary globalization (Ahmad, *On Communalism*, 95). A neoliberal discourses propagates culturalism in streamlined versions of identity, positive multiculturalist images of cultural difference ("ten thousand years of tradition"), and the more negative prohibitions that inform immigration as well as criminal policies ("Barbaric Cultural Practices"). In undoing the fetish of culture, one may look to the work of Aijaz Ahmad, who wishes to reinsert political economy into notions of culturalism; Stuart Hall, who argues that, "far from being eternally fixed in some essentialised past, [cultural identities] are subject to the continuous 'play' of history, culture and power" ("Cultural Identity," 394); and Clifford Geertz, who asks us to look at the "symbolic dimensions of social actions" (*Interpretation*, 30) in conceptualizing culture. In summary, it is important to shift the object of study away from locating and describing culture to look at how notions of culture perform in a politicized arena of representations and practices that are multicontextual, including different national and transnational communitarian contexts that are interrelated in a global field of power. In this way, we may come to recognize what social, political, and economic factors are at stake in constructing the subject of agency.

2

"Forced Marriage" and a Culture of Consent

In the late twentieth and early twenty-first centuries, the issue of arranged marriage has gained a prominent place in the British mainstream public consciousness. Conjugal practices have become a point of contestation as altered patterns of South Asian immigration increase family reunification and subsequent transnational relations reshape Britain's national culture. Formulations of marriage mark the border between acceptable and disruptive cultural difference in the national context (Enright, "Choice," 337). Multicultural discourses ostensibly give equal credence to different conjugal practices that locate decision making in individual or collective hands. However, these same discourses seek to draw absolute boundaries related to personal freedom. Much of the legal, media, and policy discourse has focused on differentiating arranged and forced marriage through the presence or absence of consent. Representations of arranged marriage, in particular discussions about the presence of force in such marriages, have become a way to chart a future for Britain by producing a subject of consent that is a rational individual with free will. At the same time, legal discourses have liberalized notions of duress, extending its range to account for psychological and emotional forces that overbear will. The dominant cultural discourses concerning forced marriage have been marked by increasing protectiveness, of the female subject especially, and constructed around the idea of enabling consent. However, these bureaucratic and media discourses have not fully recognized the structural elements that circumscribe acts of consent, elements that constitute the consenting subject. Moreover, these discourses draw on reified notions of tradition, in the process eliding the gendered transnational forces that help forge this subject. This chapter explores how various agents with vested political interests imagine the South Asian immigrant through the formulation of an increasingly variable notions of duress. In analyzing this construction of the subject of consent, this chapter uncovers the ambiguities, contradictions, and limitations in its representation within several overlapping public

67

discourses. It argues that, in considering the experiences of arranged marriage, we need to look more at how tacit or explicit consent is produced or denied in the context of transnational movement and relations. Whereas this chapter focuses on the key register of consent in the production of the acceptable immigrant, the next chapter locates that citizen in the imagined nation produced through multicultural discourses.

As well as offering its own interpretation of key legal cases and the discourse around them, this chapter assembles and interprets the ideas of feminist legal scholars who have carefully charted a critical path through the forced marriage debate (see Gill and Anitha, "Introduction"; Enright, "Choice"; Gagoomal, "Margin of Appreciation"; Phillips and Dustin, "U.K. Initiatives"; Proudman, "Criminalisation"). This chapter then brings some of their conclusions into conversation with artistic productions in an effort to push pass the impasse these scholars identify within law and to more fully elaborate the transnational subject of consent within the arranged marriage discourse. Literary and filmic texts present ways to rethink the premises of mainstream media and policy-oriented discourses that simultaneously focus on individual consent and pit such an individual against a notion of tradition. This chapter and the next seek to place the British legal, state, and media discourses concerning arranged marriage, as well as the activist influences and critiques of such discourses, in relation to a body of literature and film that sometimes elaborates and sometimes contests the understandings of these discourses. Although these works of fiction and film don't explicitly challenge the focus on consent, they may be interpreted to see ways of understanding conjugal decisions within the structural conditions of national and transnational contexts. Hanif Kureishi, Monica Ali, Ayub Khan-Din, Damien O'Donnell, Simon Chambers, and Nadeem Aslam show how the conditions of immigration generate new constructions of identity clustered around marriage practices. They reveal how global economies motivate migration and marriage. Their works represent how affective transnational relations connect metropolitan centers to distant villages to mobilize decisions around marriage. These authors and filmmakers show how transnational subjects rationalize arranged marriage practices through deterritorialized notions of law, as legal concepts based in Hindu or Muslim personal law are dislocated from the South Asian national context of origin and carried into the diaspora. They depict how the conditions of immigration are expressed in gendered form. In sum, the authors and filmmakers who represent arranged marriage in contemporary Britain reveal the myriad forces that come into play in immigrant conjugal practices, exposing the construction of consent within the dynamics of globalization—and the consenting subject as a situated product of those forces.

Arranged Marriage versus Forced Marriage

Although there had been legal discussions about force in arranged marriage since the first half of the twentieth century, the term *forced marriage* entered the popular lexicon only in the 1990s, and primarily in Britain rather than in North America. Prior to then, there was little public discussion about the need to separate the terms *arranged marriage* and *forced marriage*; British media reports regularly used the terms interchangeably (Kiley, "Forced Marriages"). A series of legal cases began to chart the idea of force, without necessarily referring to a crime known as forced marriage. Earlier studies of arranged marriage had not separated arranged marriage and forced marriage but rather included a range of consent within a conception of arranged marriage. In her 1978 article "Arranged Marriages in the British Context," for example, Catherine Ballard talks about the fact that, though most young Sikhs in her study in Leeds had some say in the choice of husband or wife, "a few had no say at all, either because the marriage was rushed through after a confrontation with their parents, or because it had been arranged informally long before they reached adulthood, usually to cement a political alliance between families, or again because they had decided that if they were going to accept an arranged marriage, then it should be done entirely by their parents 'in the traditional way'" (186). Noticeably absent in Ballard's discussion is the idea of "forced marriage" as a separate phenomenon. This is also true of earlier memoirs that detail abuse, such as Sharan-Jeet Shan's memoir *In My Own Name,* which uses the term "arranged marriage" throughout to describe a horrific experience of abuse. Following the end of the Primary Purpose Rule in 1997, which required foreign nationals to prove that the primary purpose of their marriage to a British citizen was not immigration to the United Kingdom, feminist and multicultural discourses about South Asian and/or Islamic women contributed to a distinct notion of forced, as opposed to arranged, marriage during a period of intense political discussion about immigration. The next chapter discusses the entanglement of immigration debates with legislation on forced marriage and the rise of popular media representations about forced marriage as an "honor crime" against South Asian women. It argues that in this discourse about criminalizing forced marriage, the state takes on the role of surrogate parent, supplanting the extended family that is the locus of decision making.

In talking about the concept and representations of forced marriage, this analysis necessarily interweaves with a discourse that has named both "arranged" and "forced" marriage and given the concepts political valence. Thus, before going further into an analysis of the assumptions of this late-twentieth-century discourse, it might be helpful to clarify how these terms have entered into the political discourse in contemporary Britain and to revisit choices regarding language within this book discussed in the introduction. This will also provide a rough sketch for how politically interested parties either conflate these terms or set them up in a binary; the fuller analysis of this is, in part, the subject of this chapter.

Anja Bredal offers an excellent discussion about the assumptions and agendas at work as different groups use the terms "arranged marriage" and "forced marriage" ("Arranged Marriage"). Although her article focuses on arranged and forced marriage in Norway, her schematic also applies to the context of Britain. Bredal sketches the outlines of two camps engaged in a debate about conjugal practices. She asserts that the discourse around arranged marriage has mapped these two camps onto the positions of, respectively, assimilationist and multiculturalist. Members of Bredal's assimilationist group basically see arranged and forced marriage as the same thing. They view arranged marriage as a kind of collectivism that threatens the autonomy of the individual; for this group, "the potential coercion is part of the very logic of collectivism, and is therefore intrinsic to this marriage practice" (81). When an individual conforms, they see her—for the object of this gendered discourse is usually a woman—as either a victim of false consciousness or fear. The multiculturalists take pains to distinguish arranged and forced marriage. Members of this group focus on the question of volition, categorizing arranged marriage and forced marriage based on the presence of consent. They reaffirm the value of arranged marriage and sometimes even direct attention to the problems associated with what Bredal calls "self-made marriages" (79), such as a high rate of divorce. Bredal cautions that neither of these categories comprehensively encompasses the range of positions and rationales inside of each, but the conflict between them expressed in the public arena has polarized each position (81–83).

The British discourse follows Bredal's schematic about Norway in many ways. In the British context, the positions have some powerful political rationales that make for alliances between otherwise disparate groups. For example, the first group of assimilationists includes those who oppose liberal immigration laws and see arranged marriage as a culturally retrogressive marital custom that comes with new immigrants. However, this group also includes several of the authors of the "escape memoirs" analyzed in the next chapter of this book, members of the South Asian British community who wish to draw attention to the kind of force that is disguised in all types of arranged marriage. Members of this assimilationist group suggest, either implicitly or explicitly, that all arranged marriage is fundamentally coercive.

The second group, the multiculturalists, differentiates arranged from forced marriage. Their position holds that arranged marriage may represent a positive experience, whereas forced marriage exploits aspects of the arrangement process, such as the influence of the family, to the point of emotional, psychological, or physical violence. They, and this includes British judges and policy makers, have looked to the presence of consent as the most important way to mark this opposition. The state discourse about arranged marriage in Britain now invariably differentiates arranged marriage and forced marriage using the idea of consent. For example, the document produced by the British government's 2000 working group on forced marriage states, "A forced marriage is a marriage conducted without the valid consent of both parties, where duress is a factor" (Ahmed and Uddin, *A Choice by Right*); the Forced Marriage (Civil Protection) Act of 2007 states, "For the purposes of this [section] a person ('A') is forced into a marriage if another person ('B') forces A to enter into a marriage (whether with B or another person) without A's free and full consent (2)." The group that has helped make consent the central concept in thinking through force in marriage includes reformers who have attempted to create special legal provisions to end practices like kidnapping and imprisoning for the purpose of coercing someone to wed. It also includes Muslim leaders, activists, and community workers who have argued that Islamic marital practices are always based on a notion of consent and are thus inherently antagonistic to forced marriage (Ind, "Helping").

A Culture of Consent

In the mainstream media, early discussions of arranged marriage did not necessarily feature a discussion of consent. Letter writers who emphasized the notion of consent did so in the context of explaining the prerequisite for consent in Islamic marriage (Zaigham, "Letter"; Aldridge, "Thursday

Women"). In the late 1990s, articles began to distinguish arranged and forced marriage on the basis of consent. For example, a 1998 article in the *Independent* states, "Although arranged marriages, with the consent of both sides, are still the norm in many sections of the community, forced marriages appear to be increasing, resulting in many young women and men running away from home" (Boggan, "Women's Groups," 2). In 1997, the Primary Purpose Rule was abolished, and the forced marriage discourse became part of a subsequent backlash against immigrant marriages. The Primary Purpose Rule, which had been encoded in immigration law since 1983 but made national policy in 1993, had required that foreign nationals prove that the primary purpose of their marriage to a British citizen was not for immigration to the United Kingdom. In other words, although marriage for the sole purpose of migration was still considered fraud, immigrants no longer had to prove the absence of such a motive. In the culture wars that followed the end to this rule, proponents of multiculturalism looked to distinguish arranged marriage from forced marriage as a way to validate acceptable forms of difference. The *A Choice by Right* document (Ahmed and Uddin) produced by the governmental working group on forced marriage, discussed in the next chapter, influenced the public discourse by using the idea of consent as a metric for acceptability, even if it was not the first to do so. Supporting this effort, media reports have also emphasized that "arranged marriages arrived at by consent are respected by the British Government" (Gordon, "Our Rickshaw Ride," 22).

This discourse about consent has now become the dominant one in Britain. Tellingly, some authors of memoirs who did not differentiate arranged marriage from forced marriage in their original work have reframed their work using this opposition. For example, Sharan-Jeet Shan did not use the consent-based language of the contemporary forced marriage discourse in her original 1985 memoir *In My Own Name,* instead representing arranged marriage more generally as repressive. However, by 1991, she had clarified in a new preface, "Indeed, I am certain that when a marriage is arranged with the complete consent of both partners and a thorough appraisal of each other's backgrounds, it stands a very good chance of success, maybe even a better chance than 'love marriages'" (ix). The shift here arguably represents a more general cultural reframing that parses arranged from forced marriages on the basis of consent.

Consent has long been considered the basis of legitimate marriage in human rights law, in which "marriage shall be entered into only with the free and full consent of the intending spouses" (United Nations, "Convention on Consent to Marriage"), and in British law, including the Marriage Act of 1949 and the Matrimonial Causes Act of 1973. British courts upheld this perspective when considering the legality of arranged marriages: "The first essential of a valid marriage is consent," one judgment put it (*Singh v. Singh*, 1971). The turn in the 1990s was not the use of consent to determine legitimate from illegitimate marriages; rather, what was different was the concentration on the concept of consent and its mobilization. The invocation of consent became totemic such that certain state actions could be taken in the name of a national cultural value of consent, as popular sentiment was mobilized behind such measures through reference to the same. Consent went from being a legal tool to being seen as a primary measure of degrees of difference. Moreover, the range of coercion has widened, making the idea of consent even more powerful, a point discussed more in what follows.

The idea of consent has unmistakable ethical and legal implications that are foundational to the practice of law, and it is rightly considered crucial in its measure of individual rights. Consent is also a notoriously slippery philosophical concept, and locating consent definitively has troubled both legal and legislative measures in the context of forced marriage. John Kleinig reviews some common ideas and offers the following definition: consent must be granted by an agent with capacity to grant consent; in Western law, this is almost always an "of age" individual with adequate mental capabilities. Kleinig notes that in many applications of the law, the "core of consent" is a "subjective mental state" ("Nature of Consent," 10). However, for him, consent is a kind of communicative contract: "Consent requires signification—not in the sense that a state of mind is reported but in the sense that a right or entitlement is created or permission given or obligation assumed" (11). By shifting from the psychological to the communicative, Kleinig opens the door to one thing being thought or felt and another being said. Alan Wertheimer, whose work on coercion helped clarify the notion of the choice prong in which a subject must be presented with two viable options, terms this granting of consent under duress "constrained volition" (*Coercion*, 9).

The very concept of arranged marriage arguably challenges contemporary British norms of marital consent by inserting either alternate or multiple subjects into conjugal decision making. The "agent" in an arranged marriage is not always the individual but might be family elders in addition to or instead of the individual—what this book is calling a collective subject of agency. A communicative moment is not always there, as children often enter into the practices of their families without any such speech act affirming or decrying a decision. Interpreting a 2006–7 research study in the United Kingdom on changes to the age of sponsorship, Gangoli and Chantler note that there may be an experiential slippage between the categories of arranged and forced marriage and that the partner might only retroactively characterize the experience as coercion ("Protecting Victims," 269), a phenomenon Monica Ali elaborates in her novel *Brick Lane*, discussed later. Furthermore, although there are certainly clear cases of involuntary acts (kidnapping, imprisonment, rape, or other forms of physical violence), and incidents in which the agent is not considered legally of age to grant consent, much of the annulment law concerning arranged marriage has been negotiating "constrained volition," in which the force is defined as a degree and mode of persuasion that has crossed the line into coercion. These legal decisions and the discourse around them chart the continuum between consent and coercion, "between which lie degrees of socio-cultural expectation, control, persuasion, pressure, threat and force" (Anitha and Gill, "Coercion," 165). The next section turns to the mapping of that gray area by British court cases.

The Liberalization of Duress

A close reading of British legal judgments concerning annulment reveals a marked emphasis on consent, but a more ambivalent encounter with what that means in the context of arranged marriage. Although the Marriage Act of 1949 wrote individual (versus parental) consent into the law, earlier and later judgments had taken into account criteria beyond a verbal communication moment, such as consummation (*Hussein [otherwise Blitz] v. Hussein*, 1938; *Singh v. Singh*). The more recent judgments have clearly invested the notion of consent with increased significance, as consent has become the key to determining legitimate from illegitimate marriage. Unlike divorce, which allows for legal separation, an annulment questions the very validity of marriage. A decree of nullity allows the petitioner to claim to have never been married, which in South Asian cultures is important for both women and men in terms of remarriage prospects. Furthermore, in Britain, an annulment allows for immediate termination of the union, as opposed to waiting a year. Petitioners have thus sought annulments rather than divorce, and courts have turned to consent as a way to resolve questions of legitimacy. Even as the presence or absence of consent has become the lynchpin for nullity cases, however, the rulings in these cases have also exposed the continuum of coercion—and thus the changing scale of consent. Specifically, the courts have expanded the range of what might be legally considered force in a way that suggests possible further extension. In this way, the cases of common law have liberalized the notion of duress. In their entirety, the rhetoric of these judgments about the validity of marriage may be read to understand a contemporary British culture of consent and the role of this in the imagination of a contemporary nation based on the individual subject of free will. This is not to argue that Britain is the only nation to create a culture of consent around arranged marriage (indeed, as chapter 4 argues, Canada has also increasingly moved in this direction) but rather to offer a case study, to show how this process has been embroiled with a particular transnational context of South Asian immigration and assimilation.

The earliest legal interpretations of conjugal coercion dealt in relatively clear terms of physical force. In 1938, the British courts ruled on a case in which an Egyptian man allegedly threatened an eighteen-year-old girl with death unless she married him. The record cites duress as the basis of the case but also specified that the petitioner had never lived with her husband, nor was the marriage consummated *(Hussein)*. The decision made a British legal precedent by allowing for the threat of physical force to be cause for annulling the marriage. With this decision, the court determined that a marriage created under the intimidation of physical duress is null and void.

Until the early 1970s, the courts continued to interpret coercion in terms of a will "overborne by genuine and reasonably held fear caused by threat of immediate danger (for which the party is not himself responsible), to life, limb, or liberty, so that the constraint destroys the reality of consent to ordinary wedlock" (*Szechter [otherwise Karsov] v. Szechter,* 1971). In the 1971 *Singh v. Singh* case, the court cited this earlier decision to rule against a woman who was petitioning to void her marriage, as she was "induced to enter into it by duress and coercion exercised upon her by her parents" and did and could not consummate the marriage because "she evinced an invincible repugnance to him." Although the court argued that "duress depended upon a finding of fear," and did not find evidence of such fear, the proceedings referenced a broader discussion about arranged marriage, in the sense that the petitioner's agent argued for the pressure felt by a younger generation that had "revis[ed] their ideas about marriages which have been arranged by their parents" *(Singh v. Singh).* The bride asserted that she had gone through the ceremony because "she was bound by her parents, mother and father." Thus both the agent and the petitioner offered a more comprehensive vision of constraint than the one that prevailed in the legal decision. Commenting on this case shortly after, legal scholar David Pearl questioned the decision to refuse an annulment, asserting, "It is hard to see why a fear of social ostracism from the family and the community should not produce a reasonably held fear of such proportions that the will of the girl is overpowered by the will of others" ("Arranged Marriages," 207). Pearl's use of the term "overpowered" evokes the kinds of familial structural power arrangements circumscribing the question of consent here. A young woman who is "bound," but who supposedly did not express fear, is an inchoate subject around whom the question of consent becomes problematic.

Although the Matrimonial Causes Act of 1973 recognized the role of psychological, emotional, and financial coercion in compulsion to marry (Proudman, "Criminalisation," 462), it did not have enough legal impact to change the judgment in the 1981 case *Singh v. Kaur,* in which a Sikh man sought to annul his marriage to a girl from India under one section of the act. In this case, the petitioner highlighted economic and communal elements as potential causes of force: he stated that he was threatened with the family's disgrace, ostracism from home, and a subsequent loss of income unless he agreed to the marriage. Judge Ormrod held up the burden of proof set by *Singh v. Singh* and refused the petition. He noted the cultural context of Britain and the negative implications of the judgment for the many arranged marriages, opining, "It would be a very serious matter if this court were... to water down Sir Jocylen Simon's test [of immediate danger]... because there are many of these arranged marriages" *(Singh v. Kaur).*

Pearl's comments about reasonably held fears overpowering the will anticipated the trajectory of the law during the next decade, as a subsequent series of judgments elaborated the notion of a threat to liberty. The 1980s were a period of change for the courts, which adjudicated annulment cases from immigrant marriages in which there was a claim of coercion. These legal cases sought to differentiate arranged marriage from forced marriage in terms of consent. The law became especially invested in determining the nature of coercion, and cases on arranged marriage transformed legal understandings of volition and force. This was the period during which the understanding of consent underwent the most change in terms of the law. The watershed 1982 legal case of *Hirani v. Hirani* judged that coercion to marry could take place through emotional force as well as threat of bodily harm. In this case, a nineteen-year-old Hindu girl claimed that she married her parents' choice because they told her she had to or leave home, where she would have no means of support. Judge Ormrod argued, "The crucial question in these cases, particularly where a marriage is involved, is whether the threats, pressure or whatever it is, is such as to destroy the reality of consent and overbears the will of the individual" (502). This decision expanded the definition of duress by seeking a "reality of consent" and probing the construction of will; in doing so, the judgment pushed legal decision making further into a gray area. In the words of legal scholar A. Bradney, the plea for duress under family law became "a conceptual muddle" ("Duress," 963), one that was producing a different version of consent in determining the validity of marriage than used in other contract law or in criminal law (964–65).

Subsequent court cases about conjugal coercion in both England and Scotland began to account for extreme sorts of emotional pressure, such as threats of suicide by the coercer (e.g., a parent). The change here represented a displacement from threat to the body of the individual to threat to the emotional person. Take, for example, the Scottish case of *Mahmud v. Mahmud* (1994). Mahmud was a thirty-year-old man living with a non-Muslim woman with whom he had children. His family pressured him to marry for ten years, telling him it was his father's dying wish and blaming him for his father's death. After proceeding with a ceremony in Glasgow to his cousin from Pakistan, he filed a claim of falsity with immigration and appealed to the court to annul the marriage. Again the court determined the presence of consent or coercion by assessing the degree of pressure, but this time it expanded the notion of force to include different forms of familial pressure. The newspaper the *Guardian* cited the opinion of legal experts who saw the judgment for annulment to interpret duress more broadly to include emotional as well as physical stress (Jury, "Judge Annuls"). The decision also recognized the influence of such a form of coercion upon an older man: "no greater basis for expecting the male to be stronger than the female" *(Mahmud)*. In this way, the legal judgment may be distinguished from a general public one that has almost always focused on the woman, especially the Muslim woman.

Force was also registered as a threat to livelihood and domicile. In the

1993 case of *Mahmood v. Mahmood,* Shamshad Mahmood worked in her parents' shop when they arranged her marriage. Mahmood's parents threatened to disown her and send her to Pakistan if she did not proceed with a marriage to the man of their choice. The court, asserting that coercion is determined by the degree of duress, conceded that "fear of disapproval was not enough to establish lack of consent, but argued that the threat to cut off financial support and send her to Pakistan 'could be regarded as matters which could overwhelm the will of a girl of her age and cultural background'" *(Mahmood).* This decision recognized that economic coercion and physical exile may be considered comparable to physical or psychological duress.

The judgment constructs the will of a young (but over the age of consent) girl of a certain (Pakistani) "cultural background" as already overborne, even before the threat to cut her off financially. As seen in this judgment, in describing the conditions of consent, the courts have incorporated a culturalist discourse that constructs difference through a reductionist vision of unchanging national or religious culture that itself is seen as an agent of coercion. In the 2002 case of *Sohrab v. Khan,* the plaintiff argued for a lack of consent during her 1998 wedding, when the Pakistani British girl was sixteen years old. In granting her petition, the judge characterized consent as something guided by culture-based ethics, stating, "It may be that in the multicultural society in which we now live such situations will continue to arise where ancient eastern established cultural and religious ethics clash with the spirit of 21st-Century children of a new generation and western ideas, language and what these days passes for culture. There is inevitable tension and clashes will happen" *(Sohrab).* The judge's statement represents culture as something that is inherited intact by "Easterners" that is now lost in the West. As in the legal discourse as a whole, the judge turns to arranged marriage as the embodiment of that Eastern culture rather than considering it a practice shaped by the contemporary conditions of transnational migration. The next chapter returns to this assumption to challenge it with an analysis of literary and filmic works that denaturalize the idea of "ancient eastern established cultural and religious ethics" as the basis of arranged marriage.

Commenting on the use of broader notions of consent, David Bradley noted that "arranged marriages involve one important aspect of the problem of reconciling markedly different cultural values within English domestic relations law" ("Duress," 503). Ironically, the 1970s rulings used stricter notions of duress as physical threat or harm precisely to maintain what they saw as the values of an emerging ethnic community, a point supported by the cautionary remarks about the number of arranged marriages that would be impacted by changes in the law. The logic of multiculturalist discourses around the 1983 *Hirani* case works to identify and preserve difference within Britain and intervenes to distinguish a true cultural form (arranged marriage) from an oppressive form (forced marriage). The changes in law present an increased emphasis on consent, both in terms of its recalibration and in its central role marking the border between acceptable and disruptive cultural difference. What is evident here is that by the 1990s, national culture is increasingly being forged through a liberalized notion of conjugal consent built on the foundation of the free-willed, volitional individual subject.

In the annulment cases, a discussion of age of consent for marriage has played a central role in legal and popular debates about arranged marriage. The current legal age of consent to marry is sixteen in the United Kingdom, India, and Pakistan; it is eighteen in Bangladesh for women and twenty-one for men. The shift in both state responses and media representations to a focus on underage brides, especially, sought to provide clearer, less subjective criteria for determining the presence of consent: age. A Glasgow case in which a child marriage was annulled in 1992 deemed the age of consent to be a determining factor, even though the annulment was granted nine years after the marriage (Grylls, "Victory"). Such cases have used this empirical ground for assessing the presence of force in the context of an arranged marriage. Services and public campaigns in the form of posters at airports and information at schools have focused on age; perhaps in response to this, those under seventeen represent more than one-third of the applications involving recent forced marriage legislation (Anitha and Gill, "Coercion," 147).

Upon first glance, age presents as a more objective means for determining consent and coercion, but this perspective overlooks how ideas of childhood and morality have shaped the age-of-consent regulations in changing ways. Writing on the topic, Matthew Waites argues, "The concept of 'age of consent' is itself significant as a form of representation which influences understandings of the law. The concept is often taken for granted in contemporary public and political debates that ignore even its recent history, although its meaning has shifted significantly during the past century, reflecting changing assumptions about age, gender and sexual identities"

(*Age of Consent*, 1). In other words, social ideas construct the notion of age of consent, and these notions, in turn, help to constitute those ideals. Far from being objective, the discourse about age of consent in relation to forced marriage has been both gendered and culturally biased, with a history that reaches back into the colonial period.

Debates on age of conjugal consent galvanized attention in nineteenth-century Britain and India. By the nineteenth century, reform movements in India had connected marriage to willed and regularly consummated conjugal love (Sarkar, *Hindu Wife,* 49). Sarkar argues that the colonial discourse medicalized the question of consent. By this, she means that the discussion moved away from the question of whether a girl did or did not want to get married to be concerned with determining whether a girl was physically capable of consummation without bodily harm. Sarkar offers this interpretation: "It is remarkable how all strands of opinion—colonial, revivalist-nationalist, medical-reformer—agreed on a definition of consent that pegged consent to a purely physical capability, divorced entirely from free choice of partner, from sexual, emotional or mental compatibility" (218). The construction of evidence around the physical body of the girl once again displaced the subjectivity of the female—her voice—onto criteria perceived as more objective: consent became biological.

Debates in the legislature over age of consent reflected a vortex of concurrent issues at stake in the colonial context, being expressed through the question of conjugal reform. For example, in the 1860s, the Brahmo Samaj, a reform-minded movement within Brahminism, agitated for a series of marriage reforms and found a champion for their cause in Henry Maine, Law Member of the Governor General's Legislative Council. For each of these parties, the question of age of consent, which was ten for girls, was part of a larger ideological struggle. The Brahmo sought to secure their position in matrimony, which had been sidelined. Maine proposed a "Native Marriage Bill," in which those (other than Christians) who did not want to be married in accordance with rites of Hindu, Muslim, Buddhist, Parsi, or Jewish religions could be married under the state. The statesman reimagined their proposed reforms through the process of secularization that had been taking place in Europe and turned the discourse from one concerned with reforming Hindu practices to one that emphasized individualism (Mody, *Intimate State,* 229–30). Thirteen years later, the issue of marriage reform found another bill, which ultimately became Act III of 1872. Males and females under the age of twenty-one had to obtain a father's consent.

The act required two weeks prior and post registration. As Mody argues, "the law was no longer meant simply to legitimate marriages conducted with unorthodox religious rites. It instead sought to legitimate marriages for those willing to renounce altogether their profession of faith" (232). Finally, the 1875 Indian Majority Act, IX made the age of majority eighteen years. The discussions around these changes show the specific reform as part of a large set of questions on the role of the state, religion, and the individual. The civil law of the Child Marriage Restraint Act of 1929 mandated a minimum age for marriage of sixteen for males and fourteen for females; that later became twenty-one and eighteen, respectively, a law Bangladesh still has, albeit, as of a controversial 2017 law, with special provisions for a waiver when the marriage is in the "best interests" of the adolescent. The contemporary age-of-consent discourse in the United Kingdom is marked by this gendered, colonial history as well as contemporary anti-Islamic sentiments.

In the contemporary period, the *Singh v. Kaur* and *Mahmud* cases, which centered on older men, were exceptional in a discourse that continues to concern itself with females, particularly those younger than twenty, and especially those below the British age of consent. In government initiatives like the airport posters, the emphasis lies on underage South Asian females, and girls represent 82 percent of cases of the government's Forced Marriage Unit. The reason for pointing this out is not to understate the need for such services for girls or for age-of-consent legislation; rather, the objective here is to show that the image of the vulnerable South Asian girl has been mobilized in the forced marriage debate to secure the cohesion of the state. The language of the *Mahmood* judgment that singled out the overborne will of "a girl of her age and [Pakistani] cultural background" also gave the sense that a girl with a South Asian (and/or Muslim) background would be more vulnerable to such coercion. As a corollary, the decision implied that the will of a girl of a different cultural background might stand more firmly; the non-Asian European girl is arguably the invisible counterpart here. The language of this judgment was in keeping with a state discourse that mapped the incapacity for consent onto two particular subjects, the child and the South Asian female, and overlapped the ideas.

The nexus of these issues represents how age-of-consent legislation produces rather than simply reflects concepts of childhood and adulthood and, in effect, obscures some of the situated social and material processes at work that are important to consider in ending the practice. For example, transnational child marriage is an economic practice in ways not immediately apparent. UNICEF's report "Improving Children's Lives, Transforming the Future" suggests that an overwhelmingly strong determinant for child marriage in South Asia is poverty, along with a lack of education and a rural setting. Child marriage in a rural South Asian context is based on the logic that the girl leaves home at marriage for her in-laws' home, taking rather than accumulating value for her birth family because of the dowry and wedding expenses. It is also based on patriarchal notions that prize a girl's virginity as a bride, putting a postpubescent daughter more at risk of losing that "value." These beliefs foster a context in which there is high social pressure to marry a daughter young: 46 percent of South Asian girls marry under age eighteen, and 18 percent marry before age fifteen (UNICEF, 67). As well as being economically invested, the practice is also highly differentiated. In the diaspora, a girl with British citizenship does have value in a global market that exchanges marriage for work permits. Families that marry their daughters before the legal age of consent for marriage (in England and Wales, sixteen years old with parental permission; in Scotland, sixteen years old) might no longer be securing their subsistence by unloading a daughter but rather are enabling the broader community and family by marrying a daughter, a valuable commodity with British citizenship, to someone abroad. By elaborating a more complex understanding of the rationales for child marriage, and exposing the political as well as economic investments that signify in local, national, and global arenas, this discussion seeks to think through the subject of age of consent outside of a sensationalist national campaign invested in racialized global histories.

Even given these complexities, consent has continued to be the primary focal point in constructing national cultural identity and establishing state sovereignty. The power vested in consent derives from eighteenth-century European ideals of governmentality (Johnston, "History of Consent," 45), a point that connects the arranged marriage discourse (and all conjugal discourses) closely to formulations of the modern nation. According to David Johnston, Hobbes's theory of governmental authority takes root through the notion of consent: "an ideal society, all or virtually all entitlements and obligations, including those to which the members of society are subject by law, would arise out of the wills of individuals through agreements to which all had consented freely" (45). Marriage between consenting individuals becomes the cornerstone of such a state and its analog: consent is fundamental to both marriage and government, "the question of its authenticity not meant to be reopened nor its depth plumbed once consent was given" (Cott, *Public Vows,* 3). The relationship between conjugality and the nation is not only symbolic. Under evolving British immigration law, marriage also becomes the means to residency and, potentially, citizenship; thus a test of the validity of marital consent becomes a measure of legitimate citizenship. If marriage is a paradigm and a means for national belonging, and individual will is the core value of a national culture, it makes sense that conjugal consent would become an arena for struggle in an increasingly multicultural Britain. The expanding criteria for consent represents the supremacy of an individual, free-willed subject of consent as the basis for a multicultural society.

Before concluding this section on legal annulment cases, it is worth pausing to note a contradiction in this culture of consent built by legal cases focusing on individual volition. At the same time as the notion of coercion was expanded, the courts also sought to frame "reasonable" kinds of influence that form the core of society. In doing so, they produced a counternarrative that ambivalently delimits the primacy of individual will. Here the courts have acknowledged a long-standing European conjugal culture that sees an influential role for family inside of conjugal decisions. For example, in the *Mahmood* case, the judge tried to maintain the legitimacy of parental pressure in cases of marriage: "I accept entirely that parental consent is perfectly legitimate and proper ... I also accept that the consent which has to be given to marriage need not be enthusiastic consent, but even reluctant consent will suffice provided that the consent is genuine." The idea of "reluctant consent," though it falls close to Wertheimer's notion of "constrained volition," becomes here something within the scope of acceptable familial influence. This is something Prashina Gagoomal calls "consent by proxy," which "entails a balancing of the individual and family consideration that co-exist within the very same human rights instruments. It does not require trumping individual freedoms for the sake of the cultural needs of society—as has happened in other instances" ("Margin of Appreciation," 14). In *Mahmud,* the judge explicitly acknowledged the legitimacy of parental pressure of some kind and focused on the articulation of consent: "if under pressure—and perhaps very considerable pressure—a party does indeed change his or her mind and consents to a marriage with however ill a grace and however resentfully, then the marriage is in my opinion valid."

The judges' comments recall that even self-made marriages are subject to forms of influence and are not always individual decisions, despite the individualist discourse commonly generated around them. In discussing arranged marriage, these judges present alternative narratives that disrupt the coherence of a discourse about individual consent based on individual will: the rhetoric of protectionism and the idealization of family. In these legal decisions, notions of culture continually enter the frame, but in ways that ultimately deconstruct the binaries being mobilized in the discourse on consent. The law's cultural representations go far to normalize the ideal of individual consent represented by self-made marriages by assuming individual consent as culturally neutral, while presenting community or family-based consent as embedded within tradition. However, despite the way that the courts cast arranged marriage (and forced marriage) as culturally determined and naturalize self-made marriages, the courts have continued to articulate and reinforce national cultural ideals as they ascribe legitimate forms of influence. These ambivalent judgments ultimately reveal the way that cultural ideas like family, duty, personhood, and gender continually enter the British legal sphere, even as it moves rhetorically toward a dedicated culture of consent.

Structural Inequalities and the Consenting Subject: Literary Reinterpretations

Despite the liberalization of duress that seeks more nuanced understandings of coercion, these legal cases have diverted attention from influences outside interpersonal pressure, "the structural constraints under which women exercise their agency in matters of marriage" (Anitha and Gill, "Coercion," 172). In an article on coercion and consent in the forced marriage debate, Anitha and Gill persuasively argue that the focus on consent has created a false binary between free marriages and coerced marriages that disguises the other forces at work. They elaborate that in the cases of both arranged marriage and forced marriage, "little attention is given to the many ways in which all women located within a matrix of structural inequalities can face social expectations, pressure and constraint in matters of marriage" (166). Amrit Wilson also points out the problem with the forced marriage legislative initiatives that focus primarily on consent and cites the presence of both interpersonal and social duress as determining factors: "family-arranged marriage is often an arena of struggle, which may be psychological, emotional or physical, and is affected by a complex set of interacting issues, from emotional blackmail and low self-esteem to isolation and exclusion as a result of racism" ("Forced Marriage," 32). Wilson's comment shifts attention from the vague realm of cultural background to material conditions of the diaspora, such as racism or economic hardship, as well as the patriarchal family relations that have been the focal point for legal discussion. In other words, an arranged marriage might represent the desire to belong to a community, but such a desire is not only about cultural identity. The pressures of racial and economic inequality bear down upon certain South Asian immigrants in Britain and make community a viable mode of protection within the national sphere.

In looking at the evolving legal discourse on forced marriage, Anitha and Gill note that in legal and policy discourse, "the context in which consent is constructed largely remains unexplored" (165). They examine the construction of a gendered subjectivity and the structural inequalities of South Asian women in the United Kingdom. They note that the idea of consent in use in these legal cases is grounded on a notion of individuality that precedes community: "The courts in the UK have continued to apply a similar standard of individual rationality and volition, which presumes that the individual in question is a pre-social, ahistorical, self-constituting subject who does not belong to an identity-conferring community, nor values relational aspects of personhood" (177). Anitha and Gill challenge an idea central to the British legal construction of consent, which is that a rational subject with free will enters either a South Asian culture of coercive collectivity or a Euro-American culture of the free individual. In place of this understanding of subjectivity, the feminist legal scholars posit that the law assumes a subject of consent that is already constituted as part of particular sociopolitical contexts, a "notion of the free self... predicated on the normative experiences of a white man" (171). Instead, they suggest that the agent of decision making is contextual and conjunctural, constituted in interaction with competing hegemonies and "in terms of a meaningful world always presents itself as a fluid, often contested, and only partially integrated mosaic of narratives, images and signifying practices" (Comaroff and Comaroff, *Christianity*, 27).

Literary and cinematic texts elaborate these structural and affective factors and the production of this mediated subject, even as they offer portraits of interpersonal pressure within South Asian families. These works show that these expectations and constraints are primary in creating the force in forced marriage. They also offer an alternative version to the "pre-social, ahistorical, self-constituting" subject of conjugal consent by depicting the social, political, and economic forces that circumscribe the production of that subject. Literary and cinematic texts also reveal the role of narratives of love mediating this multifaceted, located subject's relation to arranged marriage. The following interprets literary and filmic works to elaborate the consenting (or nonconsenting) subject within the web of conditions, forces, and desires that constitute the subject of agency in the context of arranged marriage.

Hanif Kureishi's *The Buddha of Suburbia*

Hanif Kureishi's 1990 novel *The Buddha of Suburbia* treats arranged marriage with Kureishi's typical eye for the ridiculous, but beneath the humor lies more serious criticism of the conditions for South Asian immigrants in Britain and the pressures placed on them. The arranged marriage story centers on the protagonist Karim's good friend and occasional lover, Jamila, and her father, Anwar, who is Karim's father's close friend from India. Anwar decides to arrange a marriage for his militantly feminist daughter with "a boy eager to come and live in London as Jamila's husband" (57). Jamila at first refuses both the match and the process, before finally capitulating on her own terms. Before examining the reasons she refuses, changes her mind, and then restructures the arrangement, it is worth thinking through Anwar's motivations. Anwar runs a shop set amid graffiti-covered buildings and leads a life of drudgery sitting in a chair, "from which he looked out expressionlessly" (51) waiting for his one week off a year. Anwar acquires another laborer through his daughter's marriage to Changez, a worker who will be dependent on the family for his employment; Anwar fantasizes about him running the shop with Anwar's daughter as the father finally takes his wife to the zoo. With this representation, Kureishi shows arranged marriage as the source of transnational labor that replenishes nascent immigrant economies.

Anwar's second motivation stems from a revived identification with India. The protagonist Karim muses on this, comparing Anwar's demand to his father's discovery of Eastern philosophy: "Perhaps it was the immigrant condition living itself out through them. For years they were both happy to live like Englishmen.... Now, as they aged and seemed settled here, Anwar and Dad appeared to be returning internally to India, or at least to be resisting the English here" (65). This sentiment mirrors the idea of cultural expression often associated with arranged marriage. However, rather than simply sustaining a practice brought from the homeland, Anwar embodies what legal scholar David Bradley terms a "reactive ethnicity" ("Duress," 46), an identity that is constructed though social conflict. Though Anwar identifies the practice with the old country, Karim recognizes that these are immigrant conditions created in response to racism and alienation.

In representing Jamila's moment of consent, Kureishi reproduces elements that have been considered aspects of force in legal cases and by ethnographic studies. Anwar pressures his daughter into the marriage through a hunger strike, a kind of emotional duress that was the basis for annulment in the 1993 *Mahmood* case. Karim suggests that Jamila ultimately agrees so as not to abandon her mother, whom Jamila represents as oppressed by her father: "Every time we talked about Jamila running away from home where she could go and how we could get money to help her survive, she said, 'What about my mother?'" (72). This sense of responsibility Jamila feels for her mother echoes the concerns expressed by the main subject of Simon Chambers's documentary, discussed later, and the cases, such as *Sohrab*, in which a mother's threat of suicide becomes a recognized element of force.

Jamila does change her mind after her initial refusal but rewrites the terms of the arrangement in the sense that she refuses to consummate her relationship with Changez. Kureishi's choice to have Jamila's family arrange her marriage while she herself arranges her sexual life allows Jamila to remain within her South Asian community and family, while renegotiating its demands. It is a different decision than the "exit strategy" of leaving (or avoiding) the marriage presented in the autobiographical works discussed in the next chapter. Obviously Kureishi is not presenting a model for managing coercion in arranged marriage, but he is offering an imaginative reconception of the problem. *The Buddha of Suburbia* is a literary attempt to extract the competing kinds of forces in arranged marriage that, in the way they have been framed by state and legal discourse, have been reduced to individual consent. Kureishi's representation offers an alternative way of understanding the situation in which material and social forces circumscribe decision making. His literary representation, while not presented as a model, does show the agency of women who take or sustain arranged marriages as a way to please their families and remain in a community.

Kureishi's representation is notable in another way, in the sense that he deals explicitly with the question of consummation. Only a few court cases in which there is an argument for nullity on the basis that the marriage was not consummated, including the *Singh v. Singh* case, in which the woman argued for an "invincible repugnance," explicitly treat the question of sex within arranged marriage. Even the broader forced marriage discourse as it intersects with debates over the age of consent often elides the question of sexual consent by merging it with the question of marriage. However, one may safely assume that concerns about sexual consent mobilize the forced marriage discourse, even though other potential abuses (exploitation of labor, appropriation of property, restrictions on personal mobility or appearance, etc.) might be present. In explicitly representing Jamila's sexual agency in her marriage, Kureishi removes what many of his Western readers would find the primary problem with arranged marriage, namely, the expectation of sex with a stranger. The decision is in keeping with the larger themes of sexual agency in *The Buddha of Suburbia*; through the character of Jamila, Kureishi places that agency back into the scope of a Muslim South Asian identity. In this way, his novel differs from the next work discussed, in which such affiliations mean only sexual repression and a lack of personal freedom.

East Is East: Patriarchal Belonging and Personal Freedom

Ayub Khan-Din's 1996 play *East Is East* and Damien O'Donnell's 1999 film based on Khan-Din's screenplay locate a father's desire to arrange the marriages of two sons as the expression of cultural identity through patriarchal power. The works, treated together here, except where they differ, present this identity as both national and transnational. In *East Is East,* a father, George, attempts to arrange a marriage between his sons, who are half English and half Pakistani, and girls from the Pakistani British community. George is presented as a man with an ambivalent relationship to his own ethnic background because of his long-term residency in Britain and his marriage to a British woman, Ella. He sees arranged marriage as a way to secure himself and his family to a Pakistani identity, a desire he attempts to realize through verbal and physical abuse of his wife and children for any behavior he deems outside those cultural bounds.

Khan-Din represents George's Pakistani identity as under erasure in the global politics of the 1970s. The play takes place on the eve of the Pakistani civil war, and the political theme of separatism that forms the backdrop to the play parallels the bid for independence on the part of the Khan children. The father closely watches the news, because he has left his first wife near the border. His desire to control his new family is closely related to his fears about the vulnerability of his former nation. George's Pakistani identity is at risk because the identity of Pakistan is no longer the same. At the same time, however, his Pakistani identity has become even more fixed in his adopted home, as his Caucasian, working-class neighbors question his British identity in the context of growing anti-immigrant sentiments.

Although both the play and the film feature a backdrop of racism, O'Donnell's film develops the representation of a tense national context by showing Enoch Powell on the news and Powell supporters in the neighborhood. Powell was a Conservative MP in the 1960s and early 1970s who endorsed anti-immigrant sentiments to the point of advocating the repatriation of black (African, Caribbean, and Asian) immigrants. George's decisions and those of his children both become direct reactions to this hostile climate, but they make different choices in expressing those reactions. For George, arranged marriage becomes an attempt to secure the family's place within an immigrant community that becomes his refuge. He follows the advice of an imam, who opines, as a prelude to discussion of arranged marriage in this community, "Until your sons join the community fully, they will be a worry for you." George sits down with a group of Pakistani men in Bradford, England, to arrange the marriages of his two sons in a scene that expresses the men's centralization of control within the immigrant community. The arrangement secures their position as leaders and their relationship to each other as a support network. George is one of several men who create a male-dominated immigrant community within the broader, hostile national context as a political form of exceptionalism. Arranged marriage is represented as playing a central role in maintaining and reproducing this minority politics produced in the context of racial exclusion.

East Is East shows tradition as a means for the father to grasp power, even as the motivations for arranging marriages are continually expressed as a desire to preserve tradition. For George, the process of arranging his sons' marriages secures his place in the family through the assertion of patriarchal obedience, much like it does for Anwar in *The Buddha of Suburbia*. In both works, South Asian masculinity is asserted through the structures of arranged marriage that designate generational roles of patriarchal control and filial obedience. *East Is East* shows a man who has never managed the control over his family he thinks he should have. He sees this absence as a cultural problem—it is his British wife and the context of Britain that remove his natural role as a patriarch, as far as he is concerned.

The film engages in a discourse of rights, placing individual rights in opposition to filial obedience. "They have a right to know, George," Ella intones about the arrangements, while George counters, "What do you mean, 'right'? Pakistani believe that if father ask son marry, son follow instruction." In this conversation, one may see the question of agency being debated. Ella articulates the position that an individual has the right to be involved in the decision making about his (or her) marriage. This position is the one represented by the court decisions described earlier, which look to individual consent as the basis for a legitimate marriage. That position is also central to national belonging, in which consent is fundamental to both marriage and government (Cott, *Public Vows*, 3). For George, however, that right of decision making is a patriarchal and communal one. He rationalizes this in terms of national belonging, asserting, "Pakistani believe," and with both this statement and the nature of his argument, he positions himself in a resistant place against a dominant British identity. The position is resistant, and not outside the British identity, because it forms the basis for the patriarchal immigrant community constructed by the fathers who sit in a living room in Bradford matching their sons and daughters. *East Is East* tells the story of both the assertion and the failure of that community and its communal subject of agency.

Arranged marriage is often presented as the cause of a generational split, with the older generation embracing the practice and the younger generation refusing in favor of self-made matches that show their liberal ideology. Khan-Din avoids such easy binaries. Tariq, who has a British girlfriend, reacts violently to news of his engagement, but the reaction is not based simply on a desire to choose for himself. "There is no way I'm marrying a bloody Paki," he says, framing his refusal in terms of an affiliation to a racist Britain. All of George's children feel a similar kind of ambivalence in this national context of the 1970s that is partly due to being seen one way and feeling another. In a speech left out of the film but key to the play, Abdul recounts his first drink in a pub:

> We were sat drinking, telling jokes, playing music, telling more jokes. Jokes about sex, thick Irish men, wog jokes, chink jokes, paki jokes. And the biggest joke was me, 'cause I was laughing the hardest. And they laughed at me because I was laughing. It seemed as if the whole pub was laughing at me, one giant grinning mouth. I just sat there and watched them, and I didn't belong, I was crying, crying so hard I couldn't catch my breath, so I ran and kept on running. When I

got home, me dad was here praying, I watched him Tariq, and it was right, to be here, to be part of this place, to belong to something. It's what I want. (57)

Abdul's experience of alienation and his sense of communal belonging motivate him to accept his father's decision to arrange a marriage. "I don't want that out there, it's not who I am, it's as alien to me as me dad's world is to you" (57), he says to the brother who does not want an arranged marriage. Khan-Din locates what appears to be the affirmation or refusal of a cultural tradition represented by the two sons within the fraught context of a racist Britain and the alienation of a second generation of immigrants.

Arranged marriage is part of a politics of exclusion in the context of 1970s Britain for Abdul, as for George. The father turns to the practice of arranged marriage as a way to secure control of both his masculinity and his national identity. He does so in a racist national context, but also in a global arena in which what it means to be Pakistani is changing. Abdul, however, imagines arranged marriage as a way "to be part of this place, to belong to something" (57), in other words, as a refuge from a racist context in which he doesn't belong. Khan-Din and O'Donnell show the "politics of belonging" (Yuval-Davis, *Politics of Belonging*) to be an important motivation in decision making for all parties involved, offering a different version of cultural identity and tradition than the one that appears in legal cases. While those decisions account for the influence of tradition on the consenting (or coerced) subjects, Khan-Din's play and O'Donnell's film locate that subject in a dynamic, politically charged context that creates affiliations to different expressions of collective or individual agency.

Monica Ali's *Brick Lane* and Modes of Agency

Monica Ali's novel *Brick Lane* offers a critical representation of a transnational arranged marriage involving a Bangladeshi woman and a Bangladeshi British man. Like Kureishi and Khan-Din, Ali shows the structural conditions that surround the practice of arranged marriage. Even more than these other authors, she elaborates the moments of decision making and explores the question of agency. In this way, Ali elaborates the complexities of sociolegal notions like consent as they are lived by a young female South Asian immigrant as subjective realities.

At the beginning of the novel, Nazneen is eighteen, married by her father to the forty-year-old Chanu. Though Ali uses a third-person narrative, one sees the events through Nazneen's eyes and feels them from her perspective. The novel represents the moment in which consent is granted and shows the ways that volition and coercion remain implicit in a decision-making moment that cannot fully account for the complex nature of agreement. It is instructive to turn to this moment in the novel to consider the nature of consent. In the novel, the critical moment is described as follows:

> Soon after, when her father asked if she would like to see a photograph of the man she would marry the following month, Nazneen shook her head and replied, "Abba, it is good that you have chosen my husband. I hope I can be a good wife, like Amma." But as she turned to go she noticed, without meaning to, where her father put the photograph.
> She just happened to see it. These things happen. (5)

This passage shows the way decision making in the context of arranged marriage may have no articulated moment of consent or clear expression of force. The father chooses the spouse and arranges the marriage prior to Nazneen's consent; the young woman is not presented with a yes-or-no proposition for the marriage, though she is asked if she wants to see the photograph.

Writing on the subject of forced marriage and consent, Dina Siddiqi offers some insight into the significance of Nazneen's silence by describing the gendered discourse of consent within a Bangladeshi context:

> That a woman or girl may indicate her consent to a marriage through silence rather than speech signals a specific construction of femininity, in which modesty, passivity, and "shame" (lojja-shorom in the Bangladeshi context) outweigh action and speech. Needless to say, there are multiple interpretations of a woman's silence, including modesty and good conduct, active assent, resistance or resignation. ("Of Consent," 291)

One may interpret Nazneen's lack of verbal affirmation as signifying an appropriate response within the script of her upbringing, but that does not mean she is without the capacity to act. Force is present without articulation, but that is also true of agency. Into this ellipsis, where a question about consent to the marriage would be (but is not actually posed), Nazneen verbally affirms her father's decision. Moreover, Nazneen demonstrates a kind of agency as she happens to see the picture she claimed (with a shake of her head) she didn't need to see. Nazneen, or the narrator channeling Nazneen's perspective, displaces this agency onto denial ("without meaning to"), coincidence ("just happened)," and objectivity ("these things happen"). In this complex rendering of decision making, Nazneen does things without admitting to her own power to compel them.

Verbally, the character positions her avowal in terms of being a good daughter, reinforcing her father's role as choice maker and modeling herself on her mother. The "soon after" at the start of the passage is important to understanding motivation in this regard. The narrator describes Nazneen's sister Hasina's decision to run away from home for a love marriage and the effect on her father, who renounces her. The narrator presents Nazneen's affirmation of her father's decision immediately after in the narrative, though the exact timeline is unclear, and the juxtaposition of these events suggests that Nazneen wants to make up for her sister's actions. The author shows Nazneen's decision as structured by her gender roles. Ali does not narrate an explicit cause for Nazneen's affirmation and instead gives only a chronology of decision making that suggests that Nazneen affirms her father's decision—"it is good"—in part as reparation for her sister's action. The narrator also does not offer a privileged moment of interiority that allows the reader to assess whether Nazneen believes what she says about the arrangement being good. Her ability to veto the proposition is never fully explored. Is her affirmation redundant, in the sense that her father has already made the decision? Would he have changed the arrangement if she had refused the process at that point? Ali leaves the answers to these questions ambiguous by having neither the father ask nor Nazneen refuse. The reader is left to her own conclusions, and most readers would assume Nazneen has no choice. However, the way the passage is structured represents something beyond a patriarchal father suppressing Nazneen's fully articulated will. The young (but still of age) Nazneen never completes the actions of considering consent or its refusal. Thus Ali is presenting the reader with the incomplete synapses that are part of the consent-granting moment—a moment that legal decision making in legislative measures has relied on to determine the difference between arranged and forced marriage. The moment for Nazneen to give her consent never arrives. Because we, as readers, do not have access to her thoughts, we see only that she has not refused her father, and we must interpret how she feels about the arrangement. The only volition represented is when she looks at the photo she said she didn't need to see. Ali leaves open the question of whether she would have refused, but also whether she actually consented.

Ali represents the decision around the arranged marriage in the context of social and economic frameworks of mobility and familial protection. After the wedding and she has immigrated to London, Nazneen looks back to affirm her father's decisions: "[Her father] had made a good marriage for her. There were plates on the wall, attached by hooks and wires, which were not for eating from but on display" (9). The presence of nonessential commodities suggests a surplus of wealth and thus a good match. Ali's representation mirrors many accounts that a match that is made between a "village girl" and a man with a university education, a job, and a legal visa in the United Kingdom would be seen as a very good one. Once again, in the preceding passage, there is ambiguity: one does not know if Nazneen is convincing herself of the merits of her father's choice or whether she believes them. However, Ali is not so much showing Nazneen hiding her "true feelings" as showing them to be outside the discourses of arranged marriage mobilized in this context—discourses based on notions of filial obedience, duty, and global upward mobility.

Ali's novel demonstrates that arranged marriage may be reinterpreted as an exchange of commodities in a global marketplace rather than a tradition that must be preserved to foster identity. While the documentary *Every Good Marriage Begins with Tears*, discussed subsequently, shows the transnational migration of male wage labor, Ali's novel depicts the unpaid female domestic labor that was historically part of the arranged marriage exchange. In one scene, Nazneen walks through the emptied streets of the part of London called Brick Lane:

> But now the waiters were at home asleep, or awake being waited on themselves by wives who only served and were not served in return except with board and lodging and the provision of children whom they also, naturally, waited upon. (38)

Here the novel hints at Nazneen's husband, Chanu's, motivations for the arranged marriage, which are otherwise left unexplored. The driving forces for alienation are economic; Nazneen's unpaid domestic labor in London and her sister's paid wage labor in Bangladesh are both exploitative and alienating. One may read their fraught interpersonal relationships as outcomes of those structures rather than simply as the bounding of their free choice to pursue romantic relationships.

The novel revisits the moment of decision making later, as an older Nazneen reflects on this early period of arrangement with newfound critical knowledge:

> Why did her father marry her off to this man?
> He just wanted to be rid of me, she thought. He wanted me to go far away, so that I would not be any trouble to him. He did not care who took me off his hands. If I had known what this marriage would be, what this man would be . . . !
> What? What then? (78)

In this passage, Nazneen reinterprets her father's decision as a failure, not a fulfillment of responsibility, and her own position as having a lack of agency ("what then?"). The criticism is that of someone who has passed through a different understanding of marital consent, one this chapter identifies as an individualist consent promoted by a liberal project of multiculturalism. The limits of Nazneen's capacity for consent are now marked by an understanding of the structural issues of gender roles and political economy that precluded (and preclude) her agency. In the context of the novel, the "what then" is filled in by the story of her sister Hasina, who did refuse her match. Hasina's decision to pursue a self-made marriage takes her outside the protective sphere of her family and community, leaving her vulnerable when that marriage does not work out. Nazneen, too, would be vulnerable if she left her marriage, but Ali presents the British context of independent wage laborers as one that would potentially support the single Bangladeshi woman should she make that decision.

In terms of consent, Ali is suggesting several things. The moment of consent is not always a clear yes or no in the context of arranged marriage, as would be suggested by the legal cases resting on this decision. This is because, often, the system is not brought to the point of confrontation that would cast consent or coercion into relief. What would be acts of coercion appear primarily as demands to fulfill duty, and incipient consent appears in the form of performing that duty. Ali's novel shows the practice of arranged marriage in the context of global economies that create unpaid transnational labor in the form of wives and draw on notions of cultural obligation to disguise exploitation. In this way, her work, like that of Kureishi and Ayub Khan-Din, represents the structural conditions that circumscribe decision making in arranged marriages. Finally, by depicting a shift in the way that Nazneen understands her own consent, from a place where she acts without acknowledging her own agency (looking at the photograph) to a place where she questions others' power (why did her father marry her off to this man?), Ali shows this contemporary discourse of consent to be the product of a liberal understanding. This is the frame through which the British state looks at the question of arranged and forced marriages. In representing this perspective as acquired through assimilation, Ali denaturalizes the consenting subject and shows it to be already part of an "identity-conferring community" (Anitha and Gill, "Coercion," 177).

Simon Chambers's *Every Good Marriage Begins with Tears*

Simon Chambers's 2006 documentary *Every Good Marriage Begins with Tears*, which represents the marriage arrangements in a Bangladeshi British family in the East of London, highlights the complex nature of assent, the material conditions that mediate conjugal decision making in the context of the Bangladeshi diaspora, and the filial and romantic narratives that affectively mobilize such resolutions. The documentary features two sisters who get arranged marriages, eighteen-year-old Shahanara and her younger sister Hushnara, as well as the older sister Azirun, their parents, and, more marginally, their spouses. The film opens with Shahanara about to greet her husband, Mamun, a rural Bangladeshi man whom she had married in an arranged marriage in Bangladesh six months before and who is now rejoining her in a London airport. The film subsequently follows the fate of Shahanara's unhappy marriage, its aftermath of separation, and Hushnara's own arranged marriage to a Bangladeshi British man.

The film references and reinterprets one of the specters that haunts the forced marriage discourse, that "at a certain age teenagers would be whisked off to Bangladesh to be married" and that they "seemed to submit to this without struggle." Chambers examines the struggle that does take place, which, perhaps surprisingly, ends up being not primarily about free choice, for although his film highlights the desires of the individual, it also shows the confluence of different causes that produce consent. Shahanara's decision to enter an arranged marriage emerges directly out of her relationship with her family. Her father appears as a patriarchal force that controls the limits of resistance within the family. With his portrayal of the father, Chambers ties the issue of coercion to the patriarchal dominance within the intimate space of the family. The father structures the options for his daughter in binary form: either leave the family or consent to the marriage he has arranged with a groom from Bangladesh. The documentary film reinforces one of the central narratives of arranged marriage, also represented in *East Is East,* which is that the practice is a means for a dislocated patriarch to reinforce a sense of power undermined in the context of diaspora. If the father is a didactic force, the mother is an affective one. As a teenager, Shahanara was put into foster care "because of her Western values." As she presents it, her desire to remain in the family is premised upon her agreeing to this transnational match. Such a desire is certainly born from affective familial ties. "I only did it for my mom," she says, because she was not allowed to see her otherwise. Writing about the role of such family influence, sociologist Hannah Bradby notes that in such decisions, "in effect, [the] woman [is] balancing up a known and valued quantity—her bond with her mother—against an unknown quantity—an imagined relationship with a future husband" ("Coercion," 160). In fact, the two are not set in opposition; rather, the force of the bond with the mother is placed behind the imagined relationship with the spouse, giving it more substance.

Shahanara's desire to remain within her family is not only motivated by emotional attachments and interpersonal pressure, however; *Every Good Marriage* highlights the role of economic forces in the decision to pursue arranged marriage. Shahanara narrates how her former boyfriend gave her the financial and emotional support to survive, feeding and clothing her as well as offering her love during the time her family abandoned her. That relationship also could not endure in relation to the boyfriend's own family, and the young man, presumably from the same community, had to end it and marry, "to keep his own family." Chambers contrasts two economies, one inside the family and its financial resources, and one outside, where the Bangladeshi British youths do not have easy access to a way to sustain themselves. At one point in the film, Shahanara will step outside of the economy being constructed around the extended family to take a job as a cashier. The film represents her exhaustion as she tries to support herself, trying to "go out and make money, spend money, and live like a normal human being." To be normal here is to live a more individualistic life in the wage labor economy of Britain rather than to be integrated into the obligations of an extended family.

For the British-based family, viable arranged marriages for Shahanara and her sister mean that they will remain a respected family within a community that is fundamentally transnational. The older sister worries about the impact of her sisters' behavior on the family's reputation in the home village in Bangladesh—"in Bangladesh, people going to give us shit in our face"—but she doesn't worry about their neighborhood in London. That sentiment reflects a larger trend to shift a sense of place from the adopted country back onto the country of origin. This is not only symbolic, in the form of cultural identification, but material. As Chambers discovers, the father has been sending money back to Bangladesh to buy acres of land; there, the factory worker who in Britain barely scrapes by has become a landlord with a host of laborers working under him. The transnational arranged marriage helps to continue this presence by marrying daughters, in particular, to Bangladeshi men from this or neighboring villages.

The economic demands are even more powerful for the groom, Mamun. Shahanara becomes central to the well-being of a family in Bangladesh. After her separation from her husband, she arrives in Bangladesh for her sister's wedding. Her mother-in-law travels eight hours through floods to appeal to her; though she doesn't meet her daughter-in-law (Shahanara does not go to the actual ceremony so as to avoid her), she makes a plea through the filmmaker. In the translated voice-over, the mother-in-law moves through strategies of appeal. She first tries to appeal to the affective ties of family, telling her she loves her more than her mother and that she wants to be close to her as a daughter. She then talks of the punitive costs, saying that she can't show her face, and that neighbors will throw sticks and stones, embroidering the story of what will happen. Shahanara, when she learns of this appeal, replies, "They don't want me. They only want my passport." She is most probably correct, but this doesn't lessen the plight of the mother's family. In this context, the dependence on the son that has been the traditional structure of the Bangladeshi family has morphed through the processes of transnational labor mediated by the structures of immigration. These structures legitimate marriage as one of the only means for entrance into Britain. It offers young Bangladeshi women unprecedented power as gatekeepers, even as it forces upon them the burdens of an uneven global economy.

Although arguably driven by transnational economic contingencies, the marriage is enabled by narratives of love, romantic and otherwise. Chambers shows how the discourse of love plays an affective role in how the young men and women understand arranged marriage. En route to meet her husband at the airport, Shahanara reflects on the nature of love:

> Simon, what is love. I think when you see that person every day so much. And he starts to care for you, starts feeding you, buying you lunch, caring for you, drops you to the station. I think little bits like that grows up, builds up to a relationship.

The notion that love grows after marriage is familiar in the arranged marriage discourse, a rationale for the compatibility of love and arrangement. However, Shahanara's philosophy recalls her own history as a teenager placed into foster care and, as she presents it, more or less left to fend for herself with the help of her boyfriend. Indeed, though she is clearly thinking about her new marriage, which will soon have its first period of extended cohabitation, her thoughts turn to her ex-boyfriend. The two competing discourses of love overlap, one self-arranged (and which ended badly) and another family arranged, which she can only imagine in the context of the other. A song she sings in the car, which she translates as "the first time I saw you I hated you, then I started to love you," reflects how both ideas of love are mediated by popular discourses of romance. Although the perspective of the Bangladeshi men pursuing arranged marriages is not directly featured in the film, there is one scene in which another groom greets his prospective bride with a bouquet of red roses at the airport, a gesture that matches customs of dating with a different kind of practice. Thus, in thinking through the material exigencies that help produce transnational marriage, it is important also to consider the affective elements, such as familial love, cultural belonging, and romance, that mobilize those forces.

Chambers's film, which begins with him seeking to understand what he sees as a Bangladeshi tradition, ends with him reflecting on the nature of contemporary Britain. If one were to read Shahanara's consent regarding her arranged marriage in the way asked by the court annulment cases considered in this chapter and by the criminalization laws discussed in the next chapter, one might say she consents and then exits from an untenable marriage. However, this interpretation would miss the whole that Chambers represents. It would miss the kinds of global sociopolitical and economic forces that create the context: a British context in which a less educated Bangladeshi woman would struggle for her daily wage outside the support of her family and community, and the transnational economic context that relies on arranged marriage for labor and social relations. Moreover, a singular emphasis on consent as free and full will would miss how affective forces, including familial love and romantic desire, motivate decision making as well as the emotional pressure recognized in the versions of consent in recent annulment cases.

Conclusion

Consent is a key term in legal and ethical considerations of arranged marriage; however, an approach primarily or exclusively focused on consent falls short. The emphasis on consent that has dominated the legal discourse concerning arranged marriage in contemporary Britain is important in looking at the conditions of violence and exploitation that accompany arranged marriage, especially transnational arranged marriage. However, such a discourse misrepresents the subject of arranged marriage as an individual fully vested in both free will and the ability to articulate such a will. Feminist legal theory offers another way to think of the subject who enters into the practice of marriage already constituted by gender, race, and transnational economic forces. Literary and filmic representations by and about South Asians in Britain trouble the legal conception of an autonomous, free subject of consent in ways that offer a useful corrective as the legal notions distinguishing arranged from forced marriage are taken up by the British mainstream. Works by British writers and filmmakers convey the need to recognize subtler forms of persuasion in the context of arranged marriage. This is something the courts have done by liberalizing notions of consent, but that emphasis on a choice prong limits the conversation about a context in which, for example, a choice as such is never articulated. Literary and filmic works, in contrast, represent arranged marriage as something emerging out of the conditions of diaspora and global economies. These creative works should be interpreted for the way they reinsert the subject of consent into the social and economic contexts, both national and transnational, of its production.

3

Britain

The Politics of Belonging

The arranged marriage discourse in Britain has been a mode for working out the politics of national belonging in the context of transnational immigration. The last chapter showed how the discourse that distinguishes arranged and forced marriage has articulated a legal subject based on the fantasy of the free-willed, fully vested individual (Anitha and Gill, "Coercion," 171) who articulates his or her will through consent. Chapter 2 interpreted fictional work by Hanif Kureishi, Ayub Khan-Din, and Monica Ali and a documentary by Simon Chambers to argue that they present an alternate perspective to this primary focus on consent and thus provide an important insight into the construction of South Asian diasporic subjectivity that might inform legal discourse. These works show how the moment of consent is often never fully articulated in the practice of arranged marriage; contextualize consent within structures of power; and finally, reveal how transnational forces of economy, politics, and society mediate the constitution of the subject even before the moment of consent.

This chapter extends this discussion of contemporary Britain by considering the role of the arranged marriage discourse in the context of immigration and multiculturalism. Specifically, this chapter looks at the way national narratives have been erected through the discourse. After this first section lays out the chapter's argument, the second section examines how discourses of multiculturalism have turned to a version of culture that is presented as a pregiven, unchanging force upon the lives of immigrants— what this book calls a culturalist discourse. The argument interprets the way a series of related texts, including media representations, political speeches, state working documents, and literary memoirs, presents acceptable and disruptive forms of this culture through the concept of the "honor crime," an idea given substance and political valence by a set of narrative images that includes representations of the forced marriage of the South Asian girl. It connects this, in the third section, to the politics of immigration by aligning shifts in immigration regulations with the rise of the forced marriage discourse.

In the fourth section, the chapter identifies how, in representative political speeches by a member of Parliament active in this area, the state has called into question the justice of a first generation's parenthood. By interpreting the way an important state document formulates this claim, the section shows how the portrayal of forced marriage operates through a protectionist discourse that is naturalized by the image of the state as a just, and therefore proper, guardian. Reading the implications of this claim on policy, this section argues that the notion of guardianship functions to legitimate the "exit strategy" that has been the state's primary resolution to the violence of forced marriage (Phillips and Dustin, "U.K. Initiatives," 1). Such a strategy depends on the young woman, almost always, leaving the marriage (and often, by consequence, her community). This approach has been animated by the popular subgenre of escape memoirs that work generically by asking the reader to identify with the young woman in flight and creating a sense of urgency through suspense.

The fifth section interprets this subgenre, arguing that narratively, these memoirs go beyond negative representations to participate in constructing what are deemed acceptable and unacceptable differences within a multicultural frame. This nationalist agenda often disguises the exigencies that structure the processes of arranging marriages in favor of highlighting the problems of familial and societal patriarchal power. Autobiographies of forced marriage use the motif of self-made romance as a way to resolve these issues and model a new Britain. The mass-market memoirs envision a trajectory from the biological family to a national one by imagining an exogamous marriage (marriage outside the community). In this way, the works act as national romances to validate a diverse national constituency through love (Sommer, *Foundational Fictions*, 74). The narrative trajectory, in which the young woman leaves the private space of her immediate and extended family to enter the public space of state assistance, invests the reader in the "exit strategy."

As the final section argues, in contrast to these state discourses and mass-market memoirs, a select set of South Asian fictional and filmic works uses the trope of the family as a way to think through a dialogic relation between South Asian communities and the British state. This chapter closes with an analysis of Nadeem Aslam's novel *Maps for Lost Lovers*, which, though it reproduces some of the same ideals of individualism and choice, also offers more complex ways to think through both the notion of culture and the possibilities of cultural change within South Asian communities. Aslam's novel questions the justness of parental control over a second generation. While still envisioning an "exit strategy" for the second generation, *Maps for Last Lovers* destabilizes the locus of Pakistani British patriarchy by representing a father character ambivalent about his powers, inauthentic in his communal identity (his father was born Hindu), and deeply troubled by both his state and his community.

Culturalism and Multiculturalism

The range of discourses and practices that has come to be known as the multiculturalist project in Britain was part of the varying response to the influx of immigrants from former colonies that has been reshaping Britain since 1945. The movement was first articulated in the late 1960s as political figures saw the need to integrate these particular, meaning nonwhite, immigrant communities into the general British polity (Rattansi, *Multiculturalism,* 9). Progressive social movements formulated multiculturalism in the 1970s and 1980s, constructing ideas of race and ethnicity through the concepts of culture and community. Those speaking under the name of multiculturalism have positioned themselves against the monoculturalism of assimilation, which would merge difference into dominant cultural values and expressions. On the surface, the multiculturalist movement has had a progressive agenda for minorities, as its proponents advocate cultural pluralism, cross-cultural understanding, and equality for minority communities.

While multiculturalists see a path toward amenable diversity by recognizing "other cultures," critics have pointed to the way that very gesture of recognition assumes power. Skeptics argue that the concept of multiculturalism encodes binaries and places cultures into a hierarchical structure. Unlike assimilation, multiculturalist projects have sought to characterize discrete identities and have done so by creating a series of oppositions. Describing criticism against this kind of construction, Nira Yuval-Davis writes, "Over the years there has been a growing critique of multicultural policies not only from the right but also from the left, as essentialist, homogenizing, reifying boundaries and inherently linked to Britain's empiric past" (*Politics,* 23). Moreover, critics contend that in validating cultural practices and understandings, multiculturalist projects have obscured the mutual constitution of cultures, for example, the way that "British" culture is also produced by people of Asian origin within that national constituency.

In talking about multiculturalism, one is necessarily referring to the ways that ideas such as diversity are appropriated and integrated into articulations, concepts, and practices. It is important to think critically about these processes by recognizing the various competing agendas at work. A. Sivanandan, a founding editor for the journal *Race and Class,* argues that commentators "fail to distinguish between the multicultural society as a fact of Britain's national make-up, arrived at through the anti-racist struggles of the 1960s and 1970s, and the multiculturalism as a cure-all for racial injustice, promoted by successive governments" (3). He argues that Margaret Thatcher's and Lord Scarman's approach toward ethnicism turned into contemporary Labour and Conservative policies of multiculturalism that helped to create ethnic enclaves by "pouring money into ethnic projects and strengthening ethnic cultures" (3). Such an approach, Sivanandan argues, is better called "culturalism."

Culture is a term with many different meanings; its fluidity is part of what makes it such a pervasive concept for understanding difference. A number of critics refer to the reified idea of unchanging, essentialized culture as a "culturalist" understanding, in which culture is excised from the material conditions that produce it and appears in the idealized form of unchanging tradition (see, e.g., Anitha and Gill, "Coercion," 128). Writing about the force of culturalism, Bhikhu Parekh argues that "in their own different ways culturalists ended up naturalizing culture, seeing it as an unalterable and ahistorical fact of life which so determined its members as to turn them into a distinct species" (*Rethinking Multiculturalism,* 11). Sivanandan opposes this culturalism to ideas of "pluralism" that were the result of the heterogeneous ideal of the antiracist struggles of the 1960s ("It's Anti-racism"). In the context of globalization, such culturalism appears, as Aijaz Ahmad argues, "not only as an integral element in social practices but as the determining instance" (*On Communalism,* 95).

The public discourse in contemporary Britain around arranged marriage offers particular insight into the ways a dynamic cultural practice may be represented through a protectionist discourse as an "unalterable and ahistorical fact of life" for a group of people. The notion of arranged marriage as a cultural institution that must be protected within a multicultural society is an idea that appears in law, literature, and popular media and culture. In fact, the terms of multiculturalism are formulated *through* the discourse of arranged marriage. One finds this culturalist discourse both in self-representations by South Asians and within more mainstream discourses like the media or the state. In looking at the way that law, the media, film, and literature center on the distinction between arranged and forced marriage, it is easy to miss how on both sides of that line, the conjugal practices are represented as primarily, if not exclusively, cultural. Texts that take up the question of cultural mobility often end up relying upon these reified notions of culture as a way to distinguish new from old cultures. For example, in her ethnography of South Asian women in East London, Kalwant Bhopal describes how her subjects emphasize cultural expectations such that "arranged marriages were considered to be part of the distinct cultural identity of South Asian people" (*Gender*, 126–27). For Bhopal's ethnographic subjects, the idea and practice of arranged marriage become a mode of affiliation to a particular constituency. That mode, Bhopal argues, functions as an ethnic and gendering force: "Entering into an arranged marriage was part of the process of being identified as an Asian woman. Strong cultural forces define South Asian women's position in society" (126). Bhopal represents arranged marriage as a kind of voluntary submission by and through culture. Notably, Bhopal herself maintains the emphasis on the cultural defined as "tradition," an unexamined term here, rather than distancing herself from the discourse of the women and representing culture as a dynamic process shaped by social, political, and material forces. The powerful rhetoric of culture here is passed from the subjects to the ethnographer, who, though she points to the patriarchy expressed by cultural forces, does not challenge the construct of culture itself, a myriad concept that disguises other kinds of forces. In the conceptions of both the subjects and the ethnographer, culture appears as an agent rather than a set of processes and ideas being actively (re)constructed in the context of the diaspora (see the introduction to this volume). The same understanding of arranged marriage as a culturalist phenomenon appears in state discourses, with culture again rendered as a given. *A Choice by Right,* produced by the Working Group on Forced Marriage, frames the discussion of conjugal practices around "the innate sense of obligation to maintain our cultures, languages, and traditions" (Ahmed and Uddin, foreword).

Arranged marriage *is* a cultural phenomenon, but it is important to be clear what is meant by culture. The public discourses often isolate culture from its historical exigencies. In contrast to this culturalism, cultural anthropologists and cultural studies critics have long seen culture as symbolic and representational (see Geertz, *Interpretation*; Hall, "Cultural"). Parekh's definition of culture reflects this, calling culture a "historically created system of meaning and significance or, what comes to the same thing, a system of beliefs and practices in terms of which a group of human beings understand, regulate and structure their individual and collective lives" (*Rethinking Multiculturalism*, 143). In this way, culture is "an active process of creating meaning, not given but constantly redefined and reconstituted" (153). Stuart Hall challenged the idea of identity as an accomplished fact represented by cultural practices. Hall suggested that we look at identity as a production constituted through representation rather than as a reflection of a given past; he argued not that culture does not exist but rather that it exists as a changing, constructed referent for being. He posited that cultural identity may be seen as a form of

> "becoming" as well as of "being." It belongs to the future as much as to the past. It is not something which already exists, transcending place, time, history and culture. Cultural identities come from somewhere, have histories. But, like everything which is historical, they undergo constant transformation. Far from being eternally fixed in some essentialised past, they are subject to the continuous "play" of history, culture and power. ("Cultural," 394)

Unlike the construction of culturalism, culture is both a dynamic and situated concept. Moreover, the reasons why people adhere to culture are variable. Parekh uses the example of Hinduism, in which "some Hindus follow the norms of their caste system because they accept its cultural authority and meaning, others because of the likely social and economic sanctions" (146). Although culture might rely on backward looking narratives, it should be read with an eye toward the work it is doing in the present. One might ask, then, what work is the arranged marriage discourse, and the forced marriage discourse in particular, doing in the context of late-twentieth- and early-twenty-first-century Britain?

The debates about forced marriage have depended upon constructed notions of Britishness as against an alternate cultural identity. In thinking about national constituency, then, "the boundary of belonging is drawn between acceptable cultural diversity and unacceptable cultural difficulty" (Enright, "Choice," 337). The discourse about arranged marriage functions to distinguish the bounds of an allowable national community. Forced marriage is presented as dangerous culture, an idea that drives the movement to criminalize forced marriage. That locus for that ethnic community might be racial (Asian), regional (South Asian), ethnic national (Pakistani, Indian, Bangladeshi), or religious (usually Muslim, Hindu, or Sikh among South Asian religions). Especially through the late 1990s, this culturalism takes place by the separation of forced marriage from arranged marriage practices. In this discourse, arranged marriage is positioned as a legitimate cultural expression, while forced marriage offers an example of deviant culture—outside the bounds of multiculturalism. In keeping with the wider conversation about arranged and forced marriage, the *A Choice by Right* report deems arranged marriage to be a legitimate cultural preference, while forced marriage is presented as a violation of the rights of an individual. Engaging in a multiculturalist discourse, the report suggests, "The tradition of arranged marriage should be respected and valued," and at another point, it admonishes, "We should celebrate our multi-cultural, multi-faith society, but we also need to make clear that difference, diversity and cultural sensitivity are not excuses for moral blindness" (Ahmed and Uddin, 4). Consistently, the report references cultural difference, framing the socioeconomic practice of arranged marriage as primarily cultural tradition.

Policy, media representations, and popular narratives consistently focus on women as the site of this cultural tradition. Both men and women are subjects of arranged marriage, but rarely do memoirs, media reports, or the anecdotes offered in legislative debates about force in marriage concern the groom of an arranged marriage. The discussion of arranged marriage in general has presented women as the locus for a practice that constitutes both masculinity and femininity through the construction of an ethnic identity. In this way, both popular and scholarly discourses on arranged marriage are gendered. The feminization of arranged marriage in the popular perspective represents the influence of a feminist discourse that concerns itself primarily with the status of women inside the practices. However, the focus on women also reproduces colonial discourses about the South Asian female (chapter 1) such that the perception of women as particularly vulnerable within the practice of arranged marriage also mobilizes the idea of women as the objects of culture.

In addition to being gendered, the culturalist understanding of arranged marriage is associated with religious practices that are, in turn, linked to particular national identities. Especially since the late 1990s, with a rise in anti-Islamic sentiment, such practices have become the marker of an Islamic South Asian community in particular. Enright writes, "The politics of belonging tends to rely on an essentialised notion of South Asian Muslim marriage practice as the product of a bounded culture which is dangerously foreign, inevitably violent and at odds with the core values which define substantive membership of the community of citizens of the United Kingdom" ("Choice," 333). This is an Orientalist discourse, produced out of the conditions of colonialism, reinvigorated as a form of national xenophobia in the late-twentieth-century context of immigration. The political discourse, as well as the memoirs, focuses on certain conjugal practices and ideas associated with Muslim communities, such as cousin marriage or marrying young (even over the age of consent), while mostly ignoring others, such as the acceptability of divorce. Representations of arranged marriage become the means for defining a British identity in opposition to a South Asian Islamic identity that is deemed deviant, if not dangerous.

The emphasis on culture and the presentation of that culture as aberrant in the representations of forced marriage are part of a larger discourse related to the honor crime. Lila Abu-Lughod argues in her article "Seductions of the Honor Crime" and in her later, related book *Do Muslim Women Need Saving?* that the "honor crime" has become a "cultural category that sucks into its web a bewildering array of events and people, gaining solidity through this assimilative process" ("Seductions," 23). While used originally to denote the murder of a woman perceived as violating a sexual code in the name of family honor (*Do Muslim*, 113), the representations of honor crimes have expanded from portraying these killings to depicting forced marriage. In both, incidences of violence (murder, kidnapping, physical and psychological abuse by a family member) that might fall under the more general category of criminal and noncriminal violence are instead attached to the domestic conditions of a specific set of non-Western cultures.

The cultural imagination of the honor crime appears in the 1990s in the mainstream media, though it has its counterparts in academic and activist discourses as well as in the popular literature presented in this chapter. The media stories galvanized public attention and presented certain communities, especially Islamic ones, as bound by traditions of honor, cultural practices that expressed themselves in violence. Media reports have been particularly concerned with "honor killing" and have tended to cluster around particular incidents, often with a young British-born or -raised woman. One such incident was the murder of Rukhsana Naz, who was strangled by her brother while her mother held her down after she became pregnant by a man other than her husband. Naz's arranged marriage at sixteen is featured in these representations, as is the older age of her groom (Chohan, "Oh Yes"). Another case is that of Tasleem Begum, who was run over with a car after purportedly falling in love with a man who was not her arranged husband (Burke, "Special Investigation"). The media articles represent the crimes as motivated by a clash of Western tradition and tradition derived from the Middle East and South Asia; for example, the *Observer* names these places and explains that "[honor killings] occur both in the rural areas, where age-old traditions, value codes and modes of justice still hold sway, and in the cities, where newer tensions have sparked increasing violence towards women" (Burke, "Special Investigation"). In another case, the murder of Anita Gindha, the *Mail on Sunday* quotes a "spate" of killings of Asian and Middle Eastern British women and cites an expert who opines, "It is about the control of women and would be anything from social ostracisation to harassment, to acts of violence against those who are seen to have stepped out of the accepted norms" (Lewis, "Arranged Marriage").

Abu-Lughod makes a point of the ways that domestic violence has been understood, in particular, culturalist ways when the victims have been women of South Asian descent, while other incidents of domestic violence perpetrated by or on white European and European American women have been ascribed to individual pathologies. Moreover, Abu-Lughod argues, noncultural circumstances of crimes on South Asian women are often elided in media representations of the violence. Writing in the same vein in her influential article "Blaming Culture for Bad Behavior," Leti Volpp argues that in the American context, both the law and the popular press have treated differently early and/or coercive marriage among whites and among people of color. In the case of whites, these situations have been treated as pathological anomalies, while in the situation of families of immigrants, such marriages are considered a reflection of cultural values (94). This reified notion of tradition denies the modernity of these practices. As Abu-Lughod argues, "the honor crime category also works through fantasy to attach people to a set of values they are made to associate strictly with modernity and the West" (*Do Muslim*, 121). She reads the construction of this hierarchical binary as playing a role in American imperial and anti-immigrant sentiments in Europe (31).

By looking at the sociohistorical conjunctures that produce understandings through the discourse of arranged marriage, one may rethink the reified notions of culture often used in discussing arranged marriage. Such rethinking would reveal how the culturalist constructions of British and

Asian are set up into binary oppositions using the discourse of arranged marriage. As the last chapter argued, such historical contextualization would also reveal how arranged marriage is better viewed as a function of transnational social, political, and economic forces in the context of diaspora. As in representations of forced marriage, the focus on tradition in these stories elides the role of transnational relationships forged by practices or the conditions of immigration that permeate diasporic contexts and shape individual lives and motivations.

Yuval-Davis writes that contemporary political projects of belonging are "always situated and always multi-layered, which serves to contextualize them both locally and globally, and affect different members of these collectivities and communities differentially" (*Politics,* vii). This book builds on her analysis of the intersectionality of immigrant practices by looking at the kinds of narratives that are produced at this juncture. In the multicultural discourse that has dominated the forced marriage discussion, discrete cultures share the space of a single governance constructed around a neoliberal ideal, but only those cultures deemed acceptable are permitted within that space. Because belonging takes place through the infrastructural regulation of the state as well as through the construction of an imagined community, this reinterpretation would see "culture" as something constructed through state practices, civil discourses, and economic and social exigencies. State, media, and literary texts in the United Kingdom narrate the dynamics of global economy, labor, and relations through the paradigm of conjugality. The next section relates arranged marriage to immigration policies before turning a critical eye to the kinds of state and popular narratives produced during the effort to criminalize forced marriage.

Immigration and Arranged Marriage

Public discourse about arranged marriage has been entangled with debates about immigration such that anti-immigrant sentiments as well as attempts to recognize those same communities within a national body politic are worked out through concurrent representations of arranged marriage. Public interest in arranged marriage, both positive and negative, has been concurrent with changes in immigration policies; the discourse reflects the construction of a national imaginary through conjugal narratives. Even when statutes have been more open to minorities, there is an enduring sense that matrimony should be based on sentiments of love rather than the desire for economic gain. Such logic comes out of a pervasive

Euro-American ideal that imagines marriage not as an arrangement of mutually beneficial terms but as an uncalculating expression of romantic love. Of course, decisions involving self-made marriages often include material considerations like property, income, status, and location, but arranged marriage practices more overtly acknowledge these considerations—they are structures in the practice. For transnational arranged marriages, which often function as a means of mobility across the seemingly unbridgeable chasm of an uneven global economy, these material investments may well be significant, if not primary.

Immigration statutes have long denoted a wariness of non-British spouses, especially those from formerly colonized countries. The Second World War brought a large migration from the colonial territories, including soldiers who had served the Crown and families that had been displaced during the war. They provided the seeds for the new waves of migration that continued through family sponsorship. The 1950s in particular saw an increase in the number of migrants from the subcontinent, who took jobs with lower pay in industries like manufacturing in the postwar boom (Ballard, "Arranged Marriages," 5). This influx, especially from the Punjab, which had been devastated by the Partition following 1947 independence, created a distinct minority from South Asia. This particular group would be followed in the 1970s by other populations after the Pakistani civil war from Pakistan and, later, Bangladesh.

Although immigration regulations were relatively open in the 1950s, popular sentiments were not always so welcoming. Against a backdrop of racist incidents targeting South Asians, a Conservative government came to power with promises of immigration strictures. A law was passed in 1962 blocking immigration from Commonwealth countries except in cases of work permits granted to highly skilled workers. This made family sponsorship a primary mode of immigration, with the number of spouse and fiancé applications rising. This was followed by related regulations concerning spouses, especially husbands. A 1969 law blocked the immigration of non-British husbands, while the sponsorship of wives became more difficult. The logic asserted here was that such men might take away jobs from British men in an economy that was not growing as quickly as in the postwar period. After a brief reprieve from this starting in 1974, the late 1970s brought strictures directed at nonwhite immigrant men, for example, allowing only British-born women to sponsor spouses and not those who acquired citizenship later.

The Primary Purpose Rule was instituted in 1993 under a Conservative government, though there had been antecedents to the law in immigration regulations long before. The rule required that, to gain entry to the United Kingdom, foreign nationals must prove that the primary purpose of their marriage to a British citizen was not immigration. The legislation was clearly directed at preventing the growth of an immigrant population from India, Pakistan, and Bangladesh through family reunification. The rule was, as subsequent Home Secretary Jack Straw put it, "arbitrary, unfair and ineffective and has penalised genuine cases, divided families and unnecessarily increased the administrative burden on the immigration system" (cited in Gupta, *From Homebreakers*, 140). Moreover, the rule assumed that the basis of a true marriage would not include the desire to migrate.

Changes in immigration policies brought an increase in media discussions of marriage fraud, but the issue of immigration fraud ultimately was less compelling than the idea that young South Asian British women were being forced into marriage as a way to sponsor grooms from the subcontinent. By the late 1990s, the discussion of forced marriage became part of the political conversation about immigration, especially immigration from Muslim countries. This public discourse has continued into the first decades of the twenty-first century, during which time legislators have sought to eradicate forced marriage through a series of controversial domestic and immigration regulations. These efforts came together in an effort to criminalize forced marriage, as opposed to primarily rendering the marriage null and void.

The Primary Purpose Rule was revoked in 1997 by the Labour government. However, the subsequent increase in marriage-related immigration, and its accompanying anti-immigrant sentiment, arguably led directly to a discussion of fraud and then the forced marriage debate. Amid media representations of immigration fraud abuses, the Foreign Affairs Select Committee investigated claims that abolishing this ban would increase the rate of nonconsensual marriage. The *Independent* claimed, "There has been a huge rise in the number of British Muslim women forced into arranged marriages following a decision by the government to liberalise the immigration laws last year" (Boggan, Abrams, and Popham, "Huge Rise"). As evidence of this, the same article cited the massive increase in the number of visa applications: "Home Office figures show that the number of Pakistani men using their wife's status to gain entry to Britain has more than doubled from 1,740 in 1995 to 3,510 last year." Citing "a critic," the *Independent* article talks about letters to the embassy by brides asking that the husband not be sponsored, a representation that again places the state into the position of more proper guardianship.

It is not the point here to dispute whether there were indeed fraudulent marriages or marriages that included coercion—there definitely were. Nor is it in dispute that women negotiate the expectations for marriage by delaying sponsoring their spouses or using divorce as a compromise (Bredal, "Arranged Marriage," 100). Rather, the focus here is on the associative connections made in talking about the intersection of immigration and forced marriage. The logic of the article conflates visa applications with forced marriage, making an associative leap that assumes that British-born Pakistani women are necessarily unenthusiastic about Pakistani-born men. Such a logic is both paternalistic and xenophobic, working against the liberalization of immigration from (other) Muslim countries while asserting the protective custody of Muslim women at home. This suspicion of male foreign nationals has shifted from an (overt) discussion of immigration to a debate about criminal laws against forced marriage, a shift related to the expanding cultural imagination of the honor crime discussed previously. One sees both the xenophobia and the fetish of matrimony in the discussion of fraud. The question of legitimate marriage has national as well as personal relevance, because immigration visas are based on proving a legitimate marriage. Helena Wray points out that the regulations guiding immigration around marriage are stricter than those guiding the legal validity of marriage. She notes that immigration policies have targeted not only marriages that are entirely motivated by the desire to migrate, with policy engaged in a discourse of abuse and fraud, but also those in which that is a partial motivation (Wray, *Regulating*, 305). The stricter policies concerning arranged marriage and immigration are part of an attempt to institutionally separate "realms subject to regulation (economic relations) from those 'protected' from such interference (the noncommercial and nonassociational)" (Haag, *Consent*, 95), and the debates surrounding such policies represent the difficulty of doing that around arranged marriage.

State as Surrogate Parent

The public discussion of forced marriage, and its related conversation about honor crimes, has positioned the state as surrogate parent in an alternate family structure. In arranged marriage, the elders in an extended family act as guardians in conjugal decision making. The state's forced marriage discussion represents the older generation of South Asians as inadequate guardians and assumes the role of true parent. Ann Cryer, a Labour MP, led the movement to criminalize arranged marriage that resulted in the British Home Office Report and represents one of the most recognizable voices in this state discourse. Cryer cited a desire to protect Muslim women from the pressure to marry South Asian men with aspirations to immigrate. She recounts her experiences with such transnational marriages as an elected official:

> "In the weeks after I was elected, quite a lot of men came to ask if I could help with visa applications for Pakistani men who had recently married their daughters," she said, "When I asked whether I could speak to their daughters, I was almost always told they were too shy.... I decided to refuse to become involved unless the daughter came to see me so I could be sure she was not forced into the marriage. Now that word of that decision has got round, I don't seem to be asked for that kind of help." (Boggan, "MPs," 5)

Cryer accuses the Pakistani fathers of coercing the hidden daughters' marriages as well as of committing immigration fraud. She positions the state as a more just and caring parent for the young South Asian woman than her biological (and cultural) families, asking "leaders of the Asian Muslim community" to "encourage their people to put their daughters' happiness, welfare and human rights first" (Cryer, "House of Commons"). In asserting herself as the protector of Pakistani daughters, she echoes a colonial discourse that seeks to guard South Asian girls from the men in their families, replacing the biological and social family with the state. The MP is implying that the just father is one who allows his daughter to have a choice, and short of that, it is the right of the state to take on that primary paternal role.

In Cryer's comments, arranged marriage becomes the focal point for what Yuval-Davis calls the politics of belonging (*Politics*, 1). It is important to recognize that in this discourse, the practice must be reformed, rather than abandoned, as a means for assimilation; in other words, difference itself is integrated to create a dynamic neoliberal globalized nation of immigrants. As Sara Ahmed argues, multiculturalism depends on this difference that demands that immigrants "refuse to keep their difference to themselves, but instead give it back to the nation, through speaking a common language and mixing with others" (Ahmed, *Cultural Politics*, 134).

Cryer's parentalism works in the service of constructing a profitable immigrant community. She envisions the transnational marriages as an economic drain on the "Muslim community" within Britain, arguing that it is the community that ultimately suffers from these arrangements:

> I want the Muslim community to be as prosperous as the Sikh and Hindu communities have become, but I believe it is being held back by marriages to men who know nothing of the culture over here, who often don't speak the language and who have to be supported because they are not entitled to benefits. (Cryer, "House of Commons")

Cryer frames the discussion in terms of the economic prosperity of a religious community, "the Muslim community," an entity that conflates multiple national origins and diverse classes into a "new 'ethnicity'" (Wilson, "Forced Marriage," 31), which then becomes a problem for contemporary Britain. She asserts that this community is being stagnated by the very conditions of immigration—a lack of cultural assimilation, a different language, and a lack of benefits. As well as being xenophobic and blaming immigrants for state-controlled conditions like benefits, Cryer's comments reveal a gender bias: it is very unlikely that men would be seen as "held back by marriages" to immigrant wives. But it is the Pakistani British woman (or, really, girl) who is the center of Cryer's vision of marriage fraud and abused women; Pakistani men are displaced as the state becomes the true father to Pakistani daughters.

Cryer's paternalistic sentiments contained in her speech find a more permanent and widely disseminated home in the official document *A Choice by Right*. The working group that published the document was made up primarily of members of the House of Lords and representatives of the Home Secretary's Race Relations Forum and immigrant women's organizations; the group consulted with a range of governmental, social service, academic, journalistic, and legal organizations as well as with individuals with direct experiences with forced marriage. The working group's report calls upon several audiences in its foreword: women and community immigrant organizations, the government, public service workers assisting the victims of forced marriage, and parents in new immigrant communities (Ahmed and Uddin, 2). The document and the process by which it was created show the complex negotiations involved in such legislation in an era that fosters both state intervention and multicultural awareness.

Lord Ahmed of Rotherham and Baroness Uddin of Bethnal Green, co-chairs of the working group and South Asians themselves, wrote the foreword to *A Choice by Right,* and this part of the document, which sets forth the rationale for the proposed legislation, offers a revealing glimpse into the assumptions and agendas at work. Ahmed and Uddin assert that the process of diaspora has created a paternal force deemed unnatural: "As many of us have migrated to Britain, the innate sense of obligation to maintain our cultures, languages, and traditions have [sic] sometimes overwhelmed our ability to develop as a natural family unit" (2). The report does not specify what would make up a natural family unit, or what would make up an ability to develop such, but the discourse more generally provides an answer. In the proposals to criminalize forced marriage, the state asserts the ability to preserve culture while maintaining personal freedom; it seeks to promote national integrity by identifying acceptable cultural practices in concordance with neoliberal ideals of free choice. This is an individualist subject of agency constructed as a "culture of choice" through neoliberal discourses (chapter 1). While elevating a multiculturalist agenda, Ahmed and Uddin prescribe a version of the family for immigrants: "a natural family unit" (2). Ahmed and Uddin frame the foreword as a pedagogical document for immigrant parents. Cautioning these immigrants on how to parent in a new nation, they make a British family unit, as they conceive it, the locus for national belonging. Children are seen as agents "who must be listened to"; thus the process is presented in terms of a generation gap. The document puts itself forward as "facilitat(ing) a dialogue between young people and their elders about their expectations" (20). While advocating for cultural importance, the authors present a teleological vision of change: "there is a rapid acceptance" (1). Rather than seeing culture, language, and tradition as dynamically produced in socioeconomic contexts, including that of diaspora, Ahmed and Uddin cast them as a duty-driven force that creates an unnatural family. The state naturalizes its role as a more just guardian through the trope of the family.

The foreword sets up a parallel between the core values often produced through religion and "new common values" within a national context. While the document highlights family's role in the construction of core values ("duty and love from their family"), it is the state, "today's Britain," that creates the new values based on "a culture of common human rights" and "responsibility among all citizens." The characters of these values are different as well, with the "timeless" core values as "right and wrong, respect, compassion, duty and love," and the "new common values" that are "based on equality and respect between men and women and between people regardless of their race, faith or ethnicity." Ahmed and Uddin are not specific about what constitutes a natural family, but they do go on to say that all parents hold a "cherished dream of untainted success" for their children. They caution that this dream may become "marred by the need to protect them from harm and what is often seen as a Western influence." Continuing to position the protective role of the state in a multicultural context, the introduction states, "The government is developing a broad strategy to ensure that all people can live without fear, whether from racist attacks on the street or from domestic violence." In this formulation, the report identifies violence on a community with violence within a community, ultimately giving the state the role of guardian for immigrant populations.

The *A Choice by Right* document as a whole shifts the discourse from the liberal ideal of full consent that had been central to previous court cases to articulate a neoliberal value of choice. The document defines *forced marriage* as "marriage without freely given consent," and the notion of consent is threaded throughout the document. This is characteristic of the legal discourse, which has also increasingly liberalized this notion of consent. We see here how the legal discourse has entered the legislation in presenting the issues. At a number of points, including in the title of the work, however, it is not consent but rather the concept of "choice" that is featured. In the foreword, choice is set against a false religious rationale: "Many parents use religious rationale to justify their use of force and violence. No religion of the world restricts choice, and we believe that good parents cannot either" (1). The statement arguably references the public debate as to whether Islam protects the freedom of the individual. Through negation, it actually invokes the "honor crime" discourse that suggests that Muslim men in particular are using force and violence on their daughters. What is significant here, though, is that it transforms the contractual notion of consent to choice. In the main body, the document states, "A clear distinction must be maintained between forced and arranged marriages. That distinction lies in the right to choose. The tradition of arranged marriage should be respected and valued" (3). From this perspective, it is not enough that the young women in the community consent to their marriages, as it had been for the courts; the practice must sustain the right to choose whether or whom to marry. The dominant discourse on forced marriage has framed feminist concerns in neoliberal terms that overlook organized struggles against oppression and focus instead on the right to choose (Wilson, "Forced Marriage," 33). Such a focus, as the preceding chapter argued, elides the structural conditions that frame decision making.

Even after *A Choice by Right* failed to bring significant legislative changes, the movement to criminalize forced marriage has continued. In 2005, a law was proposed to make forced marriage an offense but was criticized as ineffective, racist, and undermining other domestic violence legislation. A successful bill that made forced marriage a civil offense punishable through contempt of court charges, the Forced Marriage (Civil Protection) Act of 2007, was incorporated within the already existing Family Law Act of 1996 and explicitly excluded from interrupting the prosecution of other kinds of illegalities through existing law. The act made a provision "for protecting individuals against being forced to enter into marriage without their free and full consent and for protecting individuals who have been forced to enter into marriage without such consent," a scope that includes those within as well as imminent to such marriages. In clarifying the situation regulated under this law, the act relied upon the notion of consent of the individual alleged to be under such force. Entering the tricky gray area of defining force, the act stated that "'force' includes coerce [*sic*] by threats or other psychological means (and related expressions are to be read accordingly)" (2). The act was promoted as a way to streamline injunctions against marriages without consent. However, Anitha and Gill, while recognizing the importance of legal remedies in violence against women, suggest that the bill has been part of a broad movement toward national cohesion that sees forced marriage as a cultural problem and, in doing so, essentializes notions of culture ("Coercion").

The movement to criminalize forced marriage culminated in 2014 in the criminalization of a breach of the Forced Marriage (Civil Protection) Act of 2007 such that either victims or third parties (a local authority, a friend) might apply for a Forced Marriage Protection order. The government, especially the legal branch of the government, had previously approached forced marriage either by negating the validity of the marriage or by prosecuting the attendant kinds of force using already existing laws against, for example, kidnapping, while the immigration ministry looked to fraud as a way to prevent forced marriage. The criminalization names particular kinds of coercion as forced marriage and both implies and disavows an association with Islamic practices with the disclaimer in the opening, "although in the Western world, forced marriage is sometimes discussed as a religious practice" (Gay, "Forced Marriage," 1). While the disavowals show that cultural associations continue to pose a problem, several of the responses to the consultation held when the law was first proposed were concerned with specifying the nature of force. The consultation report cited responses that there "was a grey area where no actual forced was applied" (Home Office, "Forced Marriage Consultation," 9), and one even stated, "It will be almost impossible to define a crime of forced marriage, as it would have to be drawn widely" (Henna Foundation, cited in Home Office, "Forced Marriage Consultation," 10). Other critics had more pragmatic concerns, namely, that the new law would increase incidents of even younger child marriage (presumably where no such thing would yet be expected) or that the criminalization forced participants into an exit strategy who might otherwise want a noncriminal resolution and reconciliation with their families. Along with this criminalization, a controversial immigration law between 2009 and 2011 raised the age to twenty-one for those who could sponsor a spouse and those who could enter on such a visa, in an explicit attempt to forestall arranged marriage. Such tandem measures show the continued imbrication of forced marriage and immigration debates. Forced marriage legislation entered a context in which "certain narratives have traction because of an already existing script about gender, culture, immigration and Islam" (Volpp, "Blaming," 91).

The issue of forced marriage has always been sensitive political ground for immigrant women's advocacy organizations as well as for national policy makers. Feminists have walked a careful line between criticism of state policies and a concern for the well-being of young South Asian women. While maintaining the need for services for vulnerable women, especially immigrant activists have highlighted the overlap between the proposed laws and immigration biases. Among the oldest and most prominent of these organizations is the Southall Black Sisters (SBS), an antiracist feminist organization founded in 1979 and promoting issues related to women of African, Afro-Caribbean, and Asian descent; it has led the way in campaigns concerning violence against women that have highlighted the particular conditions of immigrant women as a crucible of different forces (Southall Black Sisters, "Forced Marriage Campaign"). From that early period, the SBS challenged and successfully overturned state practices that targeted South Asian women, such as the immigration virginity testing used to ensure that those women who arrived on a fiancé visa were not yet married. In the late 1980s, the SBS campaigned against religious fundamentalism and in favor of preserving a secular state. The organization has continued to highlight the intersection of South Asian women's issues and the state. In the early 1990s, it worked against the rule that required a one-year wait before giving a sponsored spouse permanent status in the United Kingdom, a delay, SBS argued, that made women in abusive relationships vulnerable, having to choose between an abusive spouse and deportation. Although the SBS and women's organizations like it present a notable exception to the more general culturalist discourse that continues to reduce oppression to "culture," how these groups named and constituted these oppressions shaped more general understandings of these conditions and their causes; that representation determined the ways in which state and local organizations responded. In the late 1990s, the SBS joined the Working Group on Forced Marriage as part of the group that put together that statement, discussed more later, but left over the question of whether the working group would advocate reconciliation through community mechanisms. The SBS argued that women would be unsafe to pursue such resolutions and, moreover, probably already had tried this by the time they sought state or nonprofit services (Southall Black Sisters, "Forced Marriage Campaign"). Moreover, they led the way in presenting resolutions. Feminist organizations like SBS named forced marriage and featured the "exit strategy" as a means for resolution—exit from the marriage and, often, the social community as well. Other immigrant women's organizations have been vocal critics of criminalization.

Officially, the government carefully avoided naming any ethnic groups of religions; in the *A Choice by Right* document, for example, the authors state under the section "Not Just an Asian Issue" that "the issue of forced marriage should not be used to stigmatise any community" (12). However, the section and the report itself name and then unname the South Asian community in particular, cautioning that "many families with a cultural background in the Indian Sub-Continent will never have come across an instance of forced marriage" (12). While mostly avoiding overt negative representations of South Asians, the official discourse concerning forced marriage frames the problem consistently in terms of culture; the *A Choice by Right* report repeatedly talks about "cultural differences" (e.g., 21).

Critics of the forced marriage legislation have pointed to the ways that the forced marriage discourse has overlapped with a policing of transnational marriages, particularly those between persons from Britain and non-Western countries. Phillips and Dustin argue that "public policy has focused almost exclusively on cases involving transcontinental marriage" ("U.K. Initiatives," 23). Amrit Wilson argues that the Home Office and Foreign and Commonwealth Offices have mainly been concerned with "the overseas dimension of forced marriage," and especially with marriage between South Asian British women and men from the subcontinent ("Forced Marriage," 32). Reforms during this period show a tightening of immigration policies around transnational marriage: the 1999 Immigration and Asylum Act imposed a duty on marriage registrars to report "suspicious marriages" of foreign nationals to the Home Office. The 2004 Asylum and Immigration (Treatment of Claimants) Act required all those subject to immigration control to apply first to the home secretary for permission to marry. This put the Home Office in the middle of deciding on valid versus invalid marriages, something that had been under ongoing discussion in the courts (see chapter 2). What had been patriarchal role, granting permission to marry, now fell inside the scope of the state. A 2012 law requires a minimum salary for those sponsoring spouses as well as a five-year wait period for citizenship. The effort to criminalize forced marriage under specific legislation has continued to be interspersed with changes to immigration laws.

Clearly the law and the media's naming of and focus on forced marriage coincide with this increased control of international marriages that connect Britain to South Asia. The relation between the move to criminalize forced marriage and a movement to forestall particular kinds of transnational marriages is fairly clear. Cryer launched the forced marriage initiative in 1999, the same year as the Immigration and Asylum Act. Immigrant rights groups accused the government of fomenting anti-Islamic attitudes through the legislation (Wilson, "Forced Marriage," 31). The effort to criminalize forced marriage became especially entangled with debates about immigration from countries with Muslim populations, such as Bangladesh and Pakistan. The 1990s and the new millennium have seen a rise in troubled international relations with nations that have a large Islamic population, as well as often contentious domestic relations with practitioners of Islam. This has led some critics to characterize the criminalization discourse as part of an anti-immigrant sentiment embedded in an imperial history. Amrit Wilson argues that initiatives on forced marriages are not empowering to women but part of the state's need to police South Asian communities for terrorism and that it has colonial roots (25). She suggests that contemporary anti-terrorist measures are directly related to neocolonial rule that extends that surveillance and intervention into South Asian practices related to women. Despite the coincidence of these changes, the transformations that gave rise to the focus on forced marriage discourse are not reducible to anti-immigrant sentiments, though they are a factor, nor to anti-Islamic sentiments, though those are there. The 1990s have also seen factors include a mainstreaming of South Asian feminist concerns that reflect a change in the national culture through a growing South Asian population. This same period has witnessed the rise of a multiculturalist discourse that has articulated patriarchal violence as a cultural problem. These too have generated the forced marriage discussion. The overlapping of these progressive and reactionary discourses is one reason why feminist immigrant rights organizations have found the issue of forced marriage legislation so difficult. It is helpful to view these overlapping agendas as what Abu-Lughod calls "articulating domains" ("Seductions," 36), or arenas where discourse shows itself in practice, and to follow Saba Mahmood's lead in sorting out how the "representations of fact, objects and events are profoundly mediated by the fields of power in which they circulate in and through which they acquire their precise shape and form" ("Feminism," 97). One such form, this chapter argues, is the trope of the family.

Forced Marriage Memoirs

Anne Phillips and Moira Dustin describe three approaches that have dominated the British state's relationship to cultural difference: regulation, dialogue, and exit. In regulation, the state creates a standard based on a universal ideal and prosecutes any deviation. Dialogue fosters a kind of ongoing dynamic between different perspectives, one of which might lead toward an intervention, but with the possibility of revision. The third strategy sidesteps direct regulation but invests in the individual's right to exit a cultural practice ("U.K. Initiatives," 1–4). Phillips and Dustin argue that this third approach has dominated the forced marriage discussion. The "exit strategy," which involves leaving the spouse (almost always a woman leaving a husband) or sometimes even cutting off ties to a family arranging the marriage, is the chosen method of resolution for forced marriages within the British state. Public political discourse and bureaucratic texts present the solution to domestic violence as exile from both the family and the community and resolution under a protective guardianship of the state.

In the popular autobiographical works about forced marriage, consent and nonconsent are the starting point in a narrative that features the right of South Asian women to choose romantic love, individual fulfillment in the form of sexual freedom, and Western education. Such works arguably animate the bureaucratic discourses about forced marriage by advocating an exit strategy imagined as a romantic escape. Like the state document *A Choice by Right,* these popular cultural works seek to reform the South Asian family into an acceptable form, but unlike that bureaucratic discourse, these sensationalist texts also appeal for a reform of state services to assist women who use the exit strategy, services that are represented as ineffectual and corrupted by South Asian networks. South Asian feminist organizations as well as legislators have actively published and promoted these memoirs as part of an effort to expand services for South Asian victims of domestic violence and/or ultimately criminalize forced marriage. *Jack and Zena: A True Story of Love and Danger* was one of the earliest of this subgenre, during the buildup to the 2000 Working Group on Forced Marriage; Ann Cryer used the Jack and Zena story, discussed later, to spearhead her forced marriage legislation ("House of Commons," 7). A second wave came about seven years later, around the time of another push for forced marriage legislation, which failed to make a criminal law but successfully led to the Forced Marriage (Civil Protection) Act of 2007. The best known of these memoirs is Jasvinder Sanghera's *Shame,* which was followed by the sequels *Daughters of Shame* (2009) and *Shame Travels: A Family Lost, a Family Found* (2011). Sanghera's family are Sikh, but most of the works published represent the lives of Muslim women, for example, Ferzanna Riley's *Unbroken Spirit: How a Young Muslim Refused to Be Enslaved by Her Culture* (2007); Saira Ahmed and Andrew Crofts's *Disgraced: Forced to Marry a Stranger, Betrayed by My Own Family, Sold My Body to Survive, This Is My Story* (2009); and Sameem Ali's *Belonging* (2008). The narratives of escape from forced marriage feature the oppression of Muslim and Sikh women by their male family members and by their national and religious communities in the diaspora. These memoirs offer affective, on-the-ground representations of oppression and the struggle for freedom as part of a broader political campaign. They also work to shape the discourse of forced marriage as a phenomenon closely attached to the representation of working-class Punjabi and Bangladeshi South Asian communities. Escape narratives work as both propaganda tools and active participants in the construction of a cultural imagination to define national identity and guide the nature of transnational relations. Leti Volpp argues that "a nation can consolidate its identity by projecting beyond its own borders the sexual practices or gender behaviors it deems abhorrent" ("Blaming Culture," 108). The sensational memoirs perform this projection by delineating these abhorrent practices in terms of patriarchal culture in the form of kidnapping, imprisonment, or rape and then reassimilating its victims into a liberal, protective nation. The individual subject of agency is contrasted to a problematic communalist one, which is represented as the embodiment of an essentially violent tradition rather than in terms of its socioeconomic position in the context of globalization (as Nadeem Aslam does in *Maps for Lost Lovers,* discussed later).

It is useful to think of most forced marriage memoirs as assemblages rather than as the true stories of individual women. Though autobiographical, these works are actually often collective works, "as told to" by South Asian British women to non–South Asian British men, who are the ghost authors. Sanghera's Shame trilogy represents a notable exception, and it is part of her project to promote South Asian women's education by presenting herself as having gained a voice. However, *Jack and Zena* is ghost written by journalist Mark McCrum, based on the testimonies of the two protagonists, and promoted by John McCarthy, who wrote the foreword and whose name is featured prominently. *Disgraced* was narrated by Saira Ahmed to Andrew Crofts. These kinds of works feature an "authentic," South Asian woman, mute in the public discourse but represented here, as she was in Cryer's remarks, by a (non–South Asian) British spokesperson. The events of forced marriage sensational literature also include the book's role promoting the forced marriage legislation and its coverage by newspapers that included the *Independent* and the *Guardian*. Although *Jack and Zena* was not a best seller in the United Kingdom, it was in Germany, and though there were earlier works in the same subgenre, such as Sharan-Jeet Shan's 1987 *In My Own Name, Jack and Zena* arguably marked a new wave of similar works produced in the first decades of the millennium. Sanghera has been the most active as a spokesperson as well as a writer. An activist with wide influence in the area of what might be called ethnic domestic violence, Sanghera's memoirs are cited in coverage of the issue, and Sanghera herself appears at forced marriage events and as an expert in documentaries on American cases, for example, the American "true crime" television show *48 Hours* (Freed and Leach, "A Family's Honor"). These memoirs are positioned as true stories of young South Asian women and depend on that for their effect as authentic "tell-alls," but they are collective propaganda tools.

Narratively, these popular writings affectively mobilize toward certain political goals and strategies of social remedy. This subgenre of writing about forced marriage functions in the form of sensationalism, investing the reader through the process of identification and suspense. As memoirs, they map the sociopolitical subject onto a life story that emphasizes the individual. Through their generic form, these narratives offer more filled-out versions of the individual subject around which the discourses of consent and choice are built. The language is simple, seemingly transparently in the voice of the character, and geared toward a popular audience. The plots are forms of the bildungsroman, tracing the trajectory of a young woman sheltered by her family into an independent adulthood that (ostensibly) leads to individual fulfillment in the form of love, education, and employment. The works help create a structure of feeling that guides their readers to a collective understanding of their own nation.

Jack and Zena is the story of an interracial couple who fled their respective homes after Zena's father arranged her marriage to a cousin in Pakistan. Zena, from a comfortably well-to-do family, watches her sister's unhappy arranged marriage and decides to make a different choice. Her self-made romantic partner is a white British man of a different religion and class. During the years recounted in the narrative, they hide from hitmen hired by Zena's family to retaliate against their unsanctioned romance. The escape route takes the couple to different parts of England, where they work with law enforcement from the local community as well as with national social services to find protection. As well as being a cross-cultural love story and an exposé of forced marriage in the Pakistani British community, the memoir is about the failure of the state to adequately handle the needs of immigrants who step out of the safety of that community. Thus there are two themes driving the *Jack and Zena* memoir: the elevation of personal choice and a call for the British state to intervene in a more assertively protectionist manner within a multicultural society.

Jack and Zena begins with a preface by John McCarthy, who legitimates the work and provides a background to the story for a British audience. The book is read in terms of the language of multiculturalism, including "cultural tradition," "multicultural society," "fight against racism," "culture clash," and "race relations" (9), with the book's role presented as a pedagogical one. McCarthy positions the book's contribution in terms of "questions about how we move on as a multiracial society" (9). In this way, McCarthy presents the function of the memoir as similar to that of the *A Choice by Right* document, which states, "We should celebrate our multi-cultural, multi-faith society, but we also need to make clear that difference, diversity and cultural sensitivity are not excuses for moral blindness" (Ahmed and Uddin, 4). McCarthy validates Zena's Islamic faith; he praises Zena's commitment to her family and community as well as Jack's openness to her difference (10). Like the government document, the memoir patrols the border between acceptable variance and disruptive difference through the trope of the family; it populates that family through the national romance.

In her work *Foundational Fictions: The National Romances of Latin America,* Doris Sommer describes the role of love narratives as solidifying the social ideals of a nation. Her work seeks to locate "an erotics of politics and to show how the variety of social ideals inscribed in the novels are all ostensibly grounded in the 'natural' romance that legitimates the nation-family through love ... this natural and familial grounding, along with its rhetoric of productive sexuality, provides a model for apparently non-violent national consolidation during periods of internecine conflict" (76). While Sommer's concept describes the construction of new Latin American nations in the nineteenth century through the trope of intercultural love, the national romances represented by forced marriage memoirs envision Britain as an imagined community made up of diverse ethnic groups cohering around a neoliberal ideal represented by choice, individual fulfillment, and national profit.

Jack and Zena incorporates a model for synthesizing a multicultural Britain in the form of a love story that becomes a way of mediating alliances to produce the modern nation (Sommer, *Foundational,* 81). Such a romance becomes a metaphor for a naturalized form of communion between disparate communities. When the romance becomes a marriage, as it does in the case of Jack and Zena, the union is sanctioned by the state. *Jack and Zena* may be read as a kind of foundational fiction for a multicultural Britain, a narrative that works discursively toward union through romance. The memoir's spatial trajectory reinforces the sense of an imagined community as the couple moves from one location to another in England. Through this imaginative geography mapped by movement, the reader is given the sense that the couple's dire situation is not localized in the immigrant-filled towns but belongs to Britain as a whole (though the couple remains in England, the narrative may arguably be read in terms of Britain because of the more general discourse framed in those terms).

There are two problems with this England, according to the memoir. First, the country appears like a dangerous place where Asians operate in a kind of underworld. Writing about the bounty hunter sent by her father and brothers to capture her, Zena states, "This bounty hunter is famous, apparently, within the Asian community. The way it works is that he gets paid a sum in advance for finding a runaway girl, and he doesn't get settlement till he's found her. He uses his own network, the Asian network that stretches across Britain like a web, though restauranteurs, shopkeepers, minicab drivers and so on" (71). The state services of the Department of Social Security are portrayed as filled with Asians with loyalties more to this network than to their jobs. A second problem with England is its inability to provide proper support services. For the most part, the state throws bureaucratic impediments in the way of their success. Moreover, as Zena faces racism, Jack faces problems because of his working-class identity. The memoir presents itself as a critique from the position of marginal identities in the national space.

In the face of these failures, the memoir asserts the validity of Jack and Zena's national belonging. Musing on why they never left, Jack states, "England is my country and, on principle, I didn't see why I should be chased out of it because I happened to have fallen in love with the wrong woman—an Englishwoman born and bred, whatever her family's origins" (113). The formulation of this claim suggests that Jack positions himself as the natural citizen who may argue for her inclusion, despite her difference ("whatever her family's origins"). Reading the message of this memoir, the story of a nation emerges, developed through the sensational narrative of an oppressed South Asian girl who must be protected by the state from her own community and legitimized (despite her British birth) by three white men—Jack, the ghost writer Mark McCrum, and the promoter John McCarthy. Even in this reformist discourse, the memoir asserts the state as the rightful protector of the girl and the exit strategy as a necessary strategy.

Jasvinder Sanghera's novel *Shame*, which has the sequels *Shame Travels* and *Daughters of Shame*, features the idea of an oppressive South Asian community driven by notions of shame and honor to the point of abdicating their custodial duties. Like *A Choice by Right*, the memoir's narrator turns to the failure of South Asian parents, asking, in *Shame*, "How could anyone turn their back on their own child for the sake of a concept? How could that be considered honorable? To me it seemed a cause of shame" (275). Sanghera does not differentiate between arranged and forced marriage in the original narrative. There is arguably no happy arranged marriage in the memoir.

Sanghera's family is Sikh and comes from the Punjab area of India. Her sisters marry grooms from their community in India when they are sixteen, and she is expected to do the same. Instead, Sanghera has an Indian British boyfriend who is from a lower caste than her family. When the family begins to arrange her marriage to a young man from India, she escapes with the help of her boyfriend, whom she later marries. In terms of plot, *Shame* tells the story of Sanghera's difficult transition and a series of romantic relationships that follow her departure, including some abusive ones. However, rather than directly criticize the isolation and vulnerability she finds in the broader national context, as does *Jack and Zena*, Sanghera directs the force of her criticism upon the community that encouraged, even expected, her arranged marriage. Of course, the two criticisms are not exclusive, but Sanghera is primarily looking for the reform of her Indian community.

Sanghera faults the Indian family for its role in her oppression, and she especially highlights her mother's role in the constraint of their daughters. Throughout the memoir, the narrator bemoans the failure of her mother to provide the kind of support and protection that she needs; she imagines her mother "looking round to check on me" (2) and admits, "The truth was I needed her." Sanghera's mother is the primary articulator of the community's mandates. She tells one of her daughters, "It is your duty to have a respectable marriage and to uphold the good name of your family" (22). When this same daughter is beaten by her husband, the mother tells them it is her duty to look after her husband. There is no evidence that Sanghera's mother questions this concept of duty, but she is shown as constrained by her reputation in the community. When Sanghera leaves the family, her mother says, "Thanks to you I can't walk the streets of Derby anymore; I can't go to the gurdwara because people are talking. People spit at me" (3). Sanghera's mother is presented as bound by the expectations of the community to the point that she relinquishes her protective role as mother. For Sanghera, that role would feature the mother–daughter bond against the community. Sanghera casts her mother, as herself, a victim of that community, who herself married her deceased sister's husband to raise her child (14). When Sanghera visits her mother dying in the hospital, and tells her mother she didn't love the husband arranged for Sanghera, her mother treats her with contempt. Sanghera tries to see things from her mother's perspective: "she was Jagir Kaur, who, at the age of fifteen, had been made to marry her dead sister's husband, my father. She had worked hard, raised eight children and led her life according to the unspoken rules of the community she feared and treasured. What did she care for love?" (165). Sanghera ultimately presents her mother as a victim of the same patriarchal values of which her mother is the primary enforcer within the family. The author frames that oppression as the denial of the ability to love.

Sanghera also faults the designated leaders of the community and the community at large for perpetrating the oppression of women. Considering a time her sister sought the advice of a religious leader, a man who tells Robina to stay with her husband, she muses, "All she'd wanted was for the rows to stop and to have some reassurance that she would be supported by her family. What she was getting was reinforcement of all her worst fears from a man of stature, a man who was speaking for the people she loved, and the whole community where Mum and Dad had to live. How could she not listen?" (143). The leaders are shown as at best uncritical of and at worst abettors of violence against women. Ultimately, however, Sanghera shows the amorphous community with its penchant for gossip and judgment, rather than just the leaders, as the true oppressor. The community teaches modes of behavior until they are internalized. When thinking about the double standard of exogamous relationships, in which an Asian boy "might have a bit of fun with white girls," but an Asian girl "would be ruined; no decent Asian man would ever want her," Sanghera describes her own interpellation within the community: "no one handed me a book of rules but I knew the particular way in which I was supposed to act, walk, talk, even breathe" (8). Community censure is a powerful trope in these memoirs, which figure the nonconformer as an outsider.

Surprisingly, given this, the most idealized alternate space is not the refuge of the British state presented in documents like *A Choice by Right*. Like *Jack and Zena*, the memoir shows alternatives to the community as a lonely place with few opportunities. Indeed, Sanghera herself gives voice to this sentiment, stating, "I'd always despised the strict censoriousness of Mum and Dad's community, but in the years alone with Jassey I'd come to understand that it did afford a safe place in the world, a clear pattern, and I'd found nothing to replace that" (168). Sanghera questions the ability of the outside community to sustain the young women who leave their families and communities, materially and emotionally, something that is true of nearly all of these memoirs, despite their ostensible support for the exit strategies. Instead, the memoir turns in resolution to the liberal space of education, as the narrator pursues a university degree that will free her from the need for any man.

What Sanghera is ultimately showing here is the inability to be a dissenting member of this South Asian community, but in this memoir, such dissent takes only the liberal, individualist vision of the "right to choose" one's own romantic partner or a British education. There is no possibility for radically transforming that community into a space of heterogeneous dissent—its inhabitants, especially those of an older generation, seem so mired in an ossified culture that such agency would be unthinkable. Moreover, it is far from Sanghera's mind to advocate for the empowerment of her immigrant community, economically and politically, such that dissenting members could sustain themselves while remaining within that community. In *Shame,* alternative behavior becomes alternative space, as the characters often exit the community to enable their alternate perspectives. Such a resolution, of exit, appears as the only solution, albeit not a very successful one. This is in contrast to literary works, such as Nadeem Aslam's *Maps for Lost Lovers* and Monica Ali's *Brick Lane,* that, while offering the same depiction of community coercion, ultimately leave at least some of their dissenting characters within the same place, albeit ambivalently. That point is discussed more subsequently. The memoirs themselves offer more contradictory depictions of personal and social resolution. Even as they participate in the government's "exit strategy," the memoirs raise important problems in the exit strategy as they detail the difficulties of the subjects to enter into a sustainable alternative community. *Jack and Zena* and *Shame* show the failure of the state to offer such a community, but they do not see an alternative in the politicization of a particular South Asian community as a whole.

Feminist support services have helped women leave dangerous situations. They have argued that such women cannot engage in resolution measures that would place them in danger (Southall Black Sisters, "Forced Marriage Campaign"). That difficulty is an important fact to remember in any critique of the policies that support women's ability to leave violent situations. However, a state policy built around generalizing the tactic of this exit has been problematic, and its discourses have been inflected by colonial antecedents. Phillips and Dustin assert that the "exit strategy" has been a problem in a few ways. The strategy oversimplifies the dichotomy between coerced and consensual marriage ("U.K. Initiatives"). That dichotomy has even been a problem for the courts, as the last chapter showed, in which the difficulty limiting forms of coercions has resulted in the liberalization of ideas around coercion, with the decisions acknowledging a range of pressures from the emotional to the economic. As even the judges in those cases concurred, consent is also more complicated than it initially appears. While the dichotomy between consent and coercion functions on a secure division between a yes and a no, sometimes even a yes might reflect significant forms of pressure, from the interpersonal to the interpellation of duty and affiliation. Those pressures become even more complex once the subject is already within the marriage, perhaps with a child. The exit strategy has not incorporated the interpersonal pressure on individuals to remain in (as opposed to enter into) an unwanted marriage (Phillips and Dustin, "U.K. Initiatives," 6).

Another problem with the "exit strategy" is socioeconomic. Exit from a marriage often means an exit from a family and even from a local community. Exiles are then forced to rely on wage labor and might not have the education or economic support structures to make this work. This is particularly true of young women, though not exclusively. "The question of what makes the exit option real has exercised virtually everyone involved in work around forced marriage," Phillips and Dustin argue ("U.K. Initiatives," 20). By "real," they mean offering a viable option. The destination for the exit has often been state support, a process that turns the state into a proxy parent. This happens literally for the young woman in Simon Chambers's documentary *Every Good Marriage Begins with Tears,* who leaves her family to enter state-sponsored foster care when she is unable to support her family's values.

The exit strategy functions in practice as a critique of immigrant communities that are represented as creating a vulnerable population of young women. It is, at its core, a protectionist discourse that infantilizes women, and not just ones under the age of consent (though that image dominates the whole), rather than creating conditions in which they might thrive in an alternative South Asian community. While no one could rightly deny the need for girls or women of any age to build their lives in the absence of violence upon their mental and bodily selves, one must also look critically at the narratives that are being produced and consider how they function within a larger sociopolitical context that includes anti-Muslim and anti-immigrant sentiment. The forced marriage discourse in Britain presents the protection of women's rights as a cultural problem rather than, for example, as related to domestic violence across culture. As Abu-Lughod argues, it takes the most extreme expression as the norm *(Do Muslim).* Moreover, the exit strategy is one that undervalues, if not precludes, the possibility of negotiation or internal intervention within the community.

Escape narrative memoirs clearly participate in the state's agenda for using the exit strategy as a resolution to what has been framed as "the forced marriage question," but they also challenge the effectiveness of the strategy. *Jack and Zena* is structured as an escape narrative; in the process, it promotes the exit strategy, but it does so as a critical participant. This memoir takes up the question of the "exit to." Sanghera also ends with a turn to a more general demand for state services on behalf of vulnerable populations of young women. Sanghera moves out from her own story to feature the stories of young women she helps after she founds a women's organization, Karma Nirvana, to work with local refuges for women. One story she tells is that of a Pakistani woman, Zainab, who has an arranged marriage at sixteen. Zainab is abused by her marital family, by a husband who rapes her, and by a mother-in-law who treats her like a servant and beats her. Unable to speak English, she swallows bleach as the ultimate exit strategy. Musing on this case, Sanghera states,

> It suddenly occurred to me that, although she must have been in Britain for two years, incarceration in her in-laws' house meant Zainab knew almost nothing of this country or its people. Her suicide had caused her to be picked up and dumped, unprepared and empty-handed, into a western way of life. She had nothing familiar to cling to. (262)

Sanghera's appeal is to educate but also, more materially, to gather political and economic support for her refuge. There is no idea of Zainab returning to a Pakistani community here; rather what is needed, from Sanghera's perspective, is a culturally sensitive British national space, something the women's shelters have not provided. Despite its awareness of the hardship of Zainab's exit from her home, Sanghera's memoir, like others within this subgenre, does not move out of the culturalist discourse of the state documents and public campaign to underscore the social, material, and economic factors operating transnationally that constitute the immigrant home.

Mapping Transnational Relations in Nadeem Aslam's *Maps for Lost Lovers*

While the state discourse and forced marriage memoirs have given a limited view of the problems regarding violence entering into or within arranged marriage, fiction and film have offered more complex understandings. The last chapter featured several of these works that present the sociopolitical, economic, and affective relations of arranged marriage, including the legal decisions on annulment, Simon Chambers's film *Every Good Marriage Begins with Tears,* and Monica Ali's novel *Brick Lane*. Another work that focuses specifically on the "honor crime" provides a similarly nuanced portrayal that brings into the discussion of force in arranged marriage the conditions of global history and transnational migration as well as the intimate relations that animate both affiliation and violence.

Maps for Lost Lovers represents a working-class Pakistani community in a town in Britain. The story is set around the disappearance of an unmarried couple, Jugnu and Chanda, who are presumed to be dead as a result of an "honor killing" on the part of the young woman's family. Much of the plot revolves around an elder couple, Jugnu's brother and sister-in-law, whose lives are affected by the disappearance. The man, Shamas, turns to an illicit relationship with a troubled young woman divorced from her husband in Pakistan, while Shamas's wife, Kaukab, recedes further into her Islamic devotion.

The British novel was published in 2004, at the height of a national fascination with honor killing, and despite its literary merits, its popularity is arguably due in part to the way it fit into this anti-Islamic cultural moment. The themes of immigration, transnational marriage, and Islam are central to the book. Aslam writes with the same didactic purpose as the forced marriage memoirs depict, and the work echoes many of the themes of the "true life" national romance narratives this chapter describes. Nearly every page provides an exposé of the corruption, small-mindedness, patriarchy, perversion, and hypocrisy that take place under the name of Islam. Aslam presents women as universally oppressed by the Islamic communities to which they belong, whether in Pakistan or Britain, and as forced into forms of sexual violation by the demands of those communities. Kaukab's devotion is a primary theme in the novel and is represented as a way of evading or disguising other kinds of troubles. Kaukab exploits her daughter Mah-Jabin's emotional vulnerability to coerce her into an arranged marriage as a way to uphold her own standing in the community, while her daughter is beaten in that same arranged marriage. One woman, separated from her arranged husband, is killed when she finds alternative love, while another, whose husband has divorced her, feels bound to prostitute herself to an older man in the hopes that he will help her negotiate a complex arrangement she believes prescribed by Islam that will allow her to see her son. Unlike Monica Ali with *Brick Lane,* Aslam presents no positive counterimage of religion and its role in the everyday lives of women, or even anyone. Pakistan is presented as a place where only a Western-raised woman with "the confidence of English life still clinging to her" would object to an uncle's rape of his fourteen-year-old niece (161). It is little wonder, then, that Lila Abu-Lughod argues that Aslam "succumbs to a pedagogical compulsion" to pit "closed-minded traditionalism" against "openness of cosmopolitanism" with its elevation of the "right to choose love against society and religious norms" ("Seductions," 35). Despite this kind of binarism, the novel arguably offers something very different than the sensational memoirs in the way it depicts the transnational affective, economic, social, and political relations that constitute the subjects of agency in an immigrant context.

In *Maps for Lost Lovers,* Aslam presents the power of patriarchy as a force wielded between generations, rather than solely that between men and women, and done so in the area of conjugality. This idea is made particularly vivid by the representation of the main character, Shamas, as having an ambivalent relationship to his own power. Although the novel emphasizes the patriarchal power that Pakistani men, including Shamas, hold over their wives to make decisions regarding where they live, how or whether they work, or even whom their children will marry, it also shows marriage as an arena in which an older generation of women exert control. Kaukab imagines a Pakistani daughter-in-law as a potential ally and continues unsuccessfully to try to bring this wish to life by arranging a marriage for one of her sons (59). Aslam presents arranged marriage in particular as a way for older women to maintain control over a younger generation. Although Kaukab's daughter Mah-Jabin agrees to an arranged marriage at one point, she is shown to be manipulated in the emotional wake of disappointed love. As that young woman comes of age, she calls arranged marriage "organized crime" (108). In Aslam's novel, women maintain this power only through their access to Pakistan and their position as archivists of Pakistani custom within the diasporic community. Marriage is seen as a way to perpetuate community values and for a woman to increase her own influence in the family.

Despite this negative portrayal of Islam as it is practiced by the represented communities in Britain, and of conjugal practices associated with the communities, Aslam's novel provides the basis for an alternative reading of culturalist understandings that have dominated the forced marriage discourse, as well as of the honor crime in general. *Maps for Lost Lovers* presents honor, and Islamic devotion in general, not as a deep, essentialized cultural understanding but as a rationale for individual pathologies and a means for maintaining transnational networks. Take the primary crime of the novel. When Chanda and Jugnu are killed by her brothers, the perpetrators represent the act as a way to preserve family honor. However, at the end of the novel, Aslam returns to this scene to show the more immediate causal factors. One brother, enraged when he finds his lover, Kiran, in bed with another man, drunkenly turns his anger on his sister and her lover. Another brother has been traumatized by the fact that he forced his wife to abort what he thought was a female fetus, only to find out the fetus was a male. The honor crime is presented as a useful cover. At the same time, like the practice of arranged marriage, the rationalized violence becomes, for Chanda's brothers, a mode of belonging, a way of being Pakistani as much as arranged marriage.

In exposing this rationale, Aslam represents how the Pakistani British community responds to its representation in the British mainstream public and sometimes even mobilizes such representations to their own ends. The brothers find this stereotype of the honor-driven Pakistani a useful tool to cover their own violence, but the more sympathetic character Shamas fears his wife's heavy-handed parenting will play into this perception and make the family vulnerable: "Shamas warned Kaukab to be careful and not lay a hand on the girl, because otherwise tomorrow the local newspaper would be carrying the headline BRITISH-BORN DAUGHTER OF PAKISTANI MUSLIM COMMUNITY LEADER BEATEN OVER MATTER OF MARRIAGE, bringing into disrepute in one fell swoop, Islam, Pakistan, the immigrant population here in England, and his place of work, which was—in the matters of race—the officially appointed conscience of the land" (122). While Aslam is reinforcing his characterization of Kaukab as someone who will beat her teenage daughter when she finds out she is in love with a local boy, he is also using Shamas's highly educated voice to question the state as a more proper custodian for that daughter. The implication here is that the community is aware of how its actions appear in the broader national context and that they experience that relationship as a kind of surveillance.

Instead of a notion of honor coming out of an essentialized version of culture, Aslam shows the real driving factor for the interpersonal violence in the Pakistani British community to be the transnational forces of migration and the national conditions of immigration. He frames the story with the conditions that prompt global migration in the first place as Pakistanis "managed to find footholds all around the globe in their search for livelihood and a semblance of dignity" (9). Aslam represents the difficult conditions for immigrants, describing the changes and increasing racism that gave rise to a ban on immigration and the repatriation of immigrants who were already there (11). This is an England in which a pig's head is left outside a mosque and a child is described as "half Pakistani and half... er...er...er...human" (10). Aslam develops a side story of two illegal immigrants so desperate they agree to be paid by the accused to pose as the dead couple and to live in such squalor that one dies in the collapse of a condemned building. There is a reason the Pakistanis call the British town "Dasht-e-Tanhaii. The Wilderness of Solitude/The Desert of Loneliness" (29), the same name as a Faiz Ahmed Faiz poem about longing. Aslam portrays Britain as a place of abject alienation for South Asian Muslim immigrants.

Although drawing on the rhetoric of tradition, Aslam's immigrant community is shown to be a modern one. These structural diasporic conditions form the backdrop for the development of a patriarchal community in Britain that garners strength from the religious hierarchies of the homeland but cultivates its vitriol from the scarcity and constraints of its new context. A new Pakistani identity emerges in Aslam's diaspora that is not so much a descendent of an original Pakistan as a source of new transnational identities that mobilize in networks across the globe. Characters move readily back and forth between Pakistan and England for labor and matrimony, and money travels from England back to Pakistan. Moreover, the legal sphere of the state moves transnationally. Investigation of the disappearance of a couple must take place transnationally through international legal agreements. The crime is rationalized under notions of shari'a, drawn from the split discourse that emerged within the postcolonial state of Pakistan, but such traditional law is given new meaning in the diaspora as the center of gravity for a displaced and disenfranchised patriarchal community. Aslam's representations of arranged and forced marriage are shaped by and shape this transnational context.

The portrayal of the sheer desperation for global migration offers the readers some rationale for the marriage arrangements that would make this possible. These are fraudulent marriages from the perspective of the state's immigration regulations, as well as from the perspective of romantic love, but they are not invalid from the perspective of self-betterment. Aslam stops short of justifying these transnational marriages driven by the prospects of British citizenship or the desire to maintain transnational relations with home villages, but his novel does explain them by laying out the socioeconomic context in which they happen. In his representations, it is only Pakistani men that are empowered through global mobility, though women secure their community connections through those same conjugal structures.

Unlike the state discourse, media representations, and the sensationalist forced marriage memoirs, which offer culturalist visions of "Muslim" identity, the novel explores alternate ways to be both Pakistani and British, while also elaborating a number of different ways characters inhabit an intersecting Pakistani British identity. Kiran, the mother, feels as though they are on borrowed space; "don't forget, this is not our country," she admonishes, though she does her best to maintain a version of Pakistan in her own home. The children move further into the British culture, away from the liminal space of their mother's home. Shamas, however, is invested in the repatriation of community members to their new home in ways compatible with their Pakistani identity. His character, who remains as an alternative voice inside his Pakistani British community, offers a challenge to the exit strategy. In this way, Aslam's literary work is what Monisha Das Gupta calls "space-making" rather than "place-making," in the sense that it agitates for viable change within a community through the restructuring of power (*Immigrants,* 9).

The representation offered by the fictional and filmic work of Aslam offers a significantly different resolution to the fraught question of national belonging than do public sphere discourses of the state, media, or popular culture. Aslam's social realist work does not offer happy resolutions, and while he too presents exit as the only viable solution for the young man of one family's younger generation, he leaves two critical perspectives, a father and daughter, inside, attempting to bring change. The shift to include the South Asian community as a dynamic form represents a departure from culturalism to culture as something that might change while retaining its identity as a locus for belonging. Against the kinds of national imaginaries offered by the public discourse and escape memoirs, this literary work gives a vision of a cultural pluralism as opposed to multiculturalism, in which a national future is imagined not as an assemblage of ahistorical, essentialized cultural forms but as a dynamic political and cultural interplay.

This chapter interprets the multiculturalist discourse in the contemporary conversation about arranged and forced marriage in Britain to show how public and official discourses about arranged marriage construct an ideal multicultural British identity that gives primacy to the state in matters of immigrant family. The political, media, bureaucratic, and autobiographical discourses challenge the guardianship of the biological and cultural family. A range of texts from these genres mobilizes anti-immigrant, especially anti-Muslim and anti-Sikh, fears through its representations of South Asian patriarchal violence reduced to culture. A critical reading of that discourse uncovers the unstable points in a national romance that is repeatedly unsettled by ways the British state has been unable to provide adequate services to those who exit from their cultural communities and by transnational forces that produce affiliations and processes that cross borders. Ironically, it is the autobiographical works themselves that offer critiques of this romantic ideal. Even though these memoirs both actively promote an exit strategy in which the young woman must leave her home and community and support the intervention of the state in an effort to criminalize forced marriage, by showing a fairly negative outcome for this exile, they present the state as a flawed custodial agent for the young South Asian British woman. While these sensationalist escape narratives do little to challenge the kind of culturalism that casts these communities as inherently violent, a social realist work, Nadeem Aslam's novel *Maps for Lost Lovers,* portrays an intersection of forces upon immigrant communities. He shows not just the expression of power but the constitution of power in violent forms in the arena of intimate familial relations. This is the kind of understanding that is needed in the forced marriage discussion as a way to move away from a discourse that repeats colonial narratives and gives form to xenophobic sentiments.

4

The United States and Canada

Individual Freedom and Community

A U.S. immigration representative sorts love letters, photographs, and hotel receipts to assess the validity of an upcoming marriage, while another official next door decides a visa based on whether a second couple belongs to a society with a long-established custom of arranged marriage. They are reviewing the I-129F U.S. immigration form for a fiancé visa entry to the country, which provides for an exemption from one of its requirements that the couple have met in person in the past two years, in the cases where such a meeting "would violate strict and long-established customs of the beneficiary's foreign culture or social practice, as where marriages are traditionally arranged" (U.S. Department of Homeland Security, "Fiancé[e] Visas"). In this imaginary scenario based on real law, evidence of the second couple's legitimacy would not be grounded in proof of individual desire or familiarity, as it would for the first couple, but on the bride's and groom's willingness to participate in a conjugal practice and the common recognition of that practice as part of a deep-rooted culture.

Representations, including media reports, autobiographical accounts, films, and fictional works, show the kind of cultural imaginary that surrounds a practice. Interpreting such an imaginary allows the critic to denaturalize a highly symbolic practice like arranged marriage so that it no longer appears as a stand-in for an unexamined notion of culture. Clifford Geertz sees culture not as a coherent "thing" that is passed down intact but as a set of beliefs and practices. He advises looking at cultural texts not just for the meaning but for how people derive meanings from the "webs of significance [humans themselves have] spun" (Geertz, *Interpretation*, 5). Culture is thus a set of representations and interpretations that enter a field of social and political practices. Moreover, as Stuart Hall argues, cultural identities are ever changing, "subject to the continuous 'play' of history, culture and power" (Hall, "Cultural Identity," 394). Following this, one should not think of arranged marriage in terms of what "it" means, because "it" is an amalgamated, changing signifier that is historically constituted. Rather, one should look at how that evolving myriad of concepts and practices function in a given community and how the community interprets this "culture" in dynamic and productive ways.

As well as identifying some of the arranged marriage narratives in North America, then, this chapter asks to what ends these positive and negative accounts that reduce notions of culture to iconic form have been mobilized. To understand the symbol of arranged marriage as a constitutive site, one must recognize the social relations that are involved and often hidden within the term *culture*. Structural and material forces shape decisions around marriage in North America, as they do elsewhere in the diaspora and in South Asia itself. Arranged marriage discourses and practices reference ancestral traditions, and certainly such practices have been long-standing both in the subcontinent and, in a more limited way, in North America. However, these representations and practices are also continually produced out of new exigencies of transnational mobility, such as immigration law, the economic ambitions or needs of a new population, reactions to forms of racism, and modes of transnational belonging. Such discourses emerge from the experiences of location through the shaping contexts of (re)settlement.

Representations of the practice of arranged marriage are situated in their own historical contingencies and imagined through different cultural forms with different effects. The discourse concerning contemporary Muslim immigration and forced marriage in the Canadian media has different goals than the mainstream U.S. media's celebration of upper-middle-class arranged marriages as fostering new kinds of love compatible with tradition. However, though the ends to which negative and positive representations have been mobilized are not unified, both kinds of representations offer responses to the condition of being marginal. As a group, this set of representations includes both narratives of assimilation and communitarian responses of differentiation. Arranged marriage appears as a staging ground for a relationship to a national identity formulated within the context of globalization, with, on one side, desire for integration and, on the other side, a desire for exceptionalism. Both sets of portrayals mobilize the idea of culture and the overdetermined symbol of arranged marriage. In the United States and Canada, narratives of arranged marriage present the wish for assimilation or refusal of the same formulated through the symbolic practice of conjugality; arranged marriage has become a marker of difference, but a difference that is not always seen as negative.

Taken as a whole, the discourse on arranged marriage turns to the institution of marriage to mark modes of national belonging. Conjugality, with its "monumental public character" (Cott, *Public Vows,* 1), empowers, and is empowered by, the nation-state that vests the institution with legitimacy; moreover, forms of conjugality represent national culture. Narratives of marriage, and their associated modes of romance, of dynastic and ethnic belonging, mobilize affectively toward political and social ends. Marital fictions produce a concept of marriage and, in in the process, "do special work in and for different types of power formations at the levels of the local, the state, and the empire" (Holzer, "Tying the Knot," 1). They present an intimate site for the exploration of belonging.

This chapter examines how a particular conjugal practice became the focal point for articulating competing subjects of agency: the individual and the community. In bringing different discursive strands together, the following discussion interrelates emic and etic, or "inside" and "outside," cultural narratives that together shape what arranged marriage means in the U.S. and Canadian diaspora. There are two arguments inherent in this method. The first is that representations *by* South Asians need to be read in conjunction with those *about* South Asians. While these might present very different political or personal perspectives that often emerge from different experiences, both South Asian and non–South Asian representations grapple with the same ideas and assumptions that circulate within national and global contexts in ways that cross over that divide. Thus, for example, Mira Nair portrays in *Monsoon Wedding* a young couple who turn away from the difficulties of interpersonal relationships in a liberalizing India and a diasporic Texas to get an arranged marriage. Isabel Coixet's film *Learning to Drive* (2014) depicts a divorcing Euro-American woman who learns about loving and being present for her family from her Sikh driving instructor in an arranged marriage. The films share a romanticized representation of arranged marriage as a return to family and substantive living. The second argument presented by this method is that the two North American nations may be read together. The reason for this is not just geographical proximity but that there are some shared histories of immigration as well as literary and filmic influences that permeate the border. With that said, the chapter shows how the overlapping but nonidentical discursive trajectories in those two nations become shaped by the conditions and structures of immigration histories in slightly different ways.

As a way of historicizing and elaborating the contemporary arranged marriage discourse in the U.S. and Canadian diaspora, this chapter begins with articulations of arranged marriage presented by early-twentieth-century immigration policy and literary works. These representations pose arranged marriage as the antithesis to the ideal of national belonging symbolized by romantic love. The chapter then turns to the alternate discourse of community belonging that, against this cultural norm of individualist assimilation, posits the value of communitarianism and reinforces the role of the family and such extended communities as religion, caste, or nation in conjugal decision making. This section reads the production of these communities in the context of minority politics, arguing that a historicized understanding of these South Asian immigrant discourses reveals the desire or necessity on the part of some South Asians to enter North America with difference. Cultural nationalists have embraced arranged marriage as a sign, using arranged marriage to create a notion of a sustained tradition that connects immigrants to the homeland. This sign should not be read as a given fact of culture, as it is in the immigration policy, but as an articulation, in that the idea of culture here promotes sociopolitical goals through the construction of communal imaginaries. People seek to reproduce community structures through endogamous practices, or marrying within the community, but that process is historically contingent and geographically located. Moreover, when these practices are constituted through concepts of caste, class, religion, ethnicity, or nationalism, they are so within the context of local and global forces that emerge from the forces of modernity and capitalist expansion (Kohsy, "Introduction," 4). This has sometimes prompted changes to the practices but has also given rise to the creation of fundamentalist formations. In the United States, a post-1965 generation solidified a narrative already present in the broader national milieu about arranged marriage as a "strict and long-established custom" around which an ethnic identity cohered, but it did so for different reasons: to refuse, reinvent, or reinvigorate such an identity.

Looking at the texts and functions of arranged marriage shows how South Asian Americans and Canadians promote new diasporic identities by returning repeatedly to the idea of arranged marriage, making arranged marriage arguably the preeminent symbol of South Asian identity. They do so not only through negation, meaning by rejecting or altering the custom; they also do so by reaffirming the notion of arranged marriage for new reasons or in new ways. In considering how the idea of community is developed, this chapter builds on the work of South Asian American studies ethnographers who have conducted fieldwork interviews about dating and marriage, but it adds to this a textual analysis of both print and digital culture. In an analysis of endogamous practices found in the categorical structures used on the matrimonial website Shaadi.com, this study finds that these structures, far from disappearing in the diaspora, have been reinvigorated by the technologies of globality.

In positing the practice of arranged marriage as the antithesis to individual freedom, both the discourses that promote assimilation and those that constitute difference through communitarian identity regularly elide the conditions within which notions of arranged marriage have emerged and become mobilized, representing conjugal forms as ahistorical embodiments of an ideological principle. The above argued for situating these portrayals in their historical contexts as a way to fill in such elisions. Another way to challenge the stories offered is to read the contradictions within the discourses themselves. One may do this across genres, from the bureaucratic and legal discourses of the state on marriage policy to the sensationalist media reports that trope the female Muslim girl as victim. However, a literary and cultural analysis lends itself particularly well to such a deconstructive read.

With an extended analysis of the South Asian feminist bildungsroman, the third part of the chapter analyzes a literary form that uses the image of arranged marriage to narrate a female subject caught between the discourses of individualism and communalism. Among liberal feminists, South Asian or otherwise, arranged marriage has become an image of oppression that unequivocally denies women agency and represents the oppressive nature of the South Asian diasporic community. Feminist literary and filmic works set the individual and community in opposition through their dramatic tension, presenting a critique of the patriarchy of communal structures. At the same time, the ambivalent resolutions of these South Asian feminist bildungsromans highlight the problem of assimilation narratives premised on a woman leaving an arranged marriage. This chapter analyzes a set of South Asian feminist bildungsromans as a way to deconstruct the binary of individual and community created around the idea of arranged marriage in the South Asian diaspora. Films, novels, and short stories by Mira Nair, Deepa Mehta, Bharati Mukherjee, and Chitra Banerjee Divakaruni have appeared to critics as indicting the patriarchal diasporic community and advocating what British feminist legal scholars call an "exit strategy." This chapter shows how, though these novels idealize individual freedom in ways similar to the feminist bildungsroman genre Rita Felski describes, the South Asian female protagonist is portrayed as unable to vest herself fully in individual freedom because of the affective ties and socioeconomic stability presented by community belonging. Jhumpa Lahiri's novel *The Namesake* does offer such a resolution for the South Asian woman in the diaspora, but in limited ways. In Lahiri's work, the conditions of diaspora make independence difficult, if not untenable, for the transnational arranged marriage bride until she has children, and the situation for the American-born one is not shown as much better. In this way, these works differ from those in chapter 5 that resolve the incompatibilities between arranged marriage narratives and neoliberal ones like choice, personal happiness, and therapeutic discourse.

Returning to the genres of media and policy, the last section of the chapter looks at the forced marriage debates in Canada to show how the politics of immigration continue to inform contemporary representations of arranged marriage. This section reads how a late-twentieth-century multicultural discourse about "values" has been radicalized by the global politics of contemporary immigration to become a discussion of "forced" and "child" marriage centered on the South Asian Muslim and Sikh girl. In the Canadian context, the last part of this chapter argues, a multicultural discourse in the mainstream media uses the language of "values" in a way that seems to validate alternate ways of being but ultimately entrenches the binary between individualist and communalist notions of agency in ways that reify cultural identities.

Arranged Marriage as Un-American

South Asian arranged marriages in North America are a relatively more recent phenomenon, because the structures of immigration prevented South Asian women from immigrating in significant numbers until the 1960s. The logistical and cultural conditions of early South Asian immigration were prohibitive to arranged marriage. As Karen Leonard, Vivek Bald, Nayan Shah, and Pawan Dhingra have shown, the various migrations to the North American West Coast, to the Gulf Coast, to the East Coast, and later to the Midwest were the site of diverse histories of labor, class relations, religious identities, and interracial relations (Leonard, *South Asian Americans*; Bald, *Bengali Harlem*; Shah, *Stranger Intimacy*; Dhingra, *Life*). However, one important commonality across these locations in early periods was that the immigration regulations shaped conjugal practices by delimiting a primarily masculine labor pool and establishing impediments to family reunification. This prevented those men from colonial India from bringing their wives or children with them. Even after Indians regained some rights to entry, the conditions of immigration, in which female immigration was not numerically significant and "only a handful of men had managed to bring their wives from India" (Hess, "Forgotten," 584), meant an interruption to arranged marriage and to endogamous (marrying within the community) practices more generally for those leaving the subcontinent.

As the channels for arranged marriage became difficult, a male community of migrant workers raised in a culture of arranged marriages (and with some members already in arranged marriages with women in India) turned to the newer practice of exogamous and self-made marriages, if they married at all. The result of this was a practice of ethnic and cultural mixing as immigration regulations fostered marriages outside of a shared national, religious, ethnic, and linguistic culture. In California's Imperial Valley, just north of Mexico, Indian men married Mexican women, creating a mixed culture (Leonard, *South Asian Americans*; Majumdar, *Marriage*; Hart, *Roots*). As well as retrieving the history of this culturally mixed community, recent scholarship has also focused on lesser-known groups that maintained a presence before and after the Punjabi migration to the West Coast: Vivek Bald describes how Bengalis who migrated to places like New York City and New Orleans in the early twentieth century mixed with other communities, especially African American ones, as they set up transnational networks of trade and migration *(Bengali Harlem)*. Sunaina Maira muses on how ignorance about early history of ethnic and cultural mixing has reinforced contemporary Indian American rules promoting marriage strictly within the Indian community *(Desis in the House,* 125). Knowledge of such mixing would presumably challenge ideas adopted by later immigrants that they, or their children, were the first to break with the endogamous practices associated with arranged marriage.

Although it is important to question the idea that all South Asian immigrant groups have always sought to marry within their communities until very recently, one must not over-romanticize this history—or the idea of marriage—for the sake of validating intercultural connections. Some of these early mixed marriages might have been unhappy, polygamous, or both. Leonard quotes a farmer's oral history in 1982: "In India, you stay together all your life. In this country, you have love" (Leonard, *South Asian Americans,* 54–55). However, as the farmer goes on to say, by the time he filed for divorce (not necessarily before the time of his second marriage), his wife in India had died. This farmer suggests he already had an arranged marriage back in India (since most marriages in India during this period would be arranged), and one gathers that he was participating in both an endogamous arranged marriage and a self-made marriage that transcended community bounds. Nayan Shah tracks the way the U.S. courts were tasked with adjudicating the legitimacy of marriages consecrated in India by considering the story of a man with a marriage in the Punjab and one in New Mexico (*Stranger Intimacy*, 165). Concluding from these examples, just as significant as the intercultural marriages is the presence of multiple forms of conjugality, including *both* an arranged and self-made marriage for some early immigrants.

The wide-sweeping prohibitions of the Asiatic Barred Zone that was enacted by the 1917 Immigrant Act in the United States effectively prevented the entrance of both men and women, cutting off the routes of transnational arranged marriage. Although citizens might sponsor wives and children, prohibitions to naturalization and citizenship for Asians in general unmanageably impeded this route. The 1923 *United States v. Bhagat Singh Thind* Supreme Court decision was a test case for Asian naturalization; the decision against Thind prevented those who were already in the United States from becoming naturalized. Thus, when the 1924 Immigrant Act expanded on the Asian exclusion policy of the 1917 act by prohibiting entry into the United States of all aliens "ineligible to citizenship," the act effectively barred new immigrants from India as well as other South and East Asian regions. Moreover, the net of prohibitive legislation made conditions for those already here even more untenable in many cases; for example, the California Alien Land Law prohibited aliens from owning land. Transnational arranged marriage became prohibitive for second-generation female Asian Americans with the 1922 Cable Act, which did not allow American women to retain their U.S. citizenship if they married a man "ineligible for citizenship," which included men from Asia (Cott 165). These early acts also prevented most Asian immigrants from bringing their families with them until after World War II and the passage of the 1946 Luce Cellar Act, which granted a small number of Indians per year entry, and the 1952 McCarran–Walter Act, which ended exclusion but maintained quotas. Still, it was not until the passage of the 1965 Hart–Cellar Act, which gave preference to professional skills and familial connections and removed the national origins quota system, that South Asians arrived in greater numbers.

Despite fewer numbers of endogamous marriages in earlier periods within these communities, the idea of arranged marriage was important in and outside of the Indian community, especially as it was used as a counterpart to an idealized romantic love. Both legal and literary discourses set arranged marriage against a national ideal of individual freedom embodied by the self-made marriage. The cultural ideal expressed freedom through individual choice and cast arranged marriage as the antithetical prehistory of such a norm. Werner Sollors argues that nineteenth-century American writers narrated the emergence of a new nation in portrayals of Native Americans by contrasting self-made love stories with images of arranged marriage, while later, European immigrant fiction used arranged marriage as a counterpart to stories of assimilation. He argues that "American allegiance, the very concept of citizenship developed in the revolutionary period, was—like love—based on consent, not on descent, which further blended the rhetoric of America with the language of love and the concept of romantic love with American identity" (*Beyond Ethnicity*, 112).

In the arena of institutional practices, while arranged marriage was made difficult by early-twentieth-century regulations that structured forms of conjugality, it was simultaneously the object of an ideological battle. A late-nineteenth-century public discourse about sex work, conjugality, and choice shaped public views about arranged marriage that remain to this day. Nancy Cott describes how in the late nineteenth century, "virtually all 'Americanizers' of the early 1900s, no matter how much they appreciated diversity among cultures, disapproved of familialy arranged marriage. Not putting love first, arranged marriage appeared to bear only a debased likeness to the real thing—akin to contract labor's travesty of consent" (*Public Vows*, 151).

As Cott argues, images of arranged marriage thus became important assertions of modernity for an evolving nation, a symbolic role the practice continues to have to this day. Moreover, the discourse on arranged marriage became the ground for an ideological vision of marriage brokered by the individual decision maker as the basis of a national identity, as opposed to a marriage arranged by kin embedded in networks of local and transnational communities.

Cott contextualizes this negative portrayal of arranged marriage as against both love and individual freedom within the context of an antiprostitution campaign that specifically targeted Asians and dominated how statesmen saw arranged marriage. The antiprostitution campaign reveals the ideological significance of sexual and conjugal practices, even as it shows how such investments were structured into the workings of a racialized state. Specific antiprostitution regulations were introduced in the Immigrant Act of 1917, and arranged marriage forms, "in which overt economic bargaining and kinship networks beyond the marrying pair played acknowledged parts" (*Public Vows*, 149), were deemed a form of prostitution. Thus being a participant in an arranged marriage, for which there was almost always an economic or kinship network aspect, was potential grounds for exclusion from citizenship and even for deportation. Pamela Haag interprets this prohibition on arranged marriage as a means to ideologically divide relationships idealized as "economically and socially interested" from those presumably free of these interests. She suggests that arranged marriage "foiled modern liberal concepts of citizenship and individual rights, which insistently partitioned off realms subject to regulation (economic relations) from those 'protected' from such interference (the noncommercial and nonassociational)" (*Consent*, 100).

Both Haag and Cott argue that this discourse on self-made versus arranged marriage was highly racialized. Haag connects the discourse of love to racial uplift, in the sense that it taught "savage" races the arts of mutual consent in their personal lives (*Consent*, 111). Cott argues that the willingness to perceive arranged marriage in this way was in part due to views that already existed against two of the communities that engaged in this practice, Asians and Jews, as racially other and un-Christian (*Public Vows*, 149). However, more than racism and anti-Semitism colored this particular discourse. The discourse around arranged marriage in the early twentieth century intersected with a central American ideal of individual agency in the form of freely held consent, an intersection that continues to structure the reception of arranged marriage today.

Cott interprets this discourse on arranged marriage and early American immigration as reinforcing notions of being American expressed through conjugal practices. Arranged marriage was deemed "un-American" because of a close relationship held between individual consent in marital practices and a form of governmentality. The basis of this was a shift between former modes of governance based in hierarchical ideals and new commitments to reciprocal rights and responsibilities (*Public Vows*, 16). Cott argues,

> Because mutual consent was intrinsic to [the American version of marriage], this form of marriage was especially congruent with

American political ideals: consent of the parties was also the hallmark of representative government. Consent was basic to both marriage and government, the question of its authenticity not meant to be reopened nor its depth plumbed once consent was given. (3)

Just as metaphors of family relations pervaded state discourse, the paradigm of consent as just governmentality infused the discourse surrounding conjugal practices. Affects of love and commitment were mobilized in service of both and could be moved from one to the other so that to be American was to have a certain kind of marriage based on consent and to have a certain kind of marriage was to be a good American. Consent was venerated as the embodiment of individual agency, as it was legitimated within a public institution in a way that made self-made marriage a way of being American. As Sollors argues, this idealization was a way of shifting power from kinship networks with marriage by "descent" to the state, with marriage by "consent" (*Beyond Ethnicity,* 111).

An early South Asian work represents arranged marriage in a way that cultivates this notion of consent but also expands it to the more general category of choice as a form of freedom. Dhan Gopal Mukerji, an Indian American author of popular acclaim in the early twentieth century, published his memoir *Caste and Outcast* in 1923. Although, as an author with a national reputation, Mukerji was from a class very different than the farm owners in Southern California's Imperial Valley who engaged in self-made relationships, his work intersects both with their intimate experiences and with the broader American discourse about self-made marriage as a form of freedom. At the same time, his memoir arguably speaks against the prohibitions on South Asian immigration through a discussion of arranged marriage. In one chapter, Mukerji deals with the subject of arranged marriage, presumably speaking to the ongoing cultural fascination with the topic in the United States. The marriage is not Mukerji's own—he later had a self-made marriage to a European American scholar—but that of his older brother when the author himself was young. In Mukerji's depiction of arranged marriage in early-twentieth-century India, young people had some choice to decide on the marriage after they were introduced with that intention. However, he writes, the idea of choice was actually an "ancient custom" in India before it was displaced by a Muslim invasion: "Now in the olden time, before the conquest of India by the Mohammedans, women chose their own husbands. It used to be called *sayamvara* meaning 'the choice'" (123). Mukerji retells the story of a princess who makes her choice of her "heart's idol" among her many suitors (123). As he continues the history, he suggests that the practice of marrying child brides spread "so that they could be protected from the Mohammedan enemy" (124). Mukerji mobilizes the concept of choice to produce a Hindu nationalist and anti-Muslim version of Indian history. He uses the language of American forms of conjugality as freedom to parallel a culturally nationalist version of India to a foundational American ideal of choice. In a political moment in which Indians were losing ground in their claims as naturalized citizens, Mukerji presents choice as an inherently Indian and specifically Hindu value, thus positing Hindu immigrants as natural Americans.

Mukerji's arguments for the Hindu as the true American fell on deaf ears, as far as the legislation was concerned. The new laws on naturalization and property made it prohibitive for many South Asians to remain in the country. The 1920s to 1940s were a period of repatriation, in which some three thousand returned to India (Hess, "Forgotten," 590). The limited migration to the United States during this interregnum included students and a group of twice displaced migrants, such as those from Britain, East Africa, and the Caribbean. This doubly displaced group of immigrants developed family structures that maintained cultural communities, including through arranged marriage, though they were not able to migrate in significant numbers until quotas were lifted. They laid the groundwork for the cultural practices of a much larger community of South Asians that arrived after 1965 in the United States. The Immigration Act of 1965 allowed certain technical professionals to enter the United States. This group of skilled workers, along with the temporary and permanent migration of students following those tracks, changed the demographics exponentially for a South Asian population and reshaped narratives of culture.

Constructions of Community: The Post-1965 Generation

There is a popular idea that South Asian immigrants have always practiced arranged marriage, and that ideal is only now breaking down with a new generation. That image falsely represents the history of conjugal arrangements and their meanings in the U.S. and Canadian diaspora. Arranged marriage is really a post-1965 phenomenon in the United States, meaning that this newish generation was the first to bring the practice from South Asia in significant numbers, and more importantly for the argument presented here, this generation was the first to give arranged marriage its contemporary meaning as a primary symbol of identity for South Asian Americans. The first generation of immigrants following the change in immigration regulations established arranged marriage as a signifier of ethnic identity rooted in history. They reinvented the idea within new historical exigencies, making arranged marriage in the South Asian diaspora a product of transnational modernity and an overdetermined symbol of culture.

The post-1965 first generation of immigrants shaped a narrative about arranged marriage as a deeply held tradition that should be maintained in the diaspora as a way to connect the transnational community to a homeland. They sustained this narrative through endogamous conjugal practices that continue to this day and the exhortations to remain true to an identity seemingly displayed by such practices. This first generation and their children have created the "imaginary homelands" Salman Rushdie famously associated with writers of the Indian diaspora, the "Indias of the mind" (*Imaginary Homelands*, 10) born of the desire to look back to the immigrant homeland. Arranged marriage, as a symbol of identity for South Asians, has played a key role in this nostalgia for different groups within the broader diverse community, even as its ongoing and evolving practices shape these diasporas. One may see this symbolic importance both in discourses that seek to define particular or more general South Asian communities through notions like the "values" inherent in arranged marriage and in the more negative representations that created and maintained the story of arranged marriage as the cultural inheritance of South Asians, but one that must be renounced.

Immigrants seek to reproduce community structures through arranged marriage, which acts as a way to organize expressions of such identities as religion, caste, language, nation, region, and ethnicity. More elite members of this community look to protect their own class and educational status through arranged marriage, expressing material interests as well as symbolic meanings through the practice. This is particularly true of the middle-class Indian immigrant community that arrived through the work permit regulations that recruited those trained in science and technology. This group was already reshaped into a national elite; Madhulika Khandelwal writes, "The well-educated Indian immigrants arriving in the 1960s and early 1970s were imbued with an Indian national identity and sophisticated pan-Indian culture that translated readily into a unitary ethnic consciousness" (*Becoming American*, 1). Such an ethnic consciousness, formed through national policies in India as well as in other South Asian nations, and given meaning in the diaspora, took form through the symbol of arranged marriage. It is among this group that arranged marriage gained its status as a sign of national culture to be preserved, even as that group assimilated into the socioeconomic structures of America like the educational system and professional workforce.

The mapping of tradition and modernity onto national locations in the subcontinent and the United States, respectively, obscures the history of modern reform in India itself. In the construction of arranged marriage produced by this post-1965 diaspora, the country of origin is perceived as a place of immobility rather than as a place itself engaged in projects of modernization that focus on conjugal practices. Speaking of Indian immigrants in an ethnographic study, Bandana Purkayastha notes that "Indian immigrant parents revert to petrified templates of dating and sexual norms in India... denying that these social mores have changed in the 'home' country since the 1960s or 1970s and clinging to their amber memories more tenaciously as their children begin to challenge them" (*Negotiating*, 159). Sunaina Maira has shown how even the younger generation of South Asians has turned to those symbols, albeit in a more selective way *(Desis in the House)*, a point discussed later in this chapter.

The matrimonial website Shaadi.com may be interpreted to see how arranged marriage practices continue to participate in endogamy in the U.S. and Canadian diaspora to mobilize community identity by reinforcing categories of identity. Shaadi.com, which was founded in 1996 by Anupam Mittal, promotes itself as the world's largest matrimonial website and claims to have served thirty million people. The website is oriented toward a South Asian membership, both in its marketing and in its categories of identity. Shaadi.com promotes self-made marriages, much like a dating website, except with the more explicit goal of matrimony; however, a significant number of profiles are posted by parents or guardians. This subset of arranged prospects most closely fits the definition of arranged marriage used in this book, in which decision making is given over to some degree. The profiles posted by guardians resemble the print ads that have been a long-standing practice in diasporic publications like *India Abroad*. Unlike those print ads, however, the structures of the interactive website appear to be read through digitally searchable identity categories.

While the profiles found on the website are prospective rather than actual matches, the statistics and structures offer a wealth of information about how South Asians in the diaspora are practicing arranged marriage. Shaadi.com offers seven choices for those who self-identify religion: Hindu, Muslim, Christian, Jain, Parsi, Buddhist, and Jewish, as well as the categories of "other," "spiritual," and "no religion." Several hundred "communities" are searchable under the religion of Hindu, fifteen for Sikhs, and twenty-one for Muslims. Gender, language, and region are searchable, as are a range of criteria like income, education, marital status, height, age, and even "special needs," including HIV status. One may also separate permanent residents or citizens of the United States and Canada and those in those countries on work or student visas, a very important pool of eligible spouses on the marriage market and by far the largest category posted by guardians.

The website and others like it both promote more transnational searches and enable endogamous practices within global matchmaking through the way they facilitate identifying and finding such mates. It is impossible to say how many who self-identify as a religion or caste would also restrict their search for a like spouse, or even how many profiles might falsely represent the subject; arguably, however, a certain consistency in the statistics allows for some provisional conclusions. First, one is struck by the sheer number of religiously identified profiles, with 5,523 Hindu-identified U.S. permanent resident and citizen female profiles and 5,376 total Hindu profiles posted for permanent residents and citizens in the United States (there is a similar ratio with lower participation for Canada). Shaadi.com seems most popular with Hindu-identified participants, with fewer than one-quarter their number of Muslim profiles, followed by one-eighth Christian and Sikh users. One of the most interesting facts gleaned from the website in searches limited to those posted by parents and guardians is how few Hindu-identified participants have "caste no bar" checked, or about 50 percent for both males and females. One may conclude that caste remains a defining community identification in the diaspora—or at least a reluctance to dismiss caste as a factor has been sustained in the arranged marriage process.

One of the striking aspects of digital matchmaking as reflected by Shaadi.com is the fact that parents and guardians of both males and females are almost equal participants in arranged marriage searches. This is despite the fact that the public discourse has been overwhelmingly preoccupied with females. It can be easy, when discussing arranged marriage, to reproduce the elisions of the discourse itself, in the sense that representations predominantly show female arranged marriage subjects, when in fact there are an equal number of males. This book attempts to fill in some of those narratives, including in the readings of Mira Nair's documentary and Jhumpa Lahiri's novel. However, as a discursive analysis, this book is more centrally concerned with how the iconic female arranged marriage subject is mobilized to social and political ends. The next section looks at how a liberal feminist discourse has articulated the promises and pitfalls of national belonging through that female subject.

Liberal Feminist Critiques of Arranged Marriage

Until very recently, when more affirmative human interest stories on arranged marriage as love marriage have appeared in the press (chapter 5), the mainstream U.S. and Canadian media represented arranged marriage as a practice that epitomized a lack of women's independence in oppressive families based on patriarchal hierarchies. A *Washington Post* article in 1993 put it this way: "Across South Asia, arranged marriages are the norm and can sometimes be the most demeaning rite of passage a woman endures" (Anderson and Moore, "Born Oppressed"). The popular understanding of arranged marriage as a point of oppression has also been a way of signifying the foreignness of South Asians (Purkayastha, *Negotiating*, 40). This representation, which posits the self-made marriage as free and the arranged marriage as compulsory, reflects a Western cultural bias, but it also draws on a liberal feminist critique of arranged marriage authored by both South Asians and non–South Asians. While this representation may sometimes simply present arranged marriage as an idea inherently oppressive to women, as in the *Washington Post* article, feminist work also contributes a structuralist analysis that locates the practice within the dynamics of power.

Liberal feminist writing presents an ideological critique that denounces the function of arranged marriage reflecting and supporting patriarchal, religious, economic, and/or heteronormative power structures. Arranged marriage is deemed violent because it becomes an opportunity for domestic violence, against women in particular, including physical or mental coercion on the part of parents or abuse by a new family, including the husband but also the extended family who compose the new home. Feminist activists have articulated the kinds of exploitation associated with arranged marriage, including compulsory sexual and other personal intimacy, economic dependency, and a lack of personal freedom. In the introduction to the seminal collection *Sisterhood Is Global,* Robin Morgan argues that because women are regarded as less than full human beings, "we are viewed in a (male-defined) sexual context with the consequent epidemic of rape, sexual harassment, forced prostitution, and sexual trafick [sic] in women, with transacted marriage, institutionalized family structures, and the denial of individual women's own sexual expression" (8). Morgan's list connects "transacted marriage," which would include arranged marriages "in which overt economic bargaining and kinship networks beyond the marrying pair played acknowledged parts" (Cott, *Public Vows*, 149), to sexual traffic and rape. Especially recently, this discourse of sex traffic has connected arranged marriage to child marriage, mobilizing anti–arranged marriage sentiments by mapping the practice onto a particular form of exploitation.

Filmic and literary representations advance the analyses begun in early feminist work, but they may also complicate understandings of women's oppression in arranged marriage as primarily a product of gender inequity. These creative works highlight the "intersectionality" of women's experience in which other dimensions besides gender shape the violence against women (Crenshaw, "Mapping," 7). Mira Nair's feminist documentary *So Far from India* (1982), for example, contextualizes the intimate power relations within a marriage and a joint family in such sociopolitico fields as rural and urban relations, changing class relations in India, and the global economies of transnational marriage. Thus, while the film does thematize the question of individual agency for the female subject in particular, it also locates both male and female arranged marriage subjects in the context of postcolonialism and globalization.

So Far from India tells the story of an arranged marriage in the context of transnational migration. Before the male subject Ashok leaves for America, where he finds work at a newspaper stand, his family in Ahmedabad arranges a marriage with a young woman named Hansa, originally from a village in Gujarat. After the wedding, Ashok stays with his wife for just a few weeks before emigrating. Hansa remains in Ashok's ancestral home with his sisters. Nair highlights how the sisters disparage the match, perhaps because it does little to further the family's social interests, and the film represents Hansa taking on the bulk of household chores. As well as featuring joint family dynamics, Nair focuses on the transnational nature of the match by interviewing Ashok in New York and his wife in Ahmedabad.

On a certain level, the documentary takes up liberal questions of individual satisfaction in representing the arranged marriage. Nair questions both the husband and wife about their happiness, but while Ashok engages her question by musing about whether he really wanted to get married,

Hansa appears resistant to assessing her life on those terms. For example, when Hansa describes how she exchanged her people for strangers who became her people, Nair asks her if she was sad—presumably about the process of relocation and marriage. Hansa smiles at her and responds that she was sad that her husband was leaving so soon. Although it is impossible to know what she felt or desired, Hansa's oblique answer proves her to be a resistant subject who remains within an alternate discourse from the filmmaker, unlike her husband. There could be a few reasons for this. One might simply be the documentary subject preserving her privacy with a new acquaintance and on such a public medium as film. Another reason might be the kinds of narratives featured in arranged marriage, in which the point of marriage is more to take one's place in a familial structure than to seek and find personal happiness. In either case, one may see in Hansa's evasion a kind of disjuncture between the documentary's narrative and the arranged marriage subject.

While Nair frames the documentary's story within the ideal of personal satisfaction that marks a liberal feminist perspective, she also highlights the social and material conditions that make the practice something more complex than a "demeaning rite of passage" (Anderson and Moore, "Born Oppressed"). During the mismatch of questions and answers about choice and happiness, another narrative appears that exposes the historical social and economic frameworks that scaffold the practice of arranged marriage in India and in transnational contexts. Hansa is disempowered by her arranged marriage not necessarily because it was arranged but because the marriage becomes an articulating point of the contradictions of community in a time of postcoloniality and globalization. The story of the family elaborates this. Ashok's family is downwardly mobile. They had been spice merchants serving the royal families of Gujarat through the colonial period, securing status through that position and gaining a relatively cosmopolitan culture. Now, though they have lost that economic position, the father and daughters retain a sense of the culture and community prestige. They turn to Ashok, as the son, to bring the family prosperity by working abroad, having him marry before he goes. Hansa, who comes from a village family, finds herself both the symbol of the family's descent and the means to connect a man to his home in the context of global migration.

Nair is exceptional in treating the particular ways that an intersection of forces comes to constitute male and female subjects of arranged marriage. The filmmaker shows the articulation of power within the domestic and intimate spheres within these national and transnational economic forces. Ashok reveals to Nair that his father initiated the marriage process so that he would not fall in love with an American woman or marry abroad, and one gets the sense that he was reluctant to marry. Arranged marriage is a way of keeping him inside the community, but it is also a stepping-stone for the community through the transnational groom. Ashok complains that many of his relatives—and presumably his wife's—have already asked him to sponsor them. A worker at a subway newsstand, Ashok does not have enough even to support his family in India, much less bring over his wife. Although the film clearly shows him as the more agential subject, Ashok is also contained by the extended family that uses its structure to increase global mobility in the context of scarce economic opportunities.

While Ashok is bound by the expectations of his family, in the patriarchal structure of marriage, Hansa's mobility is dependent on Ashok's decision making, as she waits for him to invite her abroad. Within the familial relations of the patrilocal joint family, she is positioned as interloper, a point made as the sisters exploit Hansa's labor and abuse her emotionally. Such power is deployed in intimate relations as well, as the sisters lay claim to their brother's affection against the more tenuous claims of the wife who has lived only weeks with the emigrant husband. The only way Hansa may regain that power and intimacy is in her role as mother, which it seems by the end of the film she will do.

So Far from India, Nair's first film, differs in tone from her later fictional film *Monsoon Wedding*, which focuses on a more well-to-do class participating in arranged marriages (chapter 5). While *Monsoon Wedding* offers the fantasy of an upper-middle-class family celebrating the wedding of an arranged marriage in India between a young man studying in America and a professional woman back in India, *So Far from India* gives a realist view of an arranged marriage as an articulating point of power within an impoverished family. The oppression in such a marriage, though it exists, is not reducible to the form of arrangement but rather to the way socioeconomic forces find their outlet in the domestic realm. While retaining the liberal feminist narrative of an individual subject of agency, Nair presents a version of that subject that is constituted in domestic and global spaces by the histories of postcolonial transformations and global migration as well as by patriarchal practices.

The Feminist Bildungsroman

Whereas Nair's documentary takes a realist form, many of the contemporary South Asian American fictional representations of arranged marriage fall within the genre of the feminist bildungsroman, but modify that genre with an ambivalent resolution that highlights the problem of diasporic belonging for women. Franco Moretti describes the bildungsroman as the "symbolic form of modernity" (*Way of the World*, 5) that privileges interiority while narrating the development of a youth through the motif of mobility. The classical bildungsroman ends with marriage, a resolution that becomes, for either a male or female protagonist, a "definitive and classifying act par excellence" (7). Rita Felski has defined the "feminist bildungsroman" as within the bildungsroman genre but engaged in a kind of "reworking" of some of its key characteristics, such as the marriage plot (*Beyond*, 133). Like the bildungsroman Moretti describes, these works emphasize the notion of self-discovery, but the journey for the woman is outward rather than inward. This transition from the private into the public world functions as a sign of critique of the existing social order, which is most often symbolized in the text by marriage. A woman's community mediates this transition, Felski argues, an entity which may appear in the form of a lesbian romantic relationship. While their works advance a liberal feminist critique of marriage, the South Asian American feminist writers who feature arranged marriage present culturally specific reasons why a woman enters and stays in a marriage, as well as the consequences of her leaving, by showing the intimate relation between arranged marriage and cultural belonging. This distinguishes these works from the more general feminist bildungsroman Felski describes and often leaves them with more ambivalent resolutions than total freedom.

Unlike the classical form, feminist bildungsroman novels place marriage early on in the narrative and chart the process of self-discovery as the resistance to the patriarchal structures of marriage. In the traditional bildungsroman, the romance furthers the protagonist's self-awareness, and the marriage plot allows him or her to become a functioning part of society, but this is not the case with the feminist novel, a "narrative of female self-discovery, in which access to self-knowledge is seen to require an explicit refusal of the heterosexual romance plot, the framework which has traditionally defined the meaning and direction of women's lives" (122). Felski calls this contemporary self-discovery novel form an optimistic genre in that it suggests the possibility of identifying oppression and challenging those values. The text itself becomes a kind of working-through of those oppressions in a way that parallels the development of feminist consciousness. A critical part of this is the recognition of traditional female roles as daughter, wife, and mother and the active reconstruction of these. In this way, the feminist bildungsroman is "itself an ideological site, an active process of meaning production" (126). Resistance against marriage, then, becomes both a means to and a sign of a feminist consciousness as the woman gains a sense of self while simultaneously becoming estranged from a patriarchal environment, a narrative of liberation that also imagines a possibility.

Deepa Mehta's film *Fire,* Chitra Banerjee Divakaruni's short story "Clothes" in the collection *Arranged Marriage,* and Bharati Mukherjee's novel *Wife* arguably fit within the genre of feminist bildungsroman and are interpreted at length in the following pages. Each begins with a marriage and charts the dissolution of this marriage alongside the development of the female self. In each work, the protagonist becomes gradually aware of the patriarchal structures that surround her. That recognition closes the ironic gap, the disjunction between the reader's recognition of her oppression and that of the protagonist. These are pedagogical, feminist works. For the feminist bildungsroman Felski describes, resistance to marriage becomes a way to articulate a critique of such social institutions as the dominance of the husband, the potentially restricting roles of wife and mother, the repression of female sexuality, and the constraint of female independence in general. Certainly these themes appear in what might be called the South Asian feminist bildungsroman, in the diaspora like the ones discussed here, and in subcontinental works by, for example, Bapsi Sidhwa in her novel *The Pakistani Bride,* about a woman who flees an arranged marriage. In these works, the critical representation of arranged marriage becomes a way to challenge oppressive social structures associated with the practice. These include cultural constructions of masculinity and femininity, uneven power relations between husband and wife, the potential for sexual violence within the expectations of marriage, and the hierarchical structures of the joint family that, combined with the patrilocal practice by which the bride moves into the husband's ancestral home, become points for the expression of dominance and, sometimes, violence.

Ironically, the works set in the subcontinent regularly present more viable paths for a woman leaving an arranged marriage. In Divakaruni's story "The Bats," for example, the mother finds refuge with her elderly father, though she ultimately refuses his help to return to her abusive husband. The mother in Canadian writer Anita Rau Badami's novel *Tamarind Mem* (1996) finds fulfillment in both widowhood and a personal autonomy symbolized by her journeys alone across India by train. Perhaps fitting the feminist bildungsroman genre most closely, Indian Canadian Deepa Mehta ends her 1996 film *Fire* with a lesbian relationship represented as providing an escape from the structures of patriarchy as well as a means to fulfill individual desire.

Critical interpretations of Mehta's film have focused on the film's representation of queer desire as well as its violent reception within a Hindu fundamentalist context (see Gopinath, *Impossible Desires*; Desai, "Homo"). Jigna Desai considers how global debates prompted by the film demonstrate how "processes at local, national, and transnational scales intersect to define the heteronormative communal norms that regulate women's bodies and sexualities, to facilitate the rejection of racial subjects as cultural citizens, and to encourage lesbian identity politics in non-Western locations" (66–67). Although the object of outrage for those expressing "heteronormative communal norms" is the representation of queer desire, Desai's primary interest, the protest is also aimed at the recasting of arranged marriage, which is further examined here.

The film reexamines the affective formations and structures of arranged marriage. *Fire* represents how the obligations of duty in arranged marriage overwhelm desire and are ultimately incompatible with romantic love, intimacy, and possibly even empathy between bride and groom. The film presents the romance as a counterpart by featuring a scene with the newly married couple visiting the iconographic honeymoon destination the Taj Mahal, where Sita, the young bride, describes her preference for the romantic love stories of Bollywood films. Those romantic notions are broken shortly after their marriage when Sita discovers that her new husband Jatin is still in love with his ongoing girlfriend Julie, a Chinese Indian woman who has refused to join Jatin's joint family because of the obligations that entails. As the film progresses, it is not just sentiment but physical desire and intimacy that Sita finds lacking in her arranged marriage, a condition she shares with her sister-in-law Radha. Radha's husband has committed himself to a path of spiritual enlightenment in which he renounces sex, a unilateral decision in the marriage by which his wife must abide. Sita and Radha turn to a sexual relationship with each other to find these physical and emotional components. Mehta goes beyond validating this taboo romance and same-sex orientation to show how this illicit relationship takes down the social structures as the two women give up their expected duties to their families: Sita's role caring for her elderly mother-in-law, Radha's promise to help her husband achieve ascetic transformation, and their position as "respectable" in the eyes of an observing servant. When Sita and Radha run off together, the film's narrative resolution presents arranged marriage as ultimately incompatible with the fulfillment of physical desire and emotional intimacy, and posits the formation of a lesbian relationship as its counterpart.

Mehta's film extends her liberal critique beyond the interpersonal to question the equality that is possible in the patriarchal and heteronormative communitarian structures of arranged marriage. Arranged marriage is embedded in the structures of family, including hierarchies of age that mandate duty to elders, patrilineal practices that require the bride to live with the groom's family, and shared living spaces that extend beyond the nuclear family. Sita and Radha could have never themselves had an arranged marriage, not just because they are the same sex but because their relationship, as Mehta presents it, is premised on a fulfillment of individual desire rather than being a part of this intricate social network. Although some works attempt to reconcile personal fulfillment with arranged marriage, either through a romance narrative, like Bollywood films, or through the plot device in popular diasporic fiction in which international migration sends couples far from their parents (chapter 5), none have gone so far as to completely jettison the idea of the extended family so closely tied to the idea of arranged marriage. Mehta is no different, making the only possible resolution a relationship outside of (the rest of) the family, despite the fact that, ironically, as critic Alexander Barron observes, it is the joint family structures that produce a "largely homosocial household" in which the women's affair is able to thrive ("Fire's," 66).

Mehta features the question of female agency in her works. In *Fire*, she uses representations of arranged marriage as a way to show how such agency is denied, not primarily through the interpersonal dynamics of bride and groom but by the social structures that frame arranged marriage. Mehta emphasizes the ways women secure their power over other women within the extended family as she portrays a mute but still censorious mother-in-law. By advocating an exit strategy based in a generationally bound female solidarity and intimacy, Mehta represents both arranged marriage and the traditional joint family structure as incompatible with women's need to choose, a value featured as desire in Radha's soliloquy at the end of the film.

Fire was set in India but produced by a Toronto-based company while Mehta was located in Canada. The film is in some ways a classic diasporic work in that it takes the opportunity to look back at the "imaginary homeland" and reimagine it through the "broken mirrors" Rushdie describes as "as valuable as the one supposedly unflawed" (*Imaginary Homelands,* 11). The film is a work of transnational reimagination. Although it appears more optimistic than Nair's documentary, the two films share some thematic and political commonalities. In both Nair's and Mehta's films, while the female filmic subjects are bound in place, the filmmaker, not the subject, embodies global mobility, a point that makes the works both capable of sharp critique and optimistic about the capacity for change. However, in the South Asian American feminist bildungsroman set in the diaspora, writers and filmmakers imagine different kinds of female subjects who, though they gain global mobility through transnational marriage, are arguably bound more strongly by that very process to their diasporic communities.

The South Asian American feminist works set in North America represent conjugal practices associated with the subcontinent as the antithesis of modernity in the way they sustain gender roles that constrain women. They do so by elevating the notion of individual choice as the embodiment of such modernity and the counterpart to the seeming antiquity of collective decision making. Chitra Banerjee Divakaruni, Bharati Mukherjee, and Jhumpa Lahiri reinforce American national narratives about individual agency through their portrayals of arranged marriage. At the same time, they depict arranged marriage as sometimes the only means by which a certain class of women gain such mobility. These authors emphasize how other oppressive structures come out of the conditions of diaspora, such as the isolation of the arranged wife in the new country as she leaves her home community, moves to an unfamiliar and seemingly dangerous place, and finds, in her status as wife, a specific, gendered place in a diaspora community itself besieged by racism and xenophobia. Because of these intersections, the South Asian American feminist bildungsroman highlights the sometimes fraught relationship between the critique of the feminist bildungsroman and the problem of diasporic belonging.

Although it is a product of the late twentieth century, the South Asian American female bildungsroman may be placed in a historical continuum that begins with the nineteenth-century representation described in both immigration policy and Dhan Gopal Mukerji's memoir, which portrayed arranged marriage as anathema to American values because it limited choice. In the 1990s, the subgenre became a particular incarnation of that discourse, framed by notions of women's liberation and neoliberal ideas in which a free market becomes a paradigm for personal freedom. Both the critique of patriarchy and the turn to individual choice as a resolution mobilize certain binaries of tradition and modernity by presenting culture as unchanging and coherent. The liberal feminist narrative and neoliberal story of assimilation deploy the concept of arranged marriage as a marker of authentic identity. They borrow notions of arranged marriage from an Orientalist discourse about Asian cultures "that sacrifice personal freedom to inexplicable but ancient traditions and collectivist control, unlike the individualist liberty of the rational, enlightened West" (Maira, *Desis in the House,* 153). They also build on a national concept of marriage as the ultimate expression of individual consent, a kind of consent that constitutes the American political sphere.

Inderpal Grewal has traced how neoliberal ideas have entered into South Asian American literary narratives through the trope of mobility. In this feminist fiction produced in the 1990s, a relationship to arranged marriage becomes emblematic of a split between nonassimilation and assimilation in America; such assimilation, she argues, is framed in terms of neoliberal ideals. Looking at the work of Bharati Mukherjee and Chitra Banerjee Divakaruni, Grewal argues that two figures of Asian women became visible in the 1990s in numerous narratives of South Asian women in the United States. While one figure has an abusive arranged marriage, her counterpart goes against the tradition of arranged marriage to marry a man of her selection. In these works, "arranged marriage [is] a signifier of tradition denoting the absence of choice" (*Transnational,* 77). Positing the alternative of self-made marriages, Grewal argues, "In comparison, marriage for 'love' signified passage into America through the discourse of 'choice'" (77). Grewal suggests that these literary works present women's refusal of arranged marriage as a refusal of patriarchal ideas, but the rationale reflects a commitment to the neoliberal construction of those ideals. A neoliberal discourse elevates the notion of choice, identified with a culturally Western modernity, as a route to freedom and condemns arranged marriage as denying women in particular the power to freely choose a spouse.

While it is true that arranged marriage is often presented as a symbol of constraint against an ideal of freedom, Grewal's analysis misses a few important points. Mukherjee, Divakaruni, and Lahiri bring arranged marriage more closely into alignment with these middle-class aspirations articulated as "choice" through representations of both the marriage and mobility. While the marriages represented are not "arranged love marriages," where the couple dates and then has a marriage vetted by their families, they do feature a certain degree of agency for the bride in her decisions around the marriage and in her aspirations for mobility. In Mukherjee's work, such agency appears in the false form of the global marriage market as consumerism; in Divakaruni's short story, it is the dream of a new beginning; and in Lahiri's novel, agency appears in the form of desire for something different. All three authors show transnational arranged marriage as a means, in fact the only means, for women who are not highly skilled professionals to gain a desired global mobility. Grewal rightly suggests that Mukherjee and Divakaruni present such marriages as ultimately unviable; arguably, though, Lahiri presents an alternative with a first-generation woman who finds some satisfaction in her arranged marriage, especially through the role of motherhood. For Mukherjee and Divakaruni, these marriages (and sometimes their heroines) sink under the weight of gender roles associated with an ethnic identity in diaspora—responsibilities to an extended family and a social community. However, although these works do show arranged marriage as without freedom, they also foreclose the possibility of free-choice love as viable, a second point that troubles Grewal's analysis. Departing from Grewal's claim that "choice" and national assimilation are offered as solutions in these South Asian American bildungsromans, this chapter argues that the women fail to find a viable exit strategy. To demonstrate, this discussion now turns to a close reading of Mukherjee's novel *Wife*, Divakaruni's short stories in *Arranged Marriage*, and then an outlier novel, Lahiri's *The Namesake*.

Mukherjee's *Wife* uses arranged marriage as a symbol for the constrained individual female subject, charting a protagonist's progression from a transnational arranged marriage into confinement as an immigrant wife and, ultimately, madness. However, a closer look at the character and initial motivations of Dimple Dasgupta undoes the clear opposition between arranged marriage and choice that Grewal argues shapes the novel's trajectory of assimilation. The unmarried Dimple Dasgupta introduced at the beginning of the novel sees arranged marriage as an opportunity for upward mobility: not so much a duty that must be fulfilled as yet another form of shopping. The opening lines of the novel represent the matrimonial process as procuring a professional groom: "Dimple Dasgupta had set her heart on marrying a neurosurgeon, but her father was looking for engineers in the matrimonial ads" (3). That paragraph goes on to elaborate that her reasons for wanting a neurosurgeon were so that she might achieve a certain modern lifestyle identified by its consumer products. For this class, arranged marriage and choice are initially aligned in a matrimonial market. Dimple participates, not just in the sense that she has the capacity for consent, but because arranged marriage is her opportunity for something new. The heroine pursues a form of agency as consumerism that leaves her unable to sustain herself as she slides away from the familial support structures of her parents.

Transnational mobility through arranged marriage provides Dimple with a means for change. In one dialogue, Mukherjee emphasizes how marriage becomes a primary, albeit problematic, method for women's transnational mobility. As one character says, "Any Indian girl who comes over alone is entitled to stay on any way she can. Could you have come over alone? Could any of us?" Grewal discusses how in this generation of South Asian American feminist work, "having choices" comes to stand in for feminine agency (*Transnational,* 28), and this becomes mapped onto an American identity. This is and isn't true in Mukherjee's novel. Coming to America is incidental to Dimple, who would just as soon have joined an emerging professional class in Calcutta like her best friend Pixie, but the displacement does take her away from her in-laws and exposes her to new lifestyles and opportunities that appear at first to concretize her ambitions.

The immigrant context constrains Dimple, both in the social norms of the community and because the commodities she dreamed of remain out of reach. Susan Koshy argues that Dimple replaces this extended family with an equally repressive one of the diasporic community, with the most intimate expression of that subjugation being Dimple's husband. Certainly Dimple's husband does not want her to work outside the home, but the South Asian community she encounters is a heterogeneous one and includes Indian characters who lead more liberal lives. Mukherjee focuses not as much on the outside restraints placed on Dimple as on her own interpellation into those culturally defined gender roles. When Dimple is offered a drink, her husband answers for her taste, but Mukherjee elaborates how Dimple's thoughts ultimately constrain her: "She felt that Amit was waiting for just the right answer, that it was up to her to uphold Bengali womanhood, marriage and male pride. The right answer, I do not need stimulants to feel happy in my husband's presence . . . my obligation is to my husband, seemed to dance before her eyes as though it were printed on a card" (78). Dimple attaches the proper performance of being a wife to cultural gender roles that are both duty bound and the supposed site of a scripted personal satisfaction that continues to evade her. Dimple is constrained by the narratives of self that are available to her: a nationalist version of the good wife and the "liberated" version of a commodity-bound woman. Mukherjee represents a female subject in which measures of coercion are internalized in the construction of her subjectivity as wife to the point that she is unable to articulate a no.

When Dimple seemingly kills off her husband in the end, Mukherjee offers a complex subject of agency mediated by discourses of both gender and capitalism. Grewal argues that the novel supports a neoliberal discourse in the sense that it looks to choice as a route to freedom. Yet Mukherjee shows the false way this is mapped onto consumption, both in and outside of arranged marriage. Mukherjee presents Dimple's materialism even in India and certainly later as a false outlet for fulfillment, for as she turns increasingly to the fantasy world of magazine advertisement, her reality begins to split. Dimple is looking for the "grand passion" advertised in self-help columns in the magazines she obsessively consumes. She cannot find it in the film versions of love she tries to map onto her marriage, and she cannot find it in an extramarital affair. Dimple understands her act of killing her husband through the lens of television shows about cooking, a resolution that suggests she has not found personal freedom even as she escapes her arranged marriage.

Mukherjee's *Wife* ultimately presents the American dream with ambivalence. While the narrative does show migration as reinvention, the identities of before and after are not written as the emergence of the South Asian woman from the shackles of tradition. The placing of Dimple's Indian arranged marriage into the context of a globalized India filled with advice magazines, trendy cafés, and paradigms of shopping disallows those binaries. Instead, the novel arguably traps its heroine in the double world of marriage and consumerism, showing marriage as consumerism (of status and of ethnic identity) through the portrayal of arranged marriage. Dimple's problem is not just the repression of the woman who is driven mad by domestic constraint, though there is that as well; it is that everything— traditional Indian gender roles as well as Western-style feminism—is emptied of significance in a capitalist world.

Although mobility doesn't save Dimple in Mukherjee's schematic, romance might have. In Western narratives, romantic love is consistently posited as generating a form of meaning, an "indestructible grounding for our life" (May, *Love*, 6). This first generation of South Asian American novels do not align arranged marriage and romantic love, as do those discussed in the next chapter, but show love as something more like companionship and mutual responsibility. It is worth questioning whether romantic love would have saved Dimple as it did Sita in Mehta's film *Fire*. The hints are there that it would have, as Dimple engages in an extramarital affair with a European American man, but that is foreclosed by the inability to leave the community. By cutting short the love affair and by critiquing a consumerist mind-set, Mukherjee never allows her character to pursue the "passage into America through the discourse of 'choice'" (Grewal, *Transnational America*, 77).

Chitra Banerjee Divakaruni shows arranged marriage as both the means for a woman's agency through mobility and the nexus of certain gender roles that keep her from complete fulfillment. The short story "Clothes" in the collection *Arranged Marriage* tells the story of a young woman, Sumita, from a village in India who has an arranged marriage with a young man from the United States. The story is told in first person, which offers a privileged perspective on the bride's experience of the marriage. After she arrives, the young couple begin to make plans for a new life together, one that will ostensibly allow the wife to rethink her subservient domestic role in the extended family and take part in the family-run workplace. They practice this new life in private as the wife tries on new clothes that will fit her more public self. In the story, clothes are equated with occupying different roles. Sumita and her new husband, Somesh, enjoy her experimentations with Western clothes, which she keeps hidden from her in-laws. In this way, Divakaruni presents arranged marriage as something experienced differently between the generations. While for the older generation, it represents a continuity of the duties toward the family, for the younger ones, it produces a co-conspirator and the possibility of romance. The new diasporic location produces a conflicted sense of responsibility. Sumita feels angry that her husband prioritizes his parents but then corrects herself by thinking about her own parents. However, shortly after the marriage and her migration, the husband is killed in a robbery as he works the night shift at a 7-Eleven. The status of the young woman is uncertain at the end, but the story suggests she will remain in the United States. As in *Wife*, the work's resolution does not sustain the arranged marriage, but it does preserve its accompanying mobility.

Divakaruni shows how arranged marriage functions as a means for transnational mobility for women who would otherwise not find such movement. Unlike the mobility of highly skilled labor, this kind of mobility cuts across different classes. Divakaruni ultimately shows the positive side of this, even though the marriage ends. India is represented as a place of "doves with cut-off wings" (33), while the United States represents a place of transformation through accessible education. Compelled by these narratives of migration, the story of emigration begins to frame Sumita's present even before she moves. The young woman about to leave for marriage sets up India as a kind of prehistory: "already the activities of our girlhood seem to be far in my past, the colors leached out of them, like old sepia photographs" (18). Much of her understanding remains in the realm of fantasy for the narrator, who "knows" the United States through her husband's descriptions of the 7-Eleven and imagines her future in terms of a Bollywood film that showed a British school system. In this way, the story presents her experience of mobility as mediated by representation, including fairy tales, stories told by her husband, and films. The narrator interprets her imminent marriage through the narratives of romance, for example, the fairy tales of a prince who takes his bride away to a distant kingdom (18). Divakaruni renders the unknown as experienced through the sentient. When looking at California on a metal globe, the bride "felt the excitement leap all the way up my arm like an electric shock. Then it died away, leaving only a beaten-metal coldness against my fingertips" (18). The scene anticipates the trajectory of her story, which turns from thrilling possibility to desolation. However, the marriage does allow her that movement across the globe that would otherwise be forestalled. Such mobility is placed into the narrative of arranged marriage. Divakaruni's mother understands the girl's mobility not in terms of adventure but in terms of destiny, asking, "Wasn't it every woman's destiny... to leave the known for the unknown? She had done it and her mother before her" (18). Divakaruni turns the idea that a woman must go with her husband into one that offers women the possibility for movement to new places.

These South Asian American works that begin with arranged marriages depart from the optimism of the feminist bildungsroman. Divakaruni and Mukherjee represent an exit from a marriage as an exit from a cultural community as well, and both leave their newly conscious female protagonists adrift after their critical recognition of the dominating structures of their marriages. Presented with the lack of a viable feminist South Asian community to mediate their transition from the private to the public, these heroines are left choosing between a marriage that represents cultural belonging and an independence that severs them from the South Asian community and leaves them emotionally, socially, and economically adrift.

Arranged Marriage across Generations: Jhumpa Lahiri's Bildungsroman

Lahiri's novel *The Namesake* is in many ways a departure from the feminist South Asian American bildungsroman as shaped by Mukherjee and Divakaruni, and not just because it features a young man in one of its two coming-of-age stories. In her novel, Lahiri validates the story of an arranged marriage in her portrayal of the first-generation immigrant characters Ashok and Ashima; she also questions both "self-made" relationships and modified forms of arranged marriage, represented by the romantic relationships of the second-generation protagonist Gogol. Lahiri's novel refuses the "exit strategy," in which the South Asian character must leave the community to find personal freedom, but unlike the works discussed earlier, she resolves her novel within a committed, albeit ambivalent, form of community belonging. Despite these notable differences, Lahiri's work remains within the subgenre of the South Asian American feminist bildungsroman in its overall portrayal, for whereas a first-generation arranged marriage is shown as fulfilling certain desires for mobility and family, and the male protagonist Gogol recommits to his community after his failed "arranged love marriage," both second-generation females, the more minor characters of Sonali (Sonia) and Moushimi ultimately choose self-made relationships with non-Bengali partners.

Like Divakaruni's short story "Clothes" and Mukherjee's novel *Wife*, *The Namesake* depicts arranged marriage as a primary means for female mobility. Early in the novel, Ashima is asked to greet her prospective husband in a characteristic scene in which he comes with his family for tea. She is shown to be uninvested, "in no rush to be a bride," but also approaches the meeting "obediently but without expectation" (7). Lahiri implies that Ashima will be asked for her opinion about the match after the meeting. Unlike Dimple from Mukherjee's *Wife*, Ashima is not wooed by the notion of finding a successful groom—though as a Western-educated prospect, Ashok is a very suitable boy; rather, she is compelled by a curiosity for the unknown. She sees his shoes "that were not like any she'd ever seen on the streets and trams and buses of Calcutta, or even in the windows of Bata" (8). Ashima's curiosity generates desire in one of the most memorable scenes of the novel:

Ashima, unable to resist a sudden and overwhelming urge, stepped into the shoes at her feet. Lingering sweat from the owner's feet mingled with hers, causing her heart to race; it was the closest thing she had ever experienced to the touch of a man. The leather was creased, heavy, and still warm. On the left shoe she had noticed that one of the crisscrossing laces had missed a hole, and this oversight set her at ease. (8)

The representation of Ashima's first intimate relation with her husband, a mingling of her sweat with his, is mediated by an American commodity that signifies both his difference and the possibility of change through mobility. The scene shifts erotic agency to Ashima, signifying her participation even before she enters the living room to be inspected by his mother. She later refers to this scene as "her indiscretion in her parents' corridor" (10), a conception that emphasizes the erotic nature of the encounter with a stranger's difference and her agential role in terms of both sexual desire and curiosity.

Lahiri shows how the practice of arranged marriage makes its home in the new diasporic context, becoming an important symbol and practice for both first and second generations. As a new bride in the Boston area in the 1970s, Ashima regularly meets professional young Bengali men who fly back to India to return with wives (38). It is little wonder, then, that when her son Gogol grows up, he refers to the practice of arranged marriage as "something at once unthinkable and unremarkable; nearly all their friends and relatives had been married in the same way" (138). Arranged marriage is something unthinkable to Gogol at this point in the novel because he has begun to see the familiarity of his Bengali community from the outside eyes of his European American girlfriend and her family. He acquires a view of love as romance and arranged marriage as a lack of freedom. Gogol pities his parents "for having no experience of being young and in love" (117) and "is astonished by his parents' courage, the obedience that must have been involved in doing such a thing" (222). Although his parents make little effort to arrange his own match, they also do not want him dating outside the community. Lahiri represents the greater pressure placed on the young Bengali girl Moushumi, perhaps because of her family but more likely because her sexuality as a young woman would be more vigilantly patrolled. Moushumi looks back on this history resentfully: "From the onset of adolescence [Moushumi] had been subjected to a series of unsuccessful schemes; every so often a small group of unmarried Bengali men materialized in the house, young colleagues of her father's.... During summer visits to Calcutta, strange men mysteriously appeared in the sitting room of her grandparents' flat.... 'Aren't you going to arrange a wedding for her?' relatives would ask her parents" (213). Gogol's and Moushumi's distance from arranged marriage, as represented by their parents' generation, emphasizes a shift between the generations around the practice.

The Namesake sets up two narratives of arranged marriage in two generations of the same family. Whereas the parents' marriage was a transnational one between a groom studying in the United States and a nineteen-year-old bride from Calcutta, their son Gogol has what some people call an "arranged love marriage," in which he first dates the woman his mother introduces him to with the idea that they will marry. By representing these two marriages, Lahiri arguably both works within the trope of intergenerational conflict and challenges the idea of a linear progression from arranged marriage as tradition to a self-made marriage as assimilation. The novel questions the absolute nature of this break by having the younger generation find their way back into the community through arranged marriage. When Gogol later attempts to return to his community in the midst of mourning his father, he does so through a newer form of arranged marriage: Gogol and Moushumi are introduced by their mothers and subsequently date and decide to get married. This might seem like being "set up" and like self-made marriage, but what makes it an "arranged love marriage" or "semi-arranged marriage" is both the family involvement from the beginning in arranging the match and the express idea that the explicit goal is marriage. Gogol himself makes this connection: "the [marriage proposal] was something expected—from the very beginning it was safely assumed by their families, and soon enough by themselves, that as long as they liked each other their courtship would not lag and they would surely wed" (226). While Gogol tries to return to reestablish an intimacy with his family and Bengali community through this marriage, Moushumi also seeks out the support of her family through a story already written for her, "an unquestioned future, of marriage, drawing them along" (250). As part of the same New England Bengali community, the couple is motivated by a sense of familiarity but also by a kind of allegiance to the Bengali community. "They had both sought comfort in each other, and in their shared world, perhaps for the sake of novelty, or out of the fear that that world was slowly dying" (284). Here the sentiment these members of the second generation express is not so much one of assimilation as it is the kind of nostalgia embedded in contradiction that Maira describes as invested in "the notion of being 'truly' or 'really' Indian" through the "possession of certain knowledge or participation in certain activities" (*Desis in the House*, 88) and their investment in those communities.

While Ashima and Ashok's form of arranged marriage does work out for the longer duration, that of Gogol and Moushumi does not. Lahiri represents this marriage as failing because it is incompatible with a female life grounded in personal desire. In a significant parallel, Moushumi's desire to escape echoes the feeling Ashima has when she puts her feet in a stranger's shoes. However, whereas Ashima finds a kind of life-changing mobility through her arranged marriage—her movement is a trajectory from home to home—Moushumi, alternatively, is forced to move outside the confines of her community to enact a more daring escape from the domestic sphere through her extramarital affair. Both escapes are shown to be alienating in some sense: Ashima's as she finds herself without her family in a strange new environment in Cambridge and Moushumi's as she leaves her marriage at the end. This is in contrast to the character Sonali, Gogol's sister, who find personal fulfillment in an intercultural self-made marriage. Lahiri's female characters are limited by arranged marriage in some ways, even if they choose it for their own reasons, and in this way, they are much like the protagonists of Mehta's, Nair's, Mukherjee's, and Divakaruni's works, in which arranged marriage, though offering distinctive forms of mobility, is ultimately presented as untenable for women within the diasporic context.

Canada, Immigration Fraud, and Arranged Marriage

This chapter has been considering the relationship between arranged marriage and South Asian immigration to both the United States and Canada in terms of the ways concepts of individual and collective agency have been mobilized through the conjugal idea and its practice. In the United States, the entrance of the technologically trained middle class into the country allowed for other immigrants representing a broader spectrum of classes to come through reunification visas. Following this group has been a third wave of Indian immigrants of working-class background (Maira, *Desis in the House*, 10). Koshy argues that the struggles of "'servitude and displacement' that characterize this new diaspora have not received enough public recognition" ("Introduction," 7). That limited attention extends to fiction; literary works in both the United States and Canada have predominantly featured the first group of highly skilled workers and their immediate families. Bakirathi Mani argues, "Popular fiction and film created by South Asian immigrants almost invariably reproduce middle-class narratives of migration, despite the heterogeneous experiences that characterize subcontinental immigrants" (*Aspiring*, 11). This is particularly true in the United States, where the contemporary literary representations of mostly Bengali middle-class arranged marriages in Mukherjee's, Divakaruni's, and Lahiri's work look quite different from the British literary representations, where literary depictions have narrated Sikh and Muslim working-class migration (chapters 2 and 3).

A deeper look at the diverse constituencies that make up the immigration history of those two nations reveals some internal demarcations within the discourse taken as a whole. No absolute line separates portrayals of different classes, religions, and countries of national origin in the arranged marriage discourse, nor is there a definitive difference between representations in the United States and Canada. However, there are tendencies that reflect the particularity of different histories of migration. Depictions by and about arranged marriage in the professional class of South Asians who entered in the late 1960s, as well as among their children, have tended to focus on questions of cultural assimilation. That is true both in literature and in the mainstream media. Although the Canadian literature and media do offer these assimilationist narratives in the form of changing matrimonial habits (see Badami, *Tamarind Mem*), since the 1980s, mainstream media portrayals of arranged marriage among Muslim and Sikh immigrants have been focused on forced marriage and immigration fraud.

This section reads this set of Canadian media images in terms of national dynamics rather than as evidence of the practices of particular communities. In this context, both those affirming and those decrying arranged marriage have too often obscured the conditions of migration that inform decisions around arranged marriage, turning conjugal decisions into statements about the seemingly conflicting "values" of family versus individual freedom rather than contextualizing such decisions in terms of the legal and socioeconomic exigencies of a minority community. Looking at these discourses in light of institutional, political, social, and economic histories that surround such conjugal decisions helps to make clear how notions of culture are being mobilized. Reading up to this present moment from a historical context, this section argues that these shifting dynamics have culminated in a neoliberal discourse of multiculturalism, much like the

British one discussed in chapter 3, in which arranged marriage is used as a register to demarcate the border between acceptable and unacceptable difference in a charged racialized context of immigration. That unacceptable difference appears as the absence of Canadian "cultural values," but that phrase arguably stands in for individual agency.

Canada was not a hospitable place for early Asian immigration. Prohibitions in the early twentieth century, like the Continuous Journey Act, which required immigrants to travel continuously from place of birth or citizenship, resulted in remigration below the border on the West Coast. The Immigration Act of 1952 allowed the government sweeping powers to reject immigrants on the basis of a range of criteria that provided the grounds to exclude Asians, including nationality and geographic origin but also perceived unsuitability to the climate or probable inability to assimilate. This was also the period in which Canada began to set a quota for immigrants from some of the decolonizing commonwealth countries, such as India, Pakistan, and Sri Lanka, creating a precedent for government-sanctioned admission of nonwhite immigrants (Troper, "Canada's Immigration Policy," 263). Even after Canada lifted general ethnic and racial restrictions in 1962, it maintained these quotas in family reunification cases (265); these kinds of cases would be a primary area for arranged marriage immigration cases.

It was only during the 1960s with a series of acts that these restrictions gradually disappeared. Since the early 1970s, Canada has been a chosen destination for both primary and secondary migrants from South Asia. Many South Asians fleeing Idi Amin's Uganda in 1972 went to Canada; secondary immigrants have also come from other former British colonies around the world, most notably the Caribbean. Canada, especially Vancouver, is home to an early Sikh population that grew after immigration strictures opened up and expanded even more after the anti-Sikh riots in 1984 India. As well as coming from India, more recent groups have come from Bangladesh and Pakistan. The discussion of arranged marriage in the media has been focused on Sikh and Muslim populations.

By the 1970s and 1980s, the Canadian discourse on arranged marriage had merged a liberal feminist agenda with a vision of a "mosaic" of different cultural identities, "where ethnic groups have maintained their distinctiveness while functioning as part of the whole" (Palmer, "Mosaic," 488). This approach has promoted a culturalist understanding of immigrant experiences. Journalists construct ideas of distinct South Asian cultural identities through images of a patriarchal society in which a younger generation must navigate a "culture" to which they are often at odds. For example, a 1980s article on arranged marriage uses the language of servitude to designate how a younger generation participates in the conjugal practices of a Sikh community:

> A strong sense of family is a tradition that dies hard within Vancouver's 50,000-member Sikh community and it was because of a respect for their elders that the Aroras bowed to the idea of an arranged marriage. (CP, "Marriage Arranged")

The article features the self-made marriage as the natural inclination for a second generation that "bow(s)" to a resistant tradition that "dies hard." Other media articles from the same decade more explicitly pose arranged marriage as the antithesis to freedom, particularly for females. For example, one article about two young women's suicides locates them as part of "an increasing number of East Indian women trying to escape arranged marriages in Canada" and cites someone saying that "Western culture looks like freedom" to young Indians (CP, "Indian Wives"). In seeming contrast to this negative portrayal, but still characterizing all arranged marriage as the site of female oppression, another article from the same decade details the life of a young male professional Indian who lounges in the living room as his mother takes care of his son and his wife prepares dinner for everyone:

> In Punjab, my mother was a homemaker, my father was a bread earner. Things are changing, mind you ... but I learned a lot in terms of values, quality of life and ethics from my parents. (*Toronto Star,* "Arranged Marriages")

In this article, one may already see the discourse of "values" that becomes a mainstay in later representations. Such values, while ostensibly endorsed on the basis of cultural (in this case, Punjabi) and filial belonging, are depicted as antagonistic to the freedom of South Asian Canadians, in particular, female ones.

By the early 1990s, articles in the Canadian press were presenting three familiar narratives about arranged marriage that continue to this day, though the language of "forced marriage" was not yet widely used. The first group featured articles, like the one discussed earlier, that attempted to explain arranged marriage to a presumed non–South Asian audience and represented arranged marriage that "dies hard" as an outdated leftover from the homeland that is culturally incompatible with Canada. A second group of articles affirmed arranged marriage as the expression of cultural "values" (Dhooma, "Arranged Marriages"). These articles, while legitimizing a match made on the basis of a similarity of backgrounds, based such worth on the ability of such arrangements to lead to love rather than, for example, on the social or material interests of family or community (Bolan, "Happy"). Finally, a third discourse emphasized the diaspora as the site for the transformation of tradition (Griffin, "Mixing") and reinforced the trope of intergenerational conflict. All three discourses have informed the contemporary depictions of arranged marriage in mainstream media, which, while alternating between a romanticization of these modified traditional practices and a sensationalist preoccupation with "forced marriage" and "child marriage," consistently elide the more material motivations that play a critical role in transnational arranged marriage in particular.

Concurrent to these multicultural discussions of "cultural values," "tradition," and "love" among South Asian Canadians, important debates about arranged marriage and the policies of immigration have made arranged marriage a flashpoint for anti-immigrant rhetoric. In the early 1990s, the Canadian media took up what was portrayed as the problem of arranged marriage as a means to immigration, while the government viewed arranged marriage as a potential site for fraud. In an effort to source out "marriages of convenience," Canadian immigration officials asked for personal letters and other evidence of familiarity. South Asians protested that this requirement did not allow for the forms of courtship associated with arranged marriage, which did not emphasize interpersonal intimacy. Some commentators saw the measures as targeting South Asians in particular. One subject interviewed relayed how "immigration officers in Canada asked him how he and his wife had met, how often they dated before marrying and the types of places they went on dates." He interpreted this in terms of a demand to justify his own culture: "'It [shouldn't be] my burden to defend my own tradition and culture to someone else,' said Tata, who has been waiting for the arrival of his wife from India for nearly two years" (*Toronto Star*, "Immigrants Angered").

In 1995, a controversial immigration decision denied a visa to a spouse in an arranged marriage in which the court deemed the couple had not had enough personal contact. The decision prompted accusations of cultural bias in the recognition of forms of courtship and racism against South

Asians in particular. This moment of protest revealed how immigration structures prioritize certain forms of conjugality. Although this is true in both Canada and the United States, Canadian debates about Indian (especially Sikh), Pakistani, and Bangladeshi immigration in the second half of the twentieth century have been more contentious and public than those in the United States and, in this way, parallel those in Britain.

As in the United Kingdom, during the 1990s, Canadian representations began to focus on the treatment of the Muslim girl as a locus for determining disruptive versus acceptable difference in a multicultural society (see chapter 3). A 1992 article in the *Toronto Star* described arranged marriage as "an extremely common practice in the South Asian culture" and characterized the plight of a young Pakistani Canadian woman named Farah thus:

> Like many South Asians, Farah is caught in the middle. She cannot accept all the values of mainstream society, yet she cannot justify some of the values of her South Asian heritage. And as she moves into adulthood, she is slowly learning the art of compromise. For her, compromise means swallowing her anger and accepting an arranged marriage. (Zaman, "Growing Pains")

A *Toronto Star* article on forced marriage reported the promise of foreign affairs minister to "stand up for these girls" (Black, "Ottawa").

The articles presented arranged marriage as an impediment to assimilation and a confrontation point between generations, in that way continuing the "mosaic" discourse from the 1980s. However, while arranged marriage continues to be represented as the embodiment of culture (even as it is viewed contemporaneously as a means for immigration fraud), such cultural practice now demands intervention. "'Parents think if they marry their daughter off to someone who was born and raised in, say, Pakistan, it will help preserve the culture,' says Mattoo. 'What they don't understand is that they are wreaking havoc on their kids' lives'" (Aulakh, "Speed Dating"). The language of "culture" that appears in this discourse is used to both renounce and defend arranged marriage and appears as a stand-in for affiliation to a religious or more general "South Asian" ethnic identity. The cultural values appear in the form of agency. On one hand, the girl who must "swallow her anger" to compromise represents individual agency, or a lack thereof. Set against that individual agency is an unspecified collectivity appearing under the name of "South Asian heritage" that has the power to force her capitulation. Arguably, the Pakistani Canadian community is being referenced here. The state, which must "stand up for her" in a way this community does not, appears to reassert her individual agency. These two examples, the debate about immigration requirements and the representation of the oppressed Muslim young woman who must be protected by the Canadian government, show how the public discussion of arranged marriage became a mode for working out the politics of national belonging and state sovereignty in the context of transnational immigration in terms of the subject of agency.

What has arguably shifted between the early 1980s and the late 1990s and the millennium is increased xenophobia toward those immigrant populations. This is also the period of a rise of a discourse of terror surrounding Sikh and Muslim populations, especially after the 1985 Air India bombing by a group of Sikh separatists. The Canadian magazine *Macleans* cited a survey that found that 54 percent of Canadians outside Quebec held an unfavorable view of Islam and 39 percent an unfavorable view of Sikhism, with the numbers significantly higher in Quebec (Geddes, "Canadian"). These are also the same decades that present a Western cultural fascination with the honor crime, which has become a "cultural category that sucks into its web a bewildering array of events and people, gaining solidity through this assimilative process" (Abu-Lughod, "Seductions," 23).

By the beginning of the millennium, an increasing number of articles on violence in arranged marriage appeared, always entangled in discussions about immigration. Often the concept of domestic abuse was tied to allegations of immigration fraud. One article titled "Women 'Victims' of Arranged Marriage: They Tell of Being Beaten, Robbed, Abandoned by Men Using Marriage to Gain Entry to Canada" discussed "innocent boys and girls whose parents arranged marriages in India and spent a lot of money on these marriages" being married to spouses who "began to complain and act mischievously and finally left the spouses. These victims have been left in a lurch and do not know what to do" (Bolan). In this example, the cultural values are those of the exploited brides and grooms (brides only in the title), but in a social service manual published by the Indo-Canadian Women's Association around the same time, the group suggests that the outdated cultural values belong to the victims: "counselors need to understand the background of women who come from male-dominated societies where they grow up learning to be helpless because their father or male relative helped them in every way when dealing with the outside world" (*International*, xiv).

The issues of domestic abuse and immigration fraud have been imbricated throughout the Canadian media's discussion of forced marriage. Forced marriage has been a means for articulating a national identity and national boundaries through the representation of conflicting "cultural values." For example, after a recent panel looked at the subject of forced marriage, a spokesperson for the Immigration Office stated, "Forced marriage is not only illegal in Canada, but is contrary to Canadian values and has no place in our country" (Star, "Ottawa"). The point here is not to challenge the prohibition of violence in or around marriage but to show the way such proscriptions are presented in cultural form, and done so by immigration officials rather than, say, the Department of Justice. More strikingly, one article on a set of recommendations made by the study of the South Asian Legal Clinic of Ontario regarding forced marriage immediately pares this discussion with a quotation from Citizenship and Immigration Canada (CIC): "We take the issue of forced marriage very seriously and will review the report's recommendations.... CIC visa officers are trained to identify all types of application fraud and work diligently to prevent it" (Star, "Ottawa"). This shows how interrelated are the question of force in arranged marriage and the issue of immigration.

The clearest evidence that forced marriage is seen as a cultural problem, while in fact entangled in immigration practices, is in Bill S-7, the Zero Tolerance for Barbaric Cultural Practices Act. This immigration act adds forced marriage to criminal code, sets the federal minimum age for marriage at sixteen, and prohibits polygamy as well as forced marriage. The name has been controversial with its use of the term "barbaric cultural practices," which appears to some to be targeting particular immigrant communities rather than Canada more generally. As in Britain, some also argue that current policies prohibiting polygamy or domestic violence already prohibit what falls beneath this law. Finally, some suggest that the government should work more on prevention and services rather than prohibition (Mackrael, "Experts").

An analysis of the forced marriage discourse in Canada benefits from being placed next to discussions of arranged marriage as they have taken shape in both the United States and Britain. As demonstrated throughout this chapter and others, conjugal forms have been a primary site for working out national assimilation. Since the nineteenth century, self-made marriage has been a symbol of progress as the seeming embodiment of individual rather than collective agency. Although South Asian literary and filmic writers have complicated the capacity for women in particular to "exit" those collectivities in sustainable ways, both that literature and mainstream media representations have held fast to that binary. However, with the rise of a multicultural discourse, the teleological narrative of assimilation has become more complex. Neoliberal discourses of multiculturalism mark a boundary within arranged marriage to distinguish acceptable from unacceptable forms of cultural difference separated by subjects of agency: the consenting individual versus the coercive collectivity. On the dangerous side of that boundary lies the cultural object of the vulnerable South Asian girl, a figure that has its origins in British colonial discourse of administration (chapter 1). Especially during the 1990s and the millennium, in which discussions of immigration fraud have coincided with discourses of terror, legal and media discourses have expressed an increasingly contentious relationship with Muslim and Sikh immigrant populations in discussions of arranged marriage as forced marriage. Culturalist understandings, in which historical conditions of global migration are elided in an essentialized version of "culture," mark legislation around forms of domestic violence. While the multicultural discourse seeks to dislocate the power of conjugal decision making from communal loci, it continues to validate dehistoricized and depoliticized cultural identities. On the acceptable side of this contemporary discourse of assimilation lie "modified cultural practices" that present a neoliberal resolution retaining individual agency. This conjuncture is the subject of the next chapter.

5

Regenerating Tradition through Transnational Popular Culture

The Cultural Revival of Arranged Marriage

Arranged marriage became an object of increasing global cultural fascination during the 1990s and 2000s. The number of media articles on arranged marriage increased exponentially between 1980 and 2000. By the mid-1990s, a characteristic split began to emerge. On one side, arranged marriage was represented as oppressive to women. Feminist commentators from both South Asian and non–South Asian communities connected arranged marriage to coercion and to domestic and sexual violence in particular. South Asian postcolonial and diasporic feminist literary works that received acclaim in the late twentieth century most often portrayed arranged marriage negatively. Bharati Mukherjee's 1975 novel *Wife*, Chitra Banerjee Divakaruni's 1996 short story collection *Arranged Marriage*, and Deepa Mehta's 1996 film *Fire* present arranged marriage as, at best, a structure that enables the repression of women and at worst itself fundamentally oppressive. These feminist works develop two important critiques of arranged marriage. First, they offer an ideological critique denouncing the function of arranged marriage reflecting and supporting patriarchal, religious, economic, and/or heteronormative power structures. Second, they participate in a liberal discourse of freedom, identified with a culturally Western modernity, and condemn arranged marriage as denying a woman, in particular, the power to freely choose her spouse. This critical account of arranged marriage continues to appear in twenty-first-century texts, especially those that represent the lives of working-class South Asian Muslim women in Britain, such as Monica Ali's *Brick Lane* and Nadeem Aslam's *Maps for Lost Lovers* (2004).

Simultaneous to this critical portrayal, a very different kind of representation in popular culture has emerged, in popular Indian film, in the mainstream Western media, and in popular South Asian (especially

Indian) women's fiction. Mira Nair's 2001 blockbuster film *Monsoon Wedding* presents an arranged marriage between a resident and nonresident Indian as the means to retie family bonds broken by illicit and abusive sexuality. Bollywood films, such as Sanjay Leela Bhansali's *Hum Dil De Chuke Sanam*, Vipul Shah's *Namastey London*, Aditya Chopra's *Rab Ne Bana Di Jodi*, Chandan Arora's *Main, Meri Patni... Aur Woh!*, and Meghna Gulzar's *Just Married* (2007), create love stories about arranged marriages for and about a nationally and globally mobile class that has consumed narratives of intimacy. These films mark a shift from Bollywood representations that elevated arranged marriage as a performance of duty, such as Sanjay Leela Bhansali's 2002 version of *Devdas,* instead emphasizing arranged marriage as a means for personal fulfillment.

Within a transnational cultural context, a literary subgenre has been expanding in the past ten years that also offers a new representation of arranged marriage: the concept of arranged marriage has been undergoing a cultural revival in transnational works that represent a mobile middle and upper middle class of South Asian women in the subcontinent and the diaspora. These popular cultural works may be read as creating what Lauren Berlant calls an "intimate public," a "porous, affective scene of identification among strangers that promises a certain experience of belonging and provides a complex of consolation, confirmation, discipline, and discussion about how to live as an x" (*Female Complaint*, viii). These literary and filmic texts mobilize the sentimental to offer an alternative perspective to progressive feminist works by constituting a transnational community of women through conjugal ideals. They present a streamlined form of culture that diminishes, rewrites, or ignores the practices and structures that have historically surrounded arranged marriage. This intimate public may be interpreted as a way to understand how women from an elite transnational class are claiming gendered South Asian identities inside and outside of liberal narratives of progress and neoliberal discourses of choice.

This movement among South Asians to validate arranged marriage has its counterpart in the broader public spheres of India and the United States and, to a lesser extent, of Britain and Canada. A particular Western media discourse represents arranged marriage as a solution to the problems of transient relationships. Sometimes these articles seek to validate the practice for South Asians; one typical feature article in Toronto explained how young South Asian women, disillusioned with dating, choose to pursue a transnational arranged marriage (Aulakh, "Speed Dating"). Other articles suggest that a more general population might themselves learn from—or even embrace—arranged marriages. The British newspaper the *Guardian* ran a story in 2011 headlined "Husband, by Arrangement: Should Love Come before Marriage, or the Other Way Around? After Five Years in India, Miranda Kennedy Was Forced to Rethink Her Western Approach to Relationships" (Kennedy, "Husband"). The same year, the *Daily Mail* offered a similar rationale with the article "Why an Arranged Marriage Is 'More Likely to Develop into Lasting Love'" (Bentley, "Why an Arranged Marriage"). In 2007, trend analyst Marian Salzman predicted that arranged marriage was an imminent trend: "Today is the era of the arranged couple who fall into love around the birth of the first child. . . . It sounds traditional, but in some ways so much of the future is back to the past, turbo-charged" (quoted in McKay, "Because Mom Said So"; see also Salzman and Matathia, *Next Now,* 102). In the popular American reality television show *Married at First Sight,* four specialists, including a sexologist, a spiritualist, a psychologist, and a sociologist, act as matchmakers for an arranged marriage in which the bride and groom meet for the first time at the wedding.

Changing Practices

Even as arranged marriage came to be a mode for expressing cultural affiliation through the celebration of endogamous marital practices, the rationales for arranged marriage began to shift by the year 2000. In India and the United States especially, a public discourse increasingly advocated for arranged marriage as a viable choice for the liberalized subject. This group underscored the changing terms of arranged marriage to represent conjugal decision making as a set of vetted options. Such a perspective would later be embraced by a mainstream media that idealizes these modified forms of arranged marriage as a practice that removes the difficulties associated with dating, highlighting the problem with too much choice. These kinds of portrayals frequently compare arranged marriage to dating sites like Match.com, in which there are preselected criteria that must be met before a prospect is given an opportunity. Websites like Shaadi.com and BharatMatrimony.com, as a social website with the explicit goal of matrimony, sustain the practice of arranged marriage through a digital network.

In an ethnographic study of middle-class Indian women's relationships to their marriage forms, Jyota Puri argues that "their narratives are both shaped by, but destabilizing to, distinctions between 'arranged' and 'love' marriages" (*Woman*, 141). Although the lines between these forms of marriage are less distinct than previously thought, the demarcations "shape women's discourse about themselves, and do so in ambiguous ways" (139). Women themselves blend these two in their discourse about their own marriages in both directions. They romanticize their arranged marriages in terms of companionship, intimacy, equality, and mutuality; conversely, they sometimes bring in the family to legitimate mutual attraction. This discursive slippage defines how women frame their lives, but representations of arranged marriage in India show that the material conditions of arranged marriage, which might include sexual activity with a near-stranger, a patrilocal practice of moving in with the husband's family, a disproportionate amount of household labor, limited mobility, lack of privacy with the spouse, and deference to the parents-in-law, sometimes give lie to this fluidity between narratives of duty and freedom. Thus Puri sees the women's narration as a way they "negotiate the mandates of wifehood" (136) rather than enable freedom within its terms.

The relative affirmation of arranged marriage among the educated, urban upper middle class in India also reflects the continuing importance of narratives of tradition in a social milieu that is otherwise eager to embrace what are perceived as Western cultural values. Looking at upwardly mobile youths in India's cities, Parveez Mody argues that they are making the choice for arranged marriages "because they believe that in the fast-paced urban world in which divorce is becoming increasingly commonplace, the idealized arranged-marriage can create stable social relations and ensure the continuity of ritual practices, kinship and gender hierarchies, religious traditions, culinary styles and moral values to the next generation" (*Intimate State*, 9). This notion that marriage becomes an idealized repository for social relations and cultural practices echoes in the diaspora.

The Discourse of Romance

Discourses of love have a long history in South Asia, with tales of passion and devotion featured in classical Hindu epics and expressions of longing and loss found in the ghazal. The popular cultural works treated in this chapter elevate arranged marriage through elements associated with the genre of romance. Romance is usually considered a Western cultural construction, for though there have certainly been vibrant expressions of love, desire, longing, and devotion from around the world, a particular genealogy of romantic love emerged in the West, and it is this one in play. Anthony Giddens links these narratives of romance to the interconnection of freedom and self-realization (*Transformation*, 40). Many scholars locate this process historically in terms of changes within the structure of the family, marking the eighteenth century as a period in European history in which shifts in conjugal practices that celebrate a new ideal of marriage among the middle class signified the ascendance of the individual over the extended family. According to a well-known formulation by Lawrence Stone, this "companionate marriage" marked a new valuation of personal autonomy and validation of individual happiness (*Family*, 273). Such marriage, while it certainly did not jettison the influence of family and community, has located the affective force of affiliation within the primary couple.

South Asian works, both critical and celebratory of arranged marriage, have historically presented arranged marriage as incompatible with romance. For advocates of arranged marriage, this perceived absence is frequently offered as a good thing. In her memoir, Anita Jain reads a sign that says, "A car runs on the road, not in a garage. Romance courses through affairs, not marriage" (*Marrying Anita*, 107). In another example, a mother in Monica Pradhan's novel *The Hindi-Bindi Club* offers a typical opinion about romantic love:

"Here, you talk about love. There, it's compatibility. Love's fickle. Compatibility endures, sustains marriages," she says. "Here, marriage is about two people on the wedding cake. Couples don't need permission slips from their parents. Families have a lower priority than the couple. But in India, marriage is the joining of two families, a strategic alliance. The couple's a lower priority than the family as a whole, and permission slips are essential." (183)

Like the sign, the mother's statement disparages romantic love as morally corrupting, unsustainable, and antagonistic to family. This conventional formulation holds romance to be the epitome of Western individualism and antithetical to arranged marriage, which is deemed a conjugal form committed to upholding the relations of kin.

In Sanjay Leela Bhansali's version of *Devdas,* one may see notions of romance used as the antithesis to arranged marriage. This version of the much-retold story depicts arranged marriage as imprisonment and self-made romance as the means to satisfy the self's desires. Some of the differences between this work and its famous predecessors, including Sarat Chandra Chattopadhyay's 1917 novel and Bimal Roy's 1955 version, bear mentioning for the way they reframe ideas about intergender relations, familial obligation, and possession using the motif of arranged marriage. In the earlier version, Devdas's father opposes the match for reasons of the families' relative social status; in Bhansali's version, the mother is made jealous when Devdas shows primary devotion to Paro, and this drives her to use the rationale that Paro's family is socially illegitimate. One of the most important differences is the representation of Paro's marriage. In the book and earlier films, Paro's older husband is pleased when Paro fulfills her role as wife, and Paro quietly assumes both her role and identity as mother. The couple's sexual relation is left unspecified. In Bhansali's film, Paro's older husband, Zaminder Bhuvan, explicitly tells her he won't have intercourse with her, making Paro and Devdas's relationship the sole object of cinematic desire. Moreover, instead of understanding her responsibilities to Devdas as a sign of her generosity, the husband in Bhansali's film drastically punishes Paro when he discovers her love for Devdas, declaring she will never step out of the house. Using the image of the locked gates of an imprisoning manor house in the final scene, Bhansali shows arranged marriage as a form of imprisonment rather than as the meaningful fulfillment of duty shown in the novel.

Although romance continues to be held in suspicion, if not contempt, by advocates of arranged marriage, and works like Bhansali's perpetuate its opposition between romance and arranged marriage, the new works celebrating arranged marriage increasingly mobilize elements of a genre of romance. In doing so, they reflect a shift in popular conceptions, which have increasingly begun to challenge the dichotomy between "love marriage" and "arranged marriage." The presence of this discourse in cultural representations marks a fluidity that Jyoti Puri argues already exists in Indian marital practices. Based on her interviews with fifty-four women in India, Puri suggests that the line between contemporary love and arranged marriages for middle-class women is less distinct than commonly thought. She argues that women themselves blend these two notions in their discourse about their own marriages. They romanticize their arranged marriages in terms of companionship, intimacy, equality, and mutuality; conversely, they sometimes bring in the family to legitimate mutual attraction. Puri sees the women's narration as a way they "negotiate the mandates of wifehood" (*Woman*, 136) through the "ambiguous ways" (139) they deploy the discourses of love and arrangement. The distinctions between "love marriage" and "arranged marriage" made by women in Puri's study, though ambiguous, are not irrelevant, nor even necessarily dissolving, since the study found that women narrated the stories of courtships and marriages using binaries between love and arrangement.

The popular cultural works on arranged marriage represent the same kind of erasure and retrenchment. Works that suture together the generic formulations of romance with arranged marriage narratives invariably alter both. In the service of a conjugal ideal signifying "tradition," these films and novels cannibalize rather than reject some of the key discourses used to oppose arranged marriage. In the process, they bring in new elements associated with love marriage, such as choice, creating an arranged marriage discourse that is compatible with neoliberal ideals that give shape to a transnational community. To examine this, this chapter looks first at Bollywood cinema before turning to popular women's fiction.

Bollywood: The Transnational Fantasy of Arranged Marriage

Bollywood film has played a significant role in producing fantasies of romance around arranged marriage. Hindi cinema in the past twenty-some years has popularized new versions of arranged marriage as well as represented and helped construct shifting notions of love in arranged marriage. Romantic plots have envisioned a way to smooth the difference between individual desire and family obligations by imagining several kinds of scenes: self-made marriages sanctioned by the family, love during an arranged marriage engagement period, and love after an arranged marriage. The kind of love here is not primarily the duty-bound affiliation historically associated with rationalizing arranged marriage but the modern discourse of romance that is the site for the construction of the individual self: "the rapture we feel for people and things that inspire in us the hope of an indestructible grounding for our life" (May, *Love*, 6).

During the 1990s, although popular films promoted the idea of self-made romances, they still upheld both the practices and values associated with arranged marriages. Sooraj R. Barjatya's *Hum Aapke Hain Koun...!* (2007) validated a love match by paralleling it to happy arranged marriages also represented in the film. Though the film gives the self-made love the suspense and the primary plot line, for the arranged marriage, the traditional romantic narrative of overcoming obstacles to achieve love was replaced by an extended scene of the wedding spectacle. Other films that narrate self-made romances alongside arranged marriage also give a significant amount of screen and dialogue time to the arranged marriage. In Karan Johar's *Kabhi Khushi Kabhie Gham* (2007), a rationale for arranged marriage is articulated by the father, who admonishes that they must honor and respect the ancestors, and that the unknown background of the girl will stand in the way of performing that duty. He questions the girl's ability to understand and uphold the values as a family and community. Self-made marriage wins, but arranged marriage gets a significant amount of rhetorical support. Popular Hindi films like *Kabhi Khushi Kabhie Gham* represent how the individualist discourse of romance must come into alignment with the symbolic force of the joint family. As Jenny Sharpe noted in her analysis of Aditya Chopra's *Dilwale Dulhane Le Jeyenge* (1995), this may be done by a kind of retrospective arrangement; in that film, the family patriarch must authorize the love match before it can be realized, symbolically handing over his daughter (Sharpe, "Gender," 69).

Since around 2000, Bollywood films, such as *Hum Dil De Chuke Sanam*, Vipul Amrutlal Shah's *Namastey London*, Aditya Chopra's *Rab Ne Bana Di Jodi*, and Meghna Gulzar's *Just Married* (2007), as well as Bollywood-inspired films like Mira Nair's *Monsoon Wedding*, have created arranged marriage romances for and about a nationally and globally mobile class that has consumed narratives of intimacy. These stories challenge the premises of the Western romance, in which, as David Shumway puts it, "romantic stories deal with love that leads to marriage or love outside marriage, but not love in marriage" (*Modern Love*, 3).

Sanjay Leela Bhansali's 1999 film *Hum Dil De Chuke Sanam* is probably the best-known Bollywood film that romanticizes arranged marriage. This film juxtaposes a self-made romance between Nandini and Sameer, with a marriage between Nandini and Vanraj. Like a number of these films, *Hum Dil De Chuke Sanam* seems to repudiate arranged marriage as an outdated custom, only to recuperate it as the film progresses. When another character runs away from her husband, Nandini's father, the patriarch of the extended family, opines that a daughter has to marry according to her father's wishes and that after a marriage, a husband means everything to a woman. Reinforcing this idea that the responsibility for a girl is transferred from elders to husband, the married women in the family suggest that a girl is like a kite that is controlled by her parents before marriage and after by her husband. Nandini's passionate romance with Sameer seems to defy these mandates and place agency in the hands of the young woman. Having gestured toward a critical stance, however, the film then uses both traditional rhetoric and affective mobilization to return the young woman to her culturally assigned role. Sameer is really the one who pays homage to his teacher, leaving when the father forbids him to continue his relationship to Nandini. Nandini, a devoted daughter, marries as her father wishes, thus maintaining her father's respect in the community. Having had her do her duty, however, the contemporary film must also produce a love narrative within those duty-bound relations. Vanraj wins her over with his devotion and sacrifice, both considered important values in arranged marriage. The film uses religious iconography and a sound track of religious chants and language (the rhetoric of Hindu conjugality in which "God makes the marriage") to synthesize romance, arranged marriage, and communal identification.

Shah's film *Namastey London* may be interpreted as a celebration of Indian nationalism through the discourse of arranged marriage. The film traces the shifting national affiliations of an Indian British young woman with a white fiancé who comes to embrace her Indian identity through her marriage to a Punjabi villager. As well as having an overt discussion of arranged marriage in the diaspora, in which the husband, Arjun, argues that Indian arranged marriages are more successful than the self-made ones, the film also romanticizes an arranged marriage that begins with coercion. Jasmeet's father "rescues" her from a dissolute life of clubbing in London, taking her back to India and setting up an arrangement that she feels she must go through with in case her fiancé is violent. The film treads lightly on this forced marriage territory by having Jasmeet put off consummation. She also claims that this wedding, a Sikh ceremony, does not make a real marriage that will be recognized by the British state. As Jasmeet finds herself wooed by a man who operates under the idea that he is in fact married, the film upholds the power of community and nation. Arjun teaches Jasmeet how to defend India to people who think India is filled with snake charmers. The India that is elevated is not the one of the past, represented by Jasmeet's frumpyish, village-born mother who never fits in, but by the highly masculinized Punjabi man who is just as at home at a posh London party as he is in a village in the Punjab. As in *Hum Dil De Chuke Sanam*, marriage is shown as a sacred right; the image of marriage is aligned with the scene of a father passing religion on to his son. The narrative of arranged marriage is one that represents culture, religion, and gender roles inflected with nationalist discourses.

Another film repeats the idea that arranged marriage love is divinely sanctioned but must still be mediated by worldly romance. Chopra's *Rab ne Bana di Jodi* synthesizes self-made romance and arranged marriage by having the middle-aged groom, Surinder, switch back and forth from his conservative self, whom Taani was obligated to marry by her dying father's wishes, and a disguise, a suave dance partner with whom Taani falls in love. The film plays out the different kinds of love that are required by the contemporary arranged marriage narrative, both duty and romance, while never allowing Taani to fully articulate her extramarital desire. Instead, the film reintegrates Taani by having the heroine come to "see the god in her husband," a statement of both patriarchal and devotional affiliation as well as a Hindu conception of marriage.

Two recent Bollywood films with smaller releases focused on what might be called a therapeutic discourse, in which the couple, to succeed, must talk things over and work through their problems rather than give way to some kind of "quality of enchantment" (Giddens, *Transformation*, 38). *Just Married* represents individuals discovering desire, overcoming impediments to love, and creating deep interpersonal connections after the marriage. The film features the idea that the arranged marriage reverses the order of a romance. In one scene, a series of couples at a honeymoon resort in Ooty compare their love stories over dinner. The protagonist, Akash, tells the table that they decided to reverse the order, getting married first. He leaves the sentence unfinished, suggesting their love story is still ahead of them, a point made several times in the film and featured as its primary theme. Similarly, in Chandan Arora's *Main, Meri Patni... Aur Woh!*, the protagonist must learn to reconcile his own insecurities about his height with his good fortune in a devoted and beautiful wife. The climax of the film does not come with him winning her heart, which he always held, but with his own self-acceptance. This is a contemporary discourse of love as the psychological development of the self.

Monsoon Wedding

Mira Nair's film *Monsoon Wedding* represents the reconciliation of liberal values of freedom and self-determination and neoliberal values centered in individual choice and personal satisfaction with the expression of Indian tradition. The film follows the lead up to the wedding of an arranged marriage between Hemant, a young Indian man studying in Texas, and Aditi, a young professional woman from Delhi. The resolution reinserts the neoliberal Indian subject into a narrative of tradition that is made authentic because it protects vulnerable females and allows for individual choice. At the beginning of the film, a group of television personalities debate "tradition" on television. The news moderator queries, "Just because India has gone global, should we embrace everything? What about our ancient culture?" The debate sets the stakes for the events that unfold during the film. Immediately, the value of such a neoliberal India is questioned, as a conservative older woman comes out to perform her role dubbing a porn film. Even the moderator who asks about ancient culture is portrayed as a hypocrite who lies to his wife as he carries on an affair with a young woman, Aditi. From the outset, the film questions the values of post–economically liberalized India. However, the film also challenges traditional practices as ones that have allowed for the exploitation of young women. In one of the major themes of the film, the notion of duty within the extended family is questioned as a seemingly benevolent uncle is exposed for taking advantage of the closeness of an extended family to molest his niece, Ria, as a young girl. In affirming the practices of tradition through a story that ends with the scene of an arranged couple circling the fire in a traditional Hindu ceremony, Nair is also narratively progressively reimagining the terms of the structures that surround such "ancient culture."

Monsoon Wedding gives voice to the different rationales for arranged marriage, articulated by different characters who embody the various perspectives of generation, class, and personal aspirations. Aditi's grandmother repeats the common Indian saying that is it God that arranges your marriage. Aditi's father and mother appear caught up in performing their obligations to their child—the father especially, with a community reputation he has had to build from the ground up as a Partition refugee. Ria, a scholarly and feminist-oriented character who wants to pursue creative writing graduate studies in the United States, queries her cousin as to why she's not marrying for love. The Christian servant Alice is enthralled by the wedding ceremonies, and though she doesn't question the form of matrimony, she herself is pursued by the wedding planner, a self-made match that forms a counterpart to the arranged one.

The film takes up the question of why arranged marriage is a viable, indeed desirable, form of conjugality in a globalizing India. Nair does little to explore Hemant's motivations other than to suggest in a scene where he visits a tea shop that he is nostalgic for the India of his college days. In one moment of anger, he does articulate the arguments that have persuaded him to take this route, as he imitates the picture that has been painted for him of two families bound close together. The match is a traditional one in the history of migration, with a male student and the sponsored visa wife, and perhaps for this reason, the film doesn't focus on his reasons for pursuing this. The primary question Nair addresses is why the modernized Indian woman who is a professional, sexually experienced, and well-to-do wants an arranged marriage. For Aditi, arranged marriage is a way of getting out of her situation as a mistress. Unlike her Tagore-reading cousin, Aditi gains her knowledge from popular women's magazines, stating about her prospects as the "other woman," "I read *Cosmopolitan*; I know the chances." Her comment shows this milieu as one in which individuals come at "traditional" decisions, like arranging a marriage, for reasons that have little to do with the earlier rationales associated with the practice, even the desire for mobility represented in just the generation before.

In the end, the discourses of choice and female agency come into play in validating arranged marriage. After an argument that nearly forces them to cancel the wedding, Hemant recommits by justifying the practice as interchangeable with dating: "Whether our parents introduce us or whether we meet in a club, what difference does it make?" What is implied here is the notion that marriage is about what comes after the wedding, when a couple must make things work. Similarly, Aditi and Hemant finally commit to the marriage in terms that equate arranged marriages with self-made ones: "Yeah, I know it is a risk, but what marriage isn't a risk?" In one important moment in between, Hemant gives over the decision making to Aditi, saying in the end that it is her decision to make. As well as affirming his own willingness, this statement echoes the discourse about the woman's right to choose.

Ladki-Lit

The popular culture subgenre of South Asian women's fiction sometimes called "ladki-lit" is a key arena for the cultural revival of arranged marriage. Ladki-lit, *ladki* meaning "girl" in Hindi, is the tongue-in-cheek name the Indian press dubbed a form of "chick-lit" with a South Asian protagonist (Kumar, "Rise of Ladki-Lit"). Chick-lit was an ironic name given to a group of popular contemporary novels marketed to women that narrate the travails of middle-class young women in their tumultuous professional and personal lives. Although the most famous chick-lit novels were set in London and New York and had white protagonists, the subgenre made inroads in South Asian markets as well, both in the subcontinent and its diaspora, with books focused on South Asian women, primarily Indian, Indian American, or Indian British women. These works called ladki-lit primarily represent Hindu women, though Kavita Daswani's *Salaam, Paris* (2006), Rekha Waheed's *A–Z Guide to Arranged Marriage* (2005), and Shelina Zahra Janmohamed's memoir *Love in a Headscarf* portray Muslim women. Ladki-lit depicts the young heterosexual woman meeting a series of romantic prospects and facing many of the same relationship "problems" as represented in Western chick-lit: married men who hide the fact, gay men who are not out to their families, and men who don't call back after a date.

In a 2008 article on South Asian American chick-lit, Pamela Butler and Jigna Desai offer an important reinterpretation of ladki-lit. They argue that previous postfeminist work on the subgenre had seen these works simply as South Asian versions of popular literature with Anglo-American characters; in doing so, this criticism had ignored defining differences structuring these works. Butler and Desai argue that South Asian American chick-lit represents race, nation, empire, and political economy through its portrayals of these differences. They make a convincing argument that these fictional works need to be read in terms of the way they produce "a (trans)national racialized feminine subject embedded within neoliberalism, heteronormativity, and racism" ("Manolos," 2). Neoliberalism may be defined more broadly as a state policy connected to the expansion of markets within the context of globalization; Aihwa Ong defines American neoliberalism in particular as "an extreme realization of the priority of market principles, which are now invading all areas of social life and exposing citizens to levels of risk from which they have heretofore been partially protected" (*Flexible*, 211). Inderpal Grewal has focused on how the discourse of American neoliberalism transforms liberal ideals, such as freedom or democracy, into market-bound concepts, such as choice and consumption, when it enters a transnational context (*Transnational*, 8–9). The following analysis builds on this work in transnational feminism to elaborate how a neoliberal subject is produced through marriage, in particular. It reinforces Butler and Desai's conclusion that arranged marriage practices are depicted as changing such that interpersonal intimacy becomes the measure of success. However, it departs from their analysis in an important way. The reading suggests that it is not only the increased presence of choice in arranged marriage practices that makes it desirable for the transnational subject but also the normativity it appears to embody. These popular novels idealize "culture as choice" within a context of transnational mobility.

Somewhat unexpectedly given its emphasis on dating, ladki-lit has offered a key arena for narrating the story of arranged marriage in a positive light. Certainly many mass-market novels still often focus on a "love match" overcoming expectations for arranged marriage; Anaju Chauhan's novel *The Zoya Factor* (2008), a best seller in India, falls into this category. What is new and characteristic of the alternate representations explored in this chapter is that arranged marriage is frequently represented as a possible solution to the pitfalls of more liberal relationships. Some of the better-known examples featuring arranged marriage include novels like Kavita Daswani's books *For Matrimonial Purposes* (2003), *The Village Bride of Beverly Hills*, and *Salaam, Paris*; Monica Pradhan's *The Hindi-Bindi Club*; Anne Cherian's *A Good Indian Wife*; and Anita Jain's best-selling 2008 memoir *Marrying Anita: A Quest for Love in the New India*. Only some of these works end with a successful arranged marriage, but all of them engage with the idea in a significant and positive way.

Works about arranged marriage include those with an arranged marriage plot, meaning those texts in which the primary love story takes place within an arrangement made by the family; they also include texts in which arranged marriage is featured in a significant way, either in the story or in the reception of the work, but the primary relationship is not arranged. The arranged marriage plot takes two distinguishable forms. Put very simply, in one version, arranged marriage ends the story, and in another, it begins the story. Both structures maintain the focus on a woman's development that characterizes the subgenre of chick-lit. In Daswani's *Salaam, Paris*, a beautiful girl from a conservative Muslim family in India goes to Paris to meet the fiancé to whom she has been promised by her grandfather. She runs away from the arrangement to find success as a runway model, becoming a celebrity while retaining her identity as a "good Muslim girl" who does not drink, have sex, or eat pork. Elements of a romantic narrative include a series of accidental meetings, impediments to love that must be overcome, and misunderstandings that create narrative tension. The character's steadfast adherence to what are deemed Muslim and Indian cultural values ultimately leads her back to the very man to whom she was affianced. Offering an alternative narrative structure to similar ends of affirming the concept, Cherian's *A Good Indian Wife* begins with an arranged marriage.

The couple passes through emotional trials as the husband maintains a relationship with an American woman, while the wife develops a kind of multicultural identity in the United States (learning to cook Mexican as well as Indian food); the story resolves with the wife's pregnancy and the death of the husband's grandfather, both events marking a recommitment to family values.

Not every work about arranged marriage has an arranged marriage plot. Some of the novels and films end with the character finding a match by happenstance but develop the theme of arranged marriage through various plot devices or allusions. These also contribute to the reinvigoration of arranged marriage narratives. The memoir *Love in a Headscarf* builds the narrative around a series of prospective meetings, and though Janmohamed meets her future husband at an event in the last pages of the book, the author never dismisses the value of looking for a mate through the matchmaking processes of arranged marriage. *The Hindi-Bindi Club* ends in a relationship between an Indian American and a European American that is "just like a traditional arranged marriage" (Pradhan, 344), because her mother introduces her to the young man. Chauhan's *The Zoya Factor* involves an arranged love marriage in which the family sanctions a love match and the affirmation is discursively connected to the practice of arranged marriage. The importance of such sanction is discussed more fully later in this chapter.

The marketing and reception of these novels, as well as their plots, promote the concept of arranged marriage. Reviews and marketing materials emphasize the theme of arranged marriage in the reception of books that do not begin or end with arranged marriage. For example, Jain's *Marrying Anita* is a well-marketed and reviewed memoir that narrates the travails of a professional Indian American woman who decides to return to India to work as a journalist as she pursues an arranged marriage. Like others of this contemporary genre, the memoir relates the difficulties of dating for the young professional Indian, especially the Indian woman. The author of *Marrying Anita* is left single after a series of meetings with her parents' choices. Yet the idea that a cosmopolitan New Yorker would embrace arranged marriage—indeed, write a book about it—has dominated the book's reception. Published reviews of Jain's book emphasize the author's decision to ask her parents to arrange a marriage rather than the chance encounters that continue to follow this decision. Lori Gottlieb's review for the *New York Times* is typical in turning this into a reflection on the universal lessons of arranged marriage: "Ultimately, Jain seems to be asking, Is modernization really progress? After all, if with choice comes freedom, then why do so many single women feel imprisoned by their loneliness?" ("Arrangement," 9). A review in an Indian newspaper suggests that Jain's decision to pursue an arranged marriage mediates the divide between modernity and antiquity, "strik[ing] a chord with young Indian women who have to straddle two worlds—the new one in which the Western concept of dating rules and the old one where marriage is a tribal alliance with a member of the same caste, creed and community" (Thomas, "What's Love").

Works of ladki-lit are written primarily by and for Indian women in the subcontinent and abroad; arguably, however, their market extends more broadly to a South Asian professional class. An online article by someone who attended the Karachi Literary Festival suggests that young, presumably educated middle- and upper-class Pakistanis enjoy reading popular women's fiction written in India (Soofi, "Pakistan Diary"). An opinion piece in a major Bangladeshi English-language newspaper looks to a popular Indian writer's self-help book on maintaining marriage (Shopna, "A New Year Gift"). The market also includes a more general, mostly female Western readership. Readers' reviews on Amazon.com suggest that these novels draw readers across ethnicities: "I was her—only not Indian," one reader wrote about *Marrying Anita*. This chapter focuses on the relationship of these texts to a transnational, South Asian, professional-class, female readership, with an awareness that these works might play a very different role for non–South Asians.

Ladki-lit is a transnational phenomenon. These works are issued by transnational publishers in the United States, Britain, and India, including G. P. Putnam and Plume (Daswani), Bantam Dell/Bloomsbury/Penguin India (Daswani, Jain), and HarperCollins India (Chauhan). There are certainly differences in the experiences and cultural resources these writers draw upon: Monica Pradhan and Kavita Daswani grew up outside India; Anita Jain relocated to India in her thirties; and Anuja Chauhan has retained a permanent residence in India. But the markets and readership in the emerging popular genre of ladki-lit are not fixed by the national origins or locations of the authors, and neither is the content determined by these factors. An article in *Indian Express* cites a senior editor at Penguin Books India describing how the category of "Indian chick-lit" has exploded in demand (Kumar, "Rise of Ladki-Lit"). Minneapolis-based Kavita Daswani's *Salaam, Paris* appeared as number eight in fiction on an Indian best-seller list in May 2007 (Guha, "Ian McEwan"), while the memoir of Delhi-based Indian American Jain reached India's number four in nonfiction in September 2008 (Thaindian News, "The Secret"). The presence of these works on Indian best-seller lists suggests that markets and readership are shared between India, the United Kingdom, North America, and other English-language locations. The popularity of such literature in the diaspora is more difficult to trace, either in the more general national context or within the South Asian community, but both Daswani's novels and Jain's books have been featured in new arrival sections in British and American bookstores and have been reviewed by publications focused on the diaspora (SAWNET, "Bookshelf").

For the young middle-class South Asian women who are the target audience of ladki-lit, this literature fosters recognition of a preexisting transnational English-speaking collectivity as it helps constitute that community. This is a mobile global class—mobile in two senses. First, within India, members of this professional group of young women might have moved away from where their parents live to go to school or take jobs. Second, as a group, this class crosses over lines of nation to include middle-class women in the subcontinent as well as in the South Asian diaspora. It includes those who move back and forth through education, work, or marriage.

As well as embodying transnational processes of production and consumption, increasingly these books represent transnational mobility through conjugal practices. Settings show two-way movement between the home country and the diaspora. Daswani's *The Village Bride of Beverly Hills* begins with the bride of an arranged marriage moving to California and returning to India, and then projects to a future residence back in the United States. Neel, the husband in Cherian's *A Good Indian Wife,* arranges his marriage while on a visit to India, while Anita Nair returns to India to find a husband. The forms of mobility are imaginative as well as literal. Arjun Appadurai argues that one of the primary transformations in this period of globalization has been in the capacity for people to imagine themselves or their children will live and work in places other than where they were born (*Modernity*, 6). These novels represent transnational mobility, both in their plots and as global commodities. In the process of inscribing this mobility, they allow a reader in Mumbai to envision another version of herself turning the page in London or New York.

An Intimate Public

Ladki-lit marks the creation of what Lauren Berlant calls an "intimate public" shaped by a commodity of book genre (*Female Complaint*, viii). Berlant's work is helpful as a way to explore what she calls "institutions of intimacy," including the popular cultural works known as women's fiction (169); this theoretical rubric offers a way to interpret how ladki-lit engages with conjugal ideals and to assess its social and political consequences. Berlant's argument takes as a starting point the notion that popular culture should be taken seriously as an object of critical inquiry, a place where the construction and reconstruction of meaning take place. One may use Berlant's study of twentieth-century American film and fiction to analyze how South Asian transnational popular women's novels organize desire and, in the process, create an identifiable (but noncoherent) public sphere formulated by affect. Affect is defined by the *Oxford English Dictionary* as "the capacity for willing or desiring; a mental state, mood, or emotion, *esp.* one regarded as an attribute of a more general state; a feeling, desire, intention." Both destabilizing and consolidating, affect mobilizes identification and affiliation. The subject of an intimate public looks to emotional knowledge as a kind of locus for its constitution within a shared community, often a community of women, but potentially also including other identities deemed marginal.

Narratives of arranged marriage gain ground in this transnational context through the affective function of romance. The new narratives incorporate elements from a romantic discourse, especially that part of the discourse David Shumway calls the "women's romance," a subgenre that foregrounds the love story and presumes an almost exclusively female audience (*Modern Love*, 33). The subgenre of women's romance structures expectations in such a way that pleasure emerges as the reader or viewer repeatedly finds narrative desire fulfilled in similar ways, for example, through the happy ending. Romantic stories mobilize affect as the reader identifies with the subject through its journey from denial to fulfillment. Not all romantic narratives deal with interpersonal love, but popular women's fiction takes this private realm as its primary subject. Within the structures of this subgenre, narrative functions affectively through suspense and catharsis as the plot revolves around a heroine overcoming obstacles to ultimately achieve love. In the process of reading, the reader invests in the "intersubjective character of romance" and is "positioned to identify with the excluded subject and experiences his or her desire, motivating and structuring the reader's attention" (15). The object of this desire is transferable, and in the context of the transnational popular cultural texts that are its focus, the transfer moves from the interpersonal (wanting the girl to get the guy) to the cultural, producing a romance of national belonging.

Although these works legitimate this passage from self to others as an intimate gesture—for example, love for the family—they often affirm the displacement as an act in the service of cultural identification. Arranged marriage becomes a diacritical marker of identity in these texts, meaning that the concept stands in for a complex series of structures and processes that surround the (re)emergence of this conjugal practice in the diaspora. Sometimes culture might take the form of religion or ethnicity, but most often, it takes the name of the nation. "Arranged marriages are probably more associated with India than any other national cultural tradition," Jyoti Puri argues (*Woman*, 138). Although she is speaking primarily about the Indian context, this association gathers new meanings in a transnational context. The meaning of that nation is not a given, nor is it identical across different historical–geographical locations. Arranged marriage might become a way to "be Indian" for a highly educated, professional man in New Jersey, and it might become a way to "be Bangladeshi" for a woman from East London working in the garment industry, but these forms of imagining the nation are mediated by the structures of gender, class, and religion. The popular cultural texts interpreted show that a certain notion of being Indian, especially, is produced for the elite in the transnational context of the global movement of people and capital. For the broader readership that includes some professional Pakistani and Bangladeshi women in the subcontinent and diaspora, that specific national identity may be reinterpreted as a more general South Asian one as the reader consumes the same book in London or Dhaka. These novels redirect the catharsis produced by a love plot to invigorate the affective experience of national cultural belonging. Put very simply, in these works, having an arranged marriage offers the way to be Indian (and sometimes, more generally, South Asian).

The following sections elaborate on the representation of arranged marriage in this popular transnational culture. In the next section, I show how narratives of arranged marriage are being altered to bring in elements associated with "love marriage." Arranged marriage has always been a crucible rearticulating the forces that constitute it. In the contemporary context of transnational movement of culture, capital, and people, depictions of arranged marriage mobilize a discourse of romance to reinforce rather than challenge the practice. In the subsequent section, I look at why these changes in narratives of arranged marriage make it more compatible with a globalized subjectivity articulated in terms of neoliberal ideals of choice. I then show how through the production of a fantasy space that resolves conflicts within this subjectivity, these narratives obscure the socioeconomic conditions historically associated with arranged marriage practices. In the final section, I explore why arranged marriage narratives are retained rather than simply abandoned in favor of other, more "Western" narrative forms. I suggest that the power of these narratives does not lie simply in their ability to be adapted; rather, the normative aspects of this practice are embraced rather than rejected. This section reads this cultural conservatism as the reinvigoration of tradition among a professional class in the context of globalization.

Ladki-lit and Neoliberalism

Popular South Asian novels and films often differentiate arranged marriage from love marriage using the notion of "choice." The idea of choice is a key signifier bringing together narratives of romance and neoliberal rhetorics of commerce that followed the opening of markets and underpin the global distribution of this book commodity. Butler and Desai, whose article focuses on this aspect of ladki-lit, call the subgenre an "exemplary site of neoliberal feminist subject-making," expressed as the heroines participate in a global consumer culture ("Manolos," 8). Although they note the increased presence of arranged love marriages, they suggest that "the South Asian American protagonist is seen as achieving social maturity by securing a 'modern' (i.e. not arranged) heterosexual romance and marriage" (18). Their argument builds on the work of Inderpal Grewal, who has argued that in the feminist diasporic novels of the 1990s, "marriage for 'love' signified passage into America through the discourse of 'choice'" (*Transnational*, 77). Indeed, some of the popular women's fiction that sets itself against arranged marriage does so with the notion that such arrangements deny choice to a new subject of liberalization—the single South Asian woman working a professional job—that is otherwise reveling in new choices of clothes, cuisines, and living arrangements. In an interview about an emerging Indian market for chick-lit, V. K. Karthika, publisher and chief editor at HarperCollins India, suggests,

This is the story of the new Indian woman in the cities. She is single, has a career and is willing to have fun, take risks and find a man her way, and not necessarily her family's way. It is a woman we have only read about in books from the Western countries and now, suddenly we are finding her on Indian roads. (Lakshmi, "India's Cheeky")

Unlike some of the recent South Asian fiction with transnational audiences, such as Aravind Adiga's *The White Tiger* (2008) and Kiran Desai's *The Inheritance of Loss* (2005), these works present a positive view of the economic liberalization that has taken place in South Asia in the past twenty years. The affirmation often takes shape as a scene of consumption or styling. Daswani's protagonist in *The Village Bride of Beverly Hills* undergoes a style makeover, learning how to wear designer clothes. Thus this subgenre of popular women's fiction includes South Asian women within this neoliberal discourse of choice through the representation of taste and consumption (Butler and Desai, "Manolos," 10).

Ostensibly arranged marriage is set in opposition to these changes. Jain states that though she'd "heard intriguing tales of this new Delhi," she came for reasons "far more resonant with the never-budging India of time past. I came to find a husband" (5). In *The Hindi-Bindi Club,* Monica Pradhan represents a similar moment of avowed traditionalism, in which Kiran, a New Jersey resident, confides,

> And right there in the Victoria's Secret dressing room, in my yuppie-chick equivalent of a midlife crisis, I allow myself to contemplate something I always deemed impossible, dismissed as cold, archaic, backward. The mate-seeking process that served my parents, most of their Indian-immigrant friends, and generations of ancestors for centuries.
> An arranged marriage. (7)

Both works contrast a consumer culture, characterized by Jain as having a "makeover," and emblemized in Pradhan's book by Victoria's Secret, with arranged marriage, which is deemed retrogressive. They then embrace that past, positing this as affiliation in the true sense of the word.

The neoliberal discourse of choice seems most compatible with the love match, yet even those works that validate arranged marriage promote a neoliberal discourse. There are two ideas at play here that are central to the compatibility of arranged marriage and a neoliberal discourse of choice. The first is the notion that one chooses an arranged marriage; the second is the notion that choice has expanded within the practice. Despite being contrasted with a new India, the presence of arranged marriage is represented as a product of liberalization, recast as a choice through romantic narratives borrowed from Western narrative traditions—it represents this new India.

The beginning of this chapter quoted a trend theorist who said, regarding arranged marriage, that "much of the future is back to the past, turbocharged" (quoted in McKay, "Because Mom Said So"); that idea of choosing the past features prominently in this neoliberal discourse of choice. While both depicting and participating in the transnational mobility of global flows, these works represent women affirming a conjugal ideal that references an idealized antiquated past while underscoring new choices. Kiran, in *The Hindi-Bindi Club,* places herself in a continuum from this antiquity on her wedding day by remembering "brides and grooms who came before, over thousands of years, who stood as we are" (Pradhan, 395). Within this intimate public, this decision to be part of the past coincides with new choices.

Although the reasons for that decision might be resonant with an image of old India, the mobility and logic that allow women to pursue this option indicate the present. In *Marrying Anita,* Jain sets the decision to pursue an arranged marriage against the backdrop of a new culture that accompanies liberalization. The tone is celebratory of a transforming capital city in a nation that "had embarked on a makeover" (3). Jain highlights what she sees as the progressive nature of this choice:

> In my mind, my decision [to find a husband in India] also overturned two conventions, which, in the lexicon of the West, could be seen as nothing less than empowering. The first convention is that of an Indian man who has grown up in the West going back to the motherland to find a traditional, virginal, "simple" bride. The second is that of a South Asian woman being dragged back by her parents—one hears of this more in the U.K. among Pakistanis and Bangladeshis—to be married off, more often than not to a domineering and narrow-minded groom who restricts the freedoms she's enjoyed in the West. I willingly—and willfully—returned to find a modern Indian husband on my own terms. (53)

Within a feminist discourse, choice is equated with feminine agency (Grewal, *Transnational*, 28). Jain describes her decision to pursue an arranged marriage as a feminist gain for women to enter the benefits of a transnational professional mobility.

The perception that choice has expanded plays an important role validating arranged marriage in terms of neoliberal ideals equating choice with freedom. Such expansion might mean that the bride or groom has a wider range of prospects and is often associated with technology. The technologies of arrangement have changed with the popularization of the Internet and increased the range of choice for arranged marriage. Unlike Internet dating, matrimonial websites have the explicit goal of marriage as the outcome and the involvement of family members, often fathers, in posting the profiles. The introduction of Internet matchmaking extends the practice of posting newspaper advertisements, and both practices show a new national and global subjectivity for the marriage mart over previous, more local spheres. Even in Internet matrimonial ads, the elements of arranged marriage that are retained are several. On the most traditional end, parents post and respond to matrimonial ads; Shaadi.com, for example, has the ability to search for profiles posted by a parent or guardian. For all the profiles, socioeconomic status (profession, income), religion, and caste are searchable categories, and though the first of these factors is also significant on dating sites, within the Indian context, it has been a central aspect of the practice of arranged marriage.

Ladki-lit's character as a postfeminist cultural phenomenon may be seen in the emphasis on consumption and the conflation of this kind of choice with individual freedom (Tasker and Negra, *Interrogating*, 2). Yvonne Tasker and Diane Negra's analysis of postfeminist culture offers useful insight here, both in terms of its conclusions and in terms of the ways ladki-lit holds to, or departs from, the Anglo-American popular culture they discuss. Chick-lit fits within a postfeminist cultural imagination that frequently proffers a retreat from the working world as its ultimate resolution. Ladki-lit departs from other kinds of popular women's fiction in the way it codes this retreat as a cultural affiliation. McRobbie argues that popular culture references feminism only to dismiss it (Tasker and Negra, *Interrogating*, 33); ladki-lit also presumes certain gains among Indian women, but characterizes these achievements as Westernization rather than feminist. Ladki-lit participates in the refusals and reactionary moves of postfeminist culture by idealizing a domestic space devoid of real tension. However, it posits this refusal as about culture—being "Indian" versus being "Western." In doing so, it taps other nationalist discourses about the domestic sphere, some of them originating as far back as the colonial period, when a nationalist movement mobilized around the question of legislating conjugal practices (Sarkar, *Hindu Wife*, 39).

"How to Live as an X"

Ladki-lit produces a fantasy space that fetishizes arranged marriage as a traditional cultural form while obscuring its historic and present-day economic and social relations. Understanding this genre is thus important as a way to conceptualize the role of fantasy in the processes of globalization and assess its political valance. In an intimate public, women work out their conditions of existence through fantasy and affect management within and through the genre of popular women's fiction while not necessarily transcending those conditions. In the case of arranged marriage, these real conditions might include the patrilocal practice of moving in with the husband's family and subsequent lack of privacy, a significant amount of household labor, dowry pressures, limited mobility, and sexual relations with a virtual stranger. Selecting from the aspects associated with arranged marriage and recasting them in terms more palatable to their audience, these popular literary and filmic works present an idealized version of the joint family, gender roles, and wedding practices. They represent strategies of management, coercion, coping, and discussion that illuminate how a professional transnational community might formulate itself through a cultural ideal that overtly confines individual choice. In the process, they promote this revival to a transnational middle class, mostly female audience, both of Indian origin and otherwise.

Ladki-lit, and other works that participate in the cultural revival, produce in aesthetic form a kind of "cultural streamlining" (Radhakrishnan, *Appropriately Indian,* 4). In an ethnographic study of Indian IT workers, Smitha Radhakrishnan argues that this transnational class has created a version of India through a process by which a simplified, modular form of Indian cultural norms is created in ways that are compatible with the economic and geographic mobility of the global economy (4–5). Radhakrishnan terms this constructed identity "appropriately Indian" and describes this character as a product of transnational conditions mediating national cultural forms and mobilities across national borders. The cultural streamlining process produces a version of an Indian identity compatible with the processes of globalization. In the arena of popular women's texts discussed here, this means that the protagonists embrace a neoliberal discourse of choice *and* an ideal of arranged marriage. Ladki-lit sometimes negotiates the disjuncture between fantasy and lived experience by imagining the reform of practices within arranged marriage, retaining familial and cultural affiliation while dispensing with some of the concurrent normative practices that have emerged with the practice. Author Kavita Daswani described this goal when talking about her novel *The Village Bride of Beverly Hills*: "It tells many young women, who face the predicaments Priya *(the heroine of her novel)* faces that they are not alone. That they don't have to stifle themselves. There are many opportunities to strengthen oneself and still be part of a traditional family" (Pais, "Rediff Interview," emphasis original). Novels make a point of talking about men who cook or families who enjoy take-out food, thus obliterating the problematic point that historically a large share of domestic responsibilities has fallen on the daughter-in-law. Other works make a fetish out of cooking as a signifier of culture but deemphasize it as an everyday labor practice. *The Hindi-Bindi Club,* for example, begins its chapters with recipes that stand in as representations of culture. Cooking becomes a kind of recreational practice, not an essential attribute of household labor.

One novel, *The Village Bride of Beverly Hills,* does focus on the domestic duties of the daughter-in-law. In that novel, Priya, the daughter-in-law, joins her new family in Los Angeles with so many responsibilities that the mail carrier mistakes her for a housekeeper. She struggles with this role, for which she has been groomed by her traditional family, as her career outside the home expands. Daswani depicts this role of wife/sister/daughter-in-law as exploitative; the author emphasizes how the family relies on the new bride as worker by having all the other characters do nothing inside the home. The narrative resolution suggests that a career outside the home (not simply wage labor) is the more appropriate trajectory for the new bride. With the end of the novel, in which Priya takes the family out to eat and the husband brings a key to a new home just for them, Daswani represents an answer that would have been unthinkable in earlier work: simply dine out and move out. The resolution emphasizes the arranged marriage couple over the joint family and glosses over the destruction of the joint family structure.

The joint family forms one of the primary sites for revision, both within

India and in the diaspora. Historically, the rhetoric of arranged marriage places the joint family at the center of the household economy, and the arranged marriage at the center of that. The joint family in South Asia considers the extended family as one household and may be simultaneously a legal entity, an economic one, and a genealogical one, meaning with a common lineage. Majumdar defines the joint family as "cooperation in economic pursuits, joint management and ownership of property, helping each unit of the family in times of crisis, and celebrating festivals, rituals, and birth, death, and marriage ceremonies comprised of several generations living with a patriarch or matriarch" (*Marriage*, 4). Arranged marriage has historically been an economic system in which the daughter-in-law contributes her unpaid or paid labor to her husband's family, often under the supervision of her mother-in-law. This is true both in South Asia and in the diaspora. These networks place the groom's mother—not the bride—at the center of power. The binary between individual desire and the joint family has played a significant role in the historical evolution of arranged marriage, argues Kakar, as families fear the "power of sexual love to overturn time-honoured norms," specifically a son's familial duty (Kakar, "Match Fixing").

Although the joint family is frequently cast as a central cultural practice with roots in antiquity, the joint family emerged as a South Asian *icon* only in the nineteenth century. Majumdar argues that the joint family became valorized through a set of practices as a form of resistance to the transformations associated with colonial modernity (*Marriage*, 210). Uberoi notes that the joint family does not always operate in this ideal form but cites a consensus among sociologists "that the joint family is, if not a fact of traditional Indian society, at least a deeply held traditional value that continues to provide the underlying principles of household-building strategies in South Asia, though differently for different regions, castes, and communities" (327). In the transnational context, the symbolic weight of the joint family remains while these household-building strategies, such as sharing the same household with elders, undergo transformation in this professional class.

In the transnational discourse about arranged marriage discussed here, the nature of the joint family has become a contested point. Butler and Desai read the Indian family as "one of the most significant sites of contestation and negotiation [between the binary of tradition and modernity]" and furthermore suggest that it is "specifically the joint Indian family that is framed as being able to withstand the onslaughts of modernity, in this case modernity as present in the romantic couple" ("Manolos," 16). Because extended families are frequently transnational, for example with parents or grandparents living in the subcontinent and children abroad for study or work, the modulation of these binaries is a global process. Cultural representations become a way to negotiate the conflicting narratives about the relationship between duty and personal fulfillment.

Romantic plots in popular South Asian culture have envisioned a way to smooth the difference between individual desire and family obligation through the "arranged love marriage." Bollywood films have led the way for other cultural expressions, including ladki-lit. This "retrospective arrangement" that combines the love and arrangement narratives appears frequently in ladki-lit. These works merge an ideal of free choice associated with romance with elements of arranged marriage, particularly familial sanction. Narratives sometimes stretch to show the compatibility of the "love" relationship with the practices of arranged marriage. In Advaita Kala's 2007 novel *Almost Single,* for example, the seemingly unsuitable boy Karan, whom Aisha has been dating, appears jokingly with the matrimonial ad posted by her mother and a serious proposal for marriage. The device signals his reentrance through the culturally acceptable route of familial arrangement.

A significant body of fictional and filmic work produced in the first decade of the twenty-first century goes beyond the "arranged love marriage" featured in works of the last decade to reinsert the role of the family. The retrospective arrangement is being replaced by the traditional arranged marriage in novels like *Salaam, Paris, The Village Bride of Beverly Hills,* and *A Good Indian Wife* and in films like *Monsoon Wedding, Namastey London,* and *Just Married.* These are narrated through the generic conventions of romance, in other words, the affective plot devices of suspense and catharsis. In *Monsoon Wedding,* Hemant and Aditi resolve a love triangle by recommitting to their arranged marriage; Hemant reinforces the interpersonal decision with a comment validating the practice as interchangeable with dating: "Whether our parents introduce us or whether we meet in a club, what difference does it make?" *Namastey London* and *Just Married* create romantic plots of individuals discovering desire, overcoming impediments to love, and creating deep interpersonal connections *after* the marriage. *Just Married* features the idea that the arranged marriage reverses the order of a romance. The tagline for the international edition reads "Marriage Was Just the Beginning."

These works also change the expectation of arranged marriage even as they promote it as a cultural fetish. They develop a discourse of interpersonal intimacy that further displaces the family. Earlier works exploring love in arranged marriage emphasized expressions of loyalty or duty by husbands or wives—a form of love is brought about through devotion. In ladki-lit, couples learn to talk about their feelings and sometimes even go to therapy. In *The Village Bride of Beverly Hills*, the protagonist goes to counseling, a process that helps motivate her decision to leave her husband—or, more specifically, to leave his family. After having a few sessions with him as well, her husband comes to realize that he must talk about his feelings with his wife in order to make the relationship work. This idea is so firmly entrenched in Western, especially American, culture that it seems like a given that a couple needs to work on communication to resolve any problems in the marriage. For arranged marriage, however, in which the idealized locus has traditionally been not the nuclear family but the extended family, the discourse of intimacy does more than open lines of communication; it shifts the resolution of any problems away from the family as a whole to an interpersonal problem within the nuclear couple. The narrative shift to the problem of intimacy hides what has previously been the rationale for the joint family, for beneath the guise of familial relations and a gendered rhetoric of duty lies the political economy of the household.

More often than offering a reformist vision, these works elide uncomfortable real-life obligations and expectations that are the focus of feminist works like Deepa Mehta's film *Fire* and Monica Ali's novel *Brick Lane*. They disavow the powerful impact of practices like patriarchy, dowry, or the joint family that have been the object of feminist scrutiny. Popular fiction offers this refuge. Mothers-in-law are absent, children are as-yet unborn, and servants are quietly taking on the duties. Once again, popular film has constructed a fantasy of how to negotiate potential conflicts. Uberoi shows the idealization of the joint family as a sign of Indian culture and values that takes place in blockbuster films like *Hum Aapke Hain Koun...!* (1994) and interprets that film as representing not so much Indian reality but a kind of collective fantasy about a joint family emptied of conflict (311). For the literary works discussed here, the joint family becomes an affective structure representing either a jealous impediment to the central love, a distant signifier of cultural affiliation, or, most commonly, simply a loving support network that affirms the central match. The economic structures of this joint family are broken apart, with the newly married couple moving out or even far away, while the symbolic force is retained. Diasporic mobility is used as a plot device in this regard, allowing certain responsibilities to remain at geographic distance. The arranged marriage between Aditi and Hemant that ends Mira Nair's film *Monsoon Wedding*, for example, will develop in Texas, away from both sets of parents and from the familial baggage that comes spilling out right before the wedding.

The Politics of Ladki-Lit

A romantic discourse emphasizes the possibility and expansion of choice within the practice of arranged marriage and promotes the idea of intimacy over duty, aligning itself with a neoliberal rhetoric of globalization. In her study of the subgenre of the Asian immigrant woman's novel of the 1990s, Grewal describes how these works set up an opposition between tradition and modernity, with the former figured as a culture of origin and the latter modeled on the United States. Grewal presents a critique of the way this discourse reconfigures freedom as choice. This chapter has described the ways ladki-lit participates in that reconfiguration by celebrating an expansion of choice *in* arranged marriage and validating arranged marriage *as* a choice. However, thinking through Berlant's observation that the "new metacultural figures of the emergent subject of history ... transact with previously ascendant patterns of normative identification" (*Transnational*, 235), one might ask whether the ideal of "choice" is necessarily the only—or even the primary—affective force behind this cultural revival. What, besides the discourse of freedom, is at play in the cultural revival of arranged marriage in the transnational context? In asking this question, this chapter moves this discussion away from the work of Grewal, Butler, and Desai to develop an analysis of marriage as a site that produces a transnational subject of globalization through a discourse of constraint *as well as* through of a discourse of choice. The popularity of plots in which the family does actually arrange the match beforehand suggests a kind of traditionalism expressed as a reaction against choice. Such a reaction needs to be contextualized in two ways. First, it is part of a discourse being propagated in the West on the problems of too much choice. This cultural context, discussed at the beginning of this chapter, in which arranged marriage is presented as an alternative to the perceived failure of Western "love matches," suggests a backlash against choice present in a neoliberal discourse. Second, this is part of an affirmation of tradition in the context of global mobility and transformation.

In the transnational context, the practice of arranged marriage becomes a site for expressing cultural affiliations that signify a homeland. The contemporary novels celebrating arranged marriage push away from the association Grewal described in the South Asian American work of the 1990s, in which love marriage mediated a kind of American identity, while retaining the logic of this association. Arranged marriage still represents "being Indian" in these contemporary works, but these novels celebrate, instead of revile, "tradition" as equal to oppression. The processes of globalization associated with modernity, including increased connectivity and mobility, have reinforced the significance of tradition as a reference point. Women from a variety of classes have always been mobile in India, primarily through the practices of marriage and education, but a new segment of young, middle-class, unmarried women is creating new pathways by moving abroad to take professional jobs. Although intimate practices are changing as a result, to include dating and sexual relations, the intimate public produced by ladki-lit suggests that these transnational subjects are turning to the concept of arranged marriage as a way to retain a value system and identity located in "tradition."

Recent scholarly work has challenged the binary between tradition and modernity, suggesting that far from overcoming tradition, the rhetoric of modernity has invigorated traditional practices. Partha Chatterjee looks back to the late-nineteenth-century context of Bengal to show the emergence of a highly symbolic domestic sphere as a by-product of nationalism (*Nation,* 120). Jenny Sharpe suggests that "modernity is less the negation of tradition than the grounds for its formation" ("Gender," 63). In the context of increased mobility, both intra- and internationally, marriage affirms cultural identity as a highly symbolic domestic practice even as it fully participates in the social, political, and economic conditions of its new context. Certain key elements have been mobilized through notions of tradition. The most prominent of these is the domestic arena discussed earlier, but religion is also regularly featured.

Religious identification appears most fundamentally in the choice of spouse, who is almost invariably the same religion, but it also appears in images of Vedic astrology *(The Village Bride of Beverley Hills),* goddess reincarnation (Sonia Singh's *Goddess for Hire,* 2004), and wedding rituals *(The Hindi-Bindi Club).* With the notable exception of Janmohamed's extended reflection on the teachings of Islam in *Love in a Headscarf,* religion takes a streamlined form. Although the discourse of religion is marginal in ladki-lit, it still has a potent effect signifying tradition as it is amalgamated into a broader notion of culture. This is especially true of Hinduism, which stands as a placeholder for a broader Indian identity in a discourse of the Hindu right and in the dissemination of India within a professional, transnational community. These popular cultural texts represent the way tradition has been reinvented in the context of contemporary globalization as a streamlined expression of identity—a concentration of culture that strengthens rather than dilutes its signifying force.

These fictional and filmic texts that validate arranged marriage elevate a normative cultural practice; they reveal the complex and sometimes contradictory workings of transnational female subjectivity. Specifically, these popular cultural works expose the role of nonlibratory practices in transnational cultural formulations. As Saba Mahmood argues, the discourses of both liberalism and feminism fix on a version of agency that is understood "as the capacity to realize one's own interests against the weight of custom, tradition, transcendental will, or other obstacles (whether individual or collective)" (*Politics,* 8). Whereas feminist literature has assumed a teleology of progress toward increased freedom, the texts discussed here validate the practice of arranged marriage, in which some degree of decision making is given over, most often to the family. In real-world arranged marriage practices, the degree to which a young man or woman hands over consent varies greatly. Marriage enforced through physical constraint appears as an absolute extreme, but other factors may be coercive, such as the emotional force of family, the economic exigencies of some transnational marriages, or the practices deemed acceptable within a community. Feminist writings have called attention to the force of these factors on young women in particular. As I have argued, these popular cultural works that elevate arranged marriage downplay, disguise, or elide these coercive elements, presenting arranged marriage as a woman's choice. In the process, they create an ambivalent representation of individual agency in which a female character overtly constrains her own decision making.

Affect constitutes identities by organizing desires in such a way that fantasy becomes a means for mapping experience and identity. In the case of ladki-lit, normative identifications and practices—gender, heterosexuality, class, caste, communal affiliation, and national community—are retained through the production of fantasy. However, this didactic quality does not overcome the conditions that first create the need for that fantasy, which in the cases discussed here might come precisely out of the failure of normative modes of love and matrimony to adequately satisfy the desires of South Asian women. Popular women's fiction allows for rearticulation but, as a fantasy space, also contains and sometimes constrains that expression. Put another way, the affective processes taking place through ladki-lit are not politically progressive ones, in the sense that they do not seek to culminate in liberation from patriarchy and other structures of power.

Ladki-lit does more than mirror a form of ideology in constituting an intimate public, but the subgenre is also not a full political response, even a subversive one that passively erodes normative strictures. It is "juxtopolitical," to use Berlant's formulation, "acting as a critical chorus that sees the expression of emotional response and conceptual recalibration as achievement enough" (*Female Complaint*, x). What, specifically, is the recalibration taking place around ladki-lit? One would think, given the adventures of these women, that the books would herald new kinds of interpersonal relationships available to young South Asian women in metropolitan cities around the world—and, indeed, to some extent, they do.

Yet surprisingly, the sentimental resolution to these novels ultimately takes a different route to validate a practice identified with tradition. Saba Mahmood analyzes progressive politics and asks whether this is "a teleology that makes it hard for us to see and understand forms of being and action that are not necessarily encapsulated by the narrative of subversion and reinscription of norms" (*Politics*, 9). When a progressive feminist discourse validates traditional concepts, she asserts, it does so for the ability of these practices to undermine dominant formulations such as patriarchy. Mahmood asks us to look at other, normative practices, not for either their potential to subvert the power structures that give rise to them nor as a political model but as a way of broadening our understanding of agency (24). In bringing Mahmood into conversation with Berlant, this chapter explicates an ambivalent agency that characterizes a privileged, gendered transnational subject.

As an intimate public is produced through the circulation and consumption of popular women's fiction, the institution of marriage has gained significance representing culture in a period of increased mobility, both within and outside of South Asia. Although this deeply rooted cultural identity is counterpoised to the liberal individual subject who is the prime site of economic liberalization, representations of arranged marriage (in literature and film as well as in popular conceptions of the practice) appropriate the discourse of choice and gain momentum through the tributaries of globalization. By representing conjugal practices, ladki-lit, along with other forms of popular culture like film and print media, mobilizes the affective function of romance in the service of another kind of affiliation—national cultural belonging. As these works yoke together competing discourses about agency, they alter the narratives of both love and tradition. Sidestepping a political response that might look for new paths to emancipation, the intimate public instead becomes a site for conversation, consolation, and evasion, as it obscures the economy (and more generally power structures) that have defined the practice of arranged marriage. This intimate public provides a valuable cultural diagnostic for understanding how transnational identities and practices are formulated through popular cultural forms that both collude with and challenge Western fundamentals of individual agency; this public reterritorializes the discourse of agency as not only about individual freedom, here in the guise of choice, but also about historical difference presented in the form of national, religious, or regional culture.

Conclusion

A Cultural Studies Approach

Ask any married South Asian and he or she will most likely tell you of being asked with some curiosity by a non–South Asian whether he or she has an arranged marriage. One of the challenges in writing about arranged marriage is to grapple with its status as an overdetermined symbol of South Asian cultures without reifying the object of analysis, and ultimately reinforcing the stereotype at work. Put simply, how does one write about arranged marriage as representing Indians, Pakistanis, or Bangladeshis without equating Indians, Pakistanis, or Bangladeshis with arranged marriage? Progressive scholars have focused on the history of self-made, intercultural marriages and other intimate relationships within those South Asian diasporic communities; they have done this, in part, to challenge the equation made between South Asians and arranged marriage and, by extension, the assumption of cultural conservatism that comes with that identification (see Leonard, *South Asian Americans*; Maira, *Desis in the House*; Shah, *Stranger Intimacy*). Their important work retrieves the varied practices of intimate relationships in the diaspora. This book has met the challenge of cultural determinism in another way, namely, by historicizing the normative idea of arranged marriage itself and using a cultural studies approach to understand how arranged marriage discourses operate as points of articulation in highly politicized national and global contexts. In both contexts, arranged marriage has become the locus of a set of liberal and communitarian discourses that articulate competing visions of individual and collective agency.

This book is the first critical discourse analysis of arranged marriage in a transnational context. *Arranging Marriage* identifies and analyzes representations of the practice among South Asians in literature, film, law, policy, and digital and print media as well as academic and theoretical genres like literary criticism, legal scholarship, ethnography, cultural studies, and philosophy. Within literature and film, the book considers how, within a wide range of texts that include social realism, romance, bildungsroman, memoir, documentary, independent cinema, and mass-market Bollywood cinema, the discourse of arranged marriage is working through the formal modes of genre. In these ways, the study breaks new ground by delineating its own object of study and by analyzing that object. Let me be clear and also give credit to some of the scholars whose work intersects with this book. Some scholarly monographs that deeply inform this one have considered the discourses of marriage in India (Majumdar, *Marriage*; Mody, *Intimate State*) or alternate conjugal practices as a global phenomenon (Constable, *Romance*). Still others have included chapters on the discourse of arranged marriage in the South Asian American diaspora (Grewal, *Transnational America*), discourses of the state in relation to immigrant conjugal practices (Cott, *Public Vows*; Haag, *Consent*), or discourses of forced marriage as a global object of interest (Abu-Lughod, *Do Muslim Women*). Several historical studies and ethnographies have analyzed South Asian American practices of arranged marriage (Shah, *Stranger Intimacy*; Leonard, *South Asian Americans*; Maira, *Desis in the House*; Shankar, *Desi Land*), and a whole body of sociological and legal journal writing considers state and immigrant discourses on forced marriage in the British context (see, e.g., Anitha and Gill, "Coercion"; Enright, "Choice"; Gagoomal, "Margin"; Wilson, "Forced Marriage"). Building on these works, *Arranging Marriage* brings together, for the first time, a wide range of different discourses on South Asian arranged marriage and reads them together to show that we are in a moment of conjugal globalization. In the process, this book identifies several clearly delineated discourses about arranged marriage that bear upon questions of consent, agency, state power, and national belonging. Without looking at how such representations saturate all sorts of fields in the contemporary moment, we miss important dimensions of these processes. Specifically, we might not understand how these discourses illuminate deep divisions in the processes of globalization that construct a fault line between individualist and collectivist agency. We also miss the way a neoliberal discourse of "culture as choice" attempts to bridge that separation, but only through reified notions of culture severed from their constitutive social, economic, and political forces.

This book began with the observation that arranged marriage is everywhere. During the years it took to research and write this book, public images and discussions of the practice have become even more ubiquitous.

The popular A&E television series *Married at First Sight* (2014–), now several seasons in, uses a team of experts—including a psychologist, a sociologist, a sexologist, and a spiritual adviser—to arrange a marriage. In the show, based on a Danish series, the experts take over the process of selection and courtship. Participants then agree to marry the selected person for a month, after which they may get divorced. The show is about arranged marriage, even though it features decision making in the hands of mostly social scientists instead of a kinship community. Episode 1 explicitly refers to the matches as an "arranged marriage," and the reasons given throughout the show to justify the practice are strikingly similar to those invoked in these pages. In the voice-over that sets up the premise in the first episode, the narrator suggests that people are overwhelmed by the excess of possibilities. This logic given for the contestants' participation is the very same used to rationalize the "arranged marriage as choice" discourse described in this book. Such a logic appears in the human-interest pages of the newspapers and in romance novels that feature arranged marriage. More strikingly, in its first episode, the show explicitly promotes religious endogamy, a powerful arranged marriage narrative (chapter 1), by citing divorce statistics that supposedly suggest that cross-religious marriages are more likely to end in divorce. *Married at First Sight* focuses primarily on non–South Asian participants, with only one woman of Indian heritage, who is matched with a non–South Asian, while South Asian "culture" is sustained as a referent, with images of hennaed hands in a description of the tradition of arranged marriage. By using social scientists as decision makers and by naming the marriage as an "experiment," the show positions itself as taking the lessons of traditionalism and remaking them for a scientific present that retains its spirituality. The fact that this show even exists, in Denmark and Australia as well as the United States, indicates a continued global fascination with arranged marriage, but, beyond that, it suggests that people are interested in circumscribing "choice," long conceptualized as the primary value of neoliberalism. This book argues that this limitation does not mean a shift away from neoliberalism; on the contrary, it argues that neoliberalism is gaining force through the fantasy and sometimes the practice of restriction (chapter 5).

For some South Asians, there is a context for this circumscription of choice that has to do with the politics of migration. The same year as the first episode of *Married at First Sight* aired, an independent documentary with wide release focused on why an American-born Indian man, Ravi

Patel, would pursue an arranged marriage. Directors Geeta and Ravi Patel's film *Meet the Patels* features the notion of arranged marriage as choice, but it positions itself as an Indian's insider account and offers the rationale of communitarianism. The film documents the experiences of Ravi Patel going through a series of arranged first meetings as well as matrimonial conventions that draw together what are deemed suitable matches in terms of region, religion, caste, income, and educational level. I interpret this film as developing the idea of arranged marriage as a resistant practice of shared marginalization. For the subject of the film, Ravi Patel, this resistance is not so much realized as political belief as it is the desire to connect himself to another Gujrati from the designated area in his ancestral region, a woman with whom he hopes he would share a set of experiences and understandings. While Patel ultimately returns to his non-Indian girlfriend, the film as a whole nevertheless arguably offers a validation of arranged marriage as a viable alternative to self-made relationships. Analyzing such a film is important to understanding the significance of arranged marriage as a strategy of identification through differentiation in diasporic belonging. For Patel's parents, and for Ravi himself to the extent he participates in the process, arranged marriage is a way to be a Patel in a diasporic context that has emptied that signifier of its previous meanings as the family name of a caste and eroded many of the values assigned to that name within India.

This emerging discussion on contemporary arranged marriage connotes something beyond the difficulties of dating, for the discussion opens for debate the subject of decision making. This book connects the popular culture discussion about the saturation of options to another, equally ubiquitous set of representations about a place where it appears that no options exist: the discourse on forced marriage. The meeting point of these two cultural representations is not simply that they both deal in some form with arranged marriage, although that is important. The overlap is in how different political projects, from multiculturalism to communalism, are turning to the question of conjugal agency in the contemporary moment as an intimate arena in which to delineate their projects and affectively mobilize behind them. The broader discourse on arranged marriage reveals a struggle over *who* controls decision making in the highly significant realm of conjugality. The stakes for that struggle, whether it is the individual or the collective that controls decision making, determine the subject of agency in a globalizing context, a subject that determines the values and strategies of people's well-being.

On one level, then, this book seeks to recognize difference. Many people in this world have registers of well-being that are not the same as degrees of freedom, measures such as duty, devotion, and responsibility (see Mahmood, *Politics of Piety*). Another difference is the locus of decision making, which may often be collective instead of individual. The goal of this book is not to promote cultural relativism, however, in the sense that it does not seek to identify and assign relative value to modular forms of culture by saying "that is their tradition, whereas this is our tradition." In fact, this book demonstrates that the recognition of difference is itself political, and projects like cultural relativism often depend on constructing uneven binaries between self and other. The more important critical project lies in understanding how a range of projects, from multiculturalism to communalism, mobilize various oppositions in the service of power—the individual versus the collective, freedom versus duty, and acceptable versus unacceptable difference.

In looking at the binary of individualist and collectivist visions, *Arranging Marriage* has advocated that we rethink the subject of agency as constituted by these discourses in order to see past reductive notions of culture to grasp the global forces of power mediating these increasingly polarized positions. The liberal legal tradition relies on the notion that the "individual in question is a pre-social, ahistorical, self-constituting subject who does not belong to an identity-conferring community, nor values relational aspects of personhood" (Anitha and Gill, "Coercion," 177). Similarly, the Western romance both reflects and elaborates these legal narratives of self-realization. This book shifts away from the notion of the preconstituted subject that chooses either to be independent or to belong to the community and instead sees a subject who participates in or refuses arranged marriage as constituted *through* national and transnational discourses.

The most significant impact of this reconception within a legal sphere is upon the idea of consent. The legal system in the United Kingdom has worked with an increasingly widening notion of coercion in granting annulments on the basis of nonconsent. In *Arranging Marriage*, I cite feminist legal scholars who have charted that shift and pointed to the way the legal changes have been limited by assuming a preconstituted subject of consent, by focusing on primarily interpersonal pressure, and by exclusively featuring an "exit strategy" (Anitha and Gill, "Coercion"; Enright, "Choice"; Phillips and Dustin, "U.K. Initiatives"). As well as delineating and characterizing this legal scholarship taken as a whole, I use a literary and filmic analysis to add to this discussion an interpretation of the nature of subjectivity in the context of conjugal consent. I identify how the effects of racism, filial obedience, dependency on community economies, limited language skills, and precarious immigration status combine with the variability of individual psychologies to produce a complex subject of consent that is structured by socioeconomic and political factors as well as interpersonal ones. Essentially, I use cultural studies to offer the vision of the mediated subject that feminist legal scholars argue is missing from law.

This approach of deconstructing the subject also introduces the element of change to notions of culture. This book has sustained a critique of culturalism, or the reduction of various processes to a reified notion of culture. This reduction characterized British colonial discourses of rule in the subcontinent that equated Indian communities with religion. That same culturalism now marks a neoliberal discourse of globalization, "which treats culture not only as an integral element in social practices but as the determining instance" (Ahmad, *On Communalism,* 95). A supposedly static tradition of arranged marriage has been embraced or reviled but rarely analyzed as an evolving discourse. By rereading narratives of arranged marriage in terms of the national and transnational social, economic, political, and imaginative processes that constitute the practice, this book shows how different agents, sometimes competing agents, are articulated through conjugal forms.

Far from static, arranged marriage discourses are, in fact, situated ones; they reflect the shaping experiences of both movement and (re)settlement. This book has tracked how arranged marriage moves people, along with their paid and unpaid (legal and illegal) labor and their capital. It has also charted the vectors and nodes of nonmaterial entities like ideas, practices, love and friendship, ethnic and national affiliations, and political solidarities and resistances. To illuminate that dynamism, this book has endeavored to keep simultaneous focus on two arenas: the national, in terms of both the state and the imagined nation, and the transnational.

The state administers the resettlements and movements that are part of both international and domestic arranged marriages. Marriage is a public, legal institution as well as one that expresses the values of a community along with the desires of the individual. Conjugality is absolutely central to the way states exert their dominion. Thus the state cannot be, but too often is, left out of the story. States have always asserted their power through conjugality; one sees this most clearly in the way states have heavily regulated marital practices, such as by age of consent, heteronormativity, or prohibitions on consanguinity. The raft of immigration regulations concerning marriage also underscores the articulation of the state *through* marriage. The same is true with legal cases of annulment. For precisely these reasons, in the United States and Canada, the question of arranged marriage has always been tightly intertwined with the regulation of immigration. In Canada, media representations and bureaucratic discourses regularly treat arranged marriage as a likely means for immigration fraud. In Britain, even a marriage partially motivated by the desire to relocate, which would include many transnational arranged marriages, is explicitly considered fraudulent (Wray, *Regulating Marriage,* 305). The construction of this opposition necessitates that states take on characterizing and measuring the validity of marriage, which is most often done by parsing nonmaterial motivations (affection, intimacy, desire, friendship, belief in custom) from material ones (economic advancement, monetary compensation, desire for opportunity). The policies attempt to separate, as Pamela Haag says of the U.S. context, "realms subject to regulation (economic relations) from those 'protected' from such interference (the noncommercial and nonassociational)" (*Consent,* 100). The determination of a valid marriage relies on endorsing the latter, or the economically uninterested, as the basis of a true marriage. Arranged marriage poses a problem for this separation and validation, because it is an explicitly material practice.

Arranged marriage narratives contain the collective imaginary of the nation produced in in literary and filmic work. In an important early-twentieth-century American discourse that spans both law and literature, lawmakers produced a racialized discourse that equated arranged marriage with prostitution, while novelists envisioned a shift from arranged marriage to self-made marriage as a way of being both modern and American (see Cott, *Public Vows*; Sollors, *Beyond Ethnicity*; Haag, *Consent*). A negative discourse about arranged marriages became a means for imagining a modern nation through the idealization of individual consent. A contemporary South Asian feminist tradition of writing about arranged marriage picks up on that older discourse to represent alternate conjugal practices as a problem for assimilation. This study reinterprets that writing to show how that "problem" reappears in more positive terms as the national subject that is differentiated from the general populace.

Diasporic representations of arranged marriage render this exceptionalism through the articulation of community, what this book has called "communitarianism." Very often this is a negative portrayal. Literary and filmic works critique the strictures of community as they show how the practice of arranged marriage entrenches the attendant structures of filial obedience and patriarchal power. This book considers how South Asian discourses about the construction of community through marriage are mediated by ideals of sexuality, gender, caste, and religion. Novelist Ayub Khan-Din and filmmaker Deepa Mehta portray the way heteronormativity patrols the border of community belonging. These writers as well as novelists Bharati Mukherjee, Chitra Banerjee Divakaruni, Anita Rau Badami, Nadeem Aslam, and Monica Ali use their creative works to explore how arranged marriage becomes a means for both men and women to sustain patriarchal power through endogamy. Jasvinder Sanghera explores prohibitions on caste in the diaspora. Sanghera, as well as Khan-Din and Aslam, offers perhaps the most vivid images of the impact of communal religious politics expressed through arranged marriage. This book argues that community is continuously produced and reproduced through these discourses that become very important to constructing the distinctiveness of a group, whether that collectivity be formed on caste, religion, linguistic/regional identity, or nationality.

Critics most often read the aforementioned fiction and film as only critical of arranged marriage, but this study interprets these works from a new vantage point to identify how they feature arranged marriage as a concept and practice that affords agency to resistant collectivities in the context of globalization. A moment in Geeta and Ravi Patel's documentary *Meet the Patels* movingly illustrates how arranged marriage becomes a means for constituting a community through notions of belonging. Struggling to find a bride suitable to both himself and his family, meaning an American-born one whose family comes from the designated region of Gujarat, Ravi talks to his sister about the comfort he would find in such a match: "there is something cool about showing up and feeling like you already know so much about the other person. Like we all have kind of the same exact upbringing. You don't have to explain anything." Ravi identifies his diasporic group through a shared set of symbols that compose a collective way of understanding and interpreting the world. Community and its practices are felt, producing emotional modes of affiliation. However, the constitution of community through arranged marriage is not always purely symbolic. This book identifies and analyzes how Khan-Din represents an impoverished Pakistani immigrant community in Britain for whom transnational arranged marriage is an important migration strategy, while Simon Chambers features a Bangladeshi British family that connects itself to a community back in Bangladesh through marriage and property.

Arranging Marriage has argued that the collective identities being constituted through the endogamy of arranged marriage need to be interpreted for the kind of affective and imaginative work they do within politicized contexts rather than simply as identity categories that are carried from the old world to the new. While this work might be normative in the sense that it buttresses traditionalist notions of practices, the politicized process of community formation should also be understood for its interventionist position in the context of diaspora. Similarly, arranged marriage should be understood as an economic strategy. Until that happens, these community formations will appear to be stubborn throwbacks to the old country rather than a strategy for belonging in the new. This book argues that when Canada passes a Zero Tolerance for Barbaric Cultural Practices Act, or when a British government working group refers to an "innate sense of obligation to maintain our cultures, languages, and traditions" (Ahmed and Uddin, *A Choice by Right*, 1), they miss the dynamism of culture as a strategy.

A Transnational, Transdisciplinary Project

As a project, *Arranging Marriage* crosses national contexts. Though it is primarily a book about the contemporary context, it draws from different historical periods, from the British colonial context in chapter 1 to the early-twentieth-century American one in chapter 4. One might well ask, as this book reads across historically situated, localized contexts, whether the object of study changes. As the cluster of discourses and practices commonly called arranged marriage moves across time and space, is this the same "thing," despite the dynamic reinvention of meaning identified earlier? For the reader, it might seem particularly counterintuitive for the book to align, on one hand, celebratory representations of arranged marriages that bring personal satisfaction while upholding, at least nominally, the tenets of familial duty, with, on the other hand, portrayals of young women who face domestic violence. As well as presenting very different visions of arranged marriage, and sometimes using the different terms of arranged and forced marriage, the celebratory and denunciatory portrayals have very different ideological goals. Positive portrayals of arranged marriage offer a vision of a culturally exotic practice that, though different, reinforces conservative values of family. Negative portrayals of arranged marriage usually envision a dangerous alterity that threatens the core values of society. The fact that these positive and negative portrayals usually fall on the fault line of socioeconomic class and religion suggests how much the validation or denunciation of arranged marriage functions as part of a national strategy of selective assimilation. Literary works, media representations, and legal discourse are far more likely to represent working-class Muslim or Sikh women in the forced marriage discourse than to portray professional Hindu, Jain, Buddhist, or Christian women. A version of *Meet the Patels* that starred a working-class Bangladeshi American woman being matched with prospects by her family would have been viewed as a story of exploitation instead of comedy.

This book argues that there is a reason to read positive and negative representations together and constructs its method around this rationale. The term *arranged marriage* is a widely used, readily identifiable referent in English. A Google search of the term garners more than 3.4 million hits. That cultural referent, however unstable, elusive, and contingent, needs to be interpreted precisely because it is ubiquitous. However, the rationale goes beyond prevalence. *Arranging Marriage* makes a case for interpreting situated discourses that express the particular conditions of a class, nationality, gender, caste, and religion, within a national context and at a particular historical moment, as a way to interpret the politics of belonging (Yuval-Davis, *Politics*). The contemporary fascination with Muslim and Sikh women as objects of forced marriage, for example, emerges from histories of colonial administration, the contemporary fraught politics of nonprofessional immigration, and anti-Muslim and anti-Sikh discourses about terrorism. Although Britain, the United States, and Canada provide the case studies in this book and Indians, Pakistanis, and Bangladeshis its subjects, the analysis has relevance for interpretations in many other diasporic locations and other South Asian groups. Australia, for example, is another place where the arranged marriage discourse has been both prevalent and highly politicized in the context of immigration politics. In the Caribbean, a history of arranged marriage was interrupted by the restrictions of indentured labor, only to return in the later twentieth century as the symbol of and means for reasserting ethnic identities. The gulf states offer a similarly intriguing site in which to interpret arranged marriage as a strategy of transnational belonging for a migrant labor force—a practice that connects men and women to their homeland. This book argues that, while these historically and geographically located discourses about arranged marriage are particular, they are also relatable, first because of the way they are working through questions of national belonging and, second, because they are part of a transnational network of representations focused on the subject of agency.

Along these lines, although this book focuses on the diaspora, the argument is not constructed around a coherent rupture that takes place with immigration; the claim here is not about a diasporic break, in the sense that there is one type of arranged marriage in the subcontinent and another in the diaspora. The book doesn't rest on such a claim because the transnational flow of ideas, images, and practices washes over any such definitive borders. Moreover, in India, Pakistan, and Bangladesh, concepts of arranged marriage continue to emerge dynamically from particular histories (see Mody, *Intimate State*). Finally, a book that focused on the diasporic rupture would miss the transnational focus brought by this approach, which highlights how discourses of arranged marriage are moving back and forth globally as part of a network of affiliations and socioeconomic relations that may be read to interpret the processes of globalization.

Taken as a whole, the set of discourses about arranged marriage has become a powerful global register; its various articulations may be interpreted for what they tell us about national and global belonging. There are important consistencies within this set of arranged marriage discourses emerging in different geographical spaces. Topically, both positive and negative representations feature narratives of family and community, and though that is in many ways true of all conjugal discourses, this is centralized in representations of arranged marriage. The set of arranged marriage discourses also highlights the question of who controls decision making within the powerful realm of conjugality, which is constituted simultaneously as private and public. In other words, though these discourses might not represent arranged marriage in the same way, nor have the same politics, they are all dealing with the subject of agency. Moreover, the different narratives about arranged marriage overlap in representations as well. A good example of this comes in Vipul Amrutlal Shah's Bollywood film *Namastey London* (2007), which, while treating the idea of arranged marriage as a village-based authentic expression of national identity, tries to navigate the forced marriage discourse that dominates the diasporic British context, sometimes in contradictory ways. In the film, an immigrant father takes his British-born daughter to India to marry her off. This is a familiar story of forced marriage represented repeatedly in the British press. In fact, the film explicitly deals with that narrative by having the characters talk about it. When the woman falls in love with her arranged husband after the wedding, Shah taps into another arranged marriage motif, this time a positive one, that love comes after arranged marriage. Far from avoiding the forced marriage discussion in its portrayal of arranged marriage, *Namastey London* rewrites it by giving the woman agency and by introducing a romance narrative. A communitarian discourse is still deeply embedded in the story, however, as the groom woos her with his proud masculinity based in a Punjabi Jat Sikh identity. Arranged marriage narratives, even ones as seemingly diametrically opposed as positive and negative representations, cross-pollinate and may be found in dialogue.

In this way, although this book has moments of comparitivism (and any of its case studies alone could have made a monograph), this is more a project on transnationalism than on comparative studies of arranged marriage's representations. Going beyond the nation, this book investigates how conjugal forms have come to play an important role in working out the cultures of globalization as an arena for individualism and communitarianism. Coming out of the division, a new rhetoric on arranged marriage as choice has emerged from the discourses of neoliberalism. Indeed, this neoliberalization of arranged marriage is one of the more striking historical conjunctures described in this book, a discourse in which previously opposed notions of individual choice and cultural affiliation have merged. This book interprets how popular cultural works are turning to this "semi-arranged marriage" to produce and consume a streamlined version of culture.

The Question of Politics

A cultural studies scholar thinks critically about discourses and exposes the work such ideas and practices are doing within their historical contexts. In other words, the critic considers how these discourses intervene in their contemporary moments as a way to reinforce, refuse, or transform social, political, and economic conditions. Cultural studies is a field shaped by analytics rather than pragmatics, a characteristic that is a limitation but also a strength. Despite the problem of not prescribing solutions, critical thinking can, and should, inform more pragmatically oriented arenas, including activism, policy, and law. It is a field in which contradiction and nuance are not necessarily a problem to be resolved through coherence but rather a rich source of understanding. It is also a field that teaches us that questions are sometimes just as important as solutions, because they can reframe a problem that seems to have no solution.

This is not always an easy vindication to uphold when one encounters an image of the child bride. I have found this one of the most difficult images to analyze, because it elicits in me a visceral rather than an analytical response. In viewing these images in literature, media reports, or photography, I am always aware that they represent real girls who are under the age of sexual consent. Yet, as a critic, I also know that the repetition of such images, like many other sensational objects, must be understood for its performative political role, which in this case is often (though not always) part of an anti-immigrant discourse that has roots in a colonial context. Even my own imagination of the trauma of her wedding night (rather than a lifetime of forced labor), or her lack of ability to consent (rather than her position as a subaltern in a community that is itself already politically and economically disenfranchised), is part of very powerful narratives that have problematic histories in colonial, neocolonial, and xenophobic national contexts. Both British colonial administrators and nationalist leaders have used the image of the child bride as a means to assert sovereignty (Sarkar, *Hindu Wife*; Mody, *Intimate State*). More recently, the image of the child bride is one that reinforces anti-Muslim sentiment in a Western context in which "certain narratives have traction because of already existing scripts about gender, culture, immigration and Islam" (Volpp, "Blaming," 91). This book does not suggest that the real girl in the representation be ignored; rather, it seeks to examine these histories and their politics for that girl to speak and be heard as a complex mediated subject rather than the object of a sensationalist campaign.

One of the most fraught political topics examined here is consent. The book's discussion of the forced marriage debate in the United Kingdom shows how consent is both mediated and not always fully articulated. Although consent matters, it is not the same as empowerment, or even well-being. I interpret the history of British annulment cases for arranged marriage as well as novelists' visions of decision making to show how consent is not necessarily fully articulated as yes or no. This is true for several reasons. First, decisions are not always articulated. Second, decision making is not always presented as such and might simply be what one does, such as performing a duty or fulfilling expectations. Third, consent is mediated by affective forces (pleasing a parent or a fiancé) and interpersonal pressure (explicit and implicit emotional threats). The structural conditions of social and economic forces circumscribe decision making in arranged marriages, from the needs of a family placed on a daughter or son to the problem of exiting a marriage without the proper skills, opportunities, or legal permission for wage labor and self-support. In handling the question of forced marriage in the United Kingdom, the courts have used annulment cases to develop an increasingly liberal version of coercion, meaning one that includes wider influences and forces that impact decision making. Yet, while such cases deal with modes of force other than whether a man or woman said yes (they almost always did, in annulment cases), for the court decisions, such points of coercion have primarily remained in the realm of interpersonal pressure. The capacity to consent is more deeply embedded in the production of the subject through affective, racialized, politicized, economic discourses and practices. By turning to the production of a consenting subject embedded in those articulations of "yes," the book suggests that these structures of inequality must also be dealt with to reach a more empowered version of volition. If there is a lesson about consent to be learned from this book (as opposed to the more ethically clear issue of nonconsent), it is that we need to look at the affective, social, and material forces that weigh on the consenting sexual subject as well as at the decision-making moment.

This book seeks a more complex understanding of the specific processes that surround violence with the hope that, by doing so, both diasporic communities and the nations that house them may find relevant ways to end such violence. Take, for example, the patriarchal sites of power occupied by both men and women. Such positions are held within a complex of minority politics, global economics, interpersonal relations, and affective desires. We have to look not just at how "culture is clashing" but at how needs, desires, and national and communal imaginaries are coming being negotiated—or not—in the politics of belonging. Such more holistic understanding would also help inform policies or political projects around ending such violence. For example, while the "exit strategy" that has been the focus of British policy around forced marriage (Phillips and Dustin, "U.K. Initiatives," 2), this book considers why leaving a community is logistically, emotionally, and politically difficult. By reading the South Asian feminist bildungsroman, this book shows how South Asian women have not been able to fully embrace the narrative of liberation from marriage because leaving the marriage has meant severing themselves from the community that supports them in various ways. These chapters do not prescribe, but they do indicate that change needs to happen within the community through the activism that already exists around immigrant communities, modes of critical consciousness, and change that have their literary equivalent in Nadeem Aslam's or Jhumpa Lahiri's work.

A critical analysis does not necessarily lead to paralysis. In fact, an interpretive study can help activists, policy makers, and lawmakers understand that to focus so primarily on consent is to miss other sites at which power is articulated and exploitation is reproduced. Throughout this book, I engage in a critical discourse analysis to show the production of a subject of agency in a series of contexts, subjects that are to various degrees embedded in national and transnational communities that are sometimes in conflict. Within these contexts, some arranged marriage narratives function as a primary site for producing social narratives within the diaspora, reinforcing a minority community's opposition to assimilation. Other narratives "speak back" to the group in ways that complicate the coherency of that collectivity. The study of culture as a dynamic process shows the active constitution of meaning around arranged marriage in ways that legitimate and reproduce long-standing narratives of the practice but also bring challenges to this. In this book, I read through the discourses of individualism and communitarianism to represent the way these polarized positions set the free will of the individual against the duty to the community. I identify a particular neoliberal discourse that appears to synthesize these positions, but only by collapsing the forces surrounding arranged marriage into the idea of culture. Offering a counterrepresentation to this neoliberal discourse, I approach the deep rift in the subject of agency that arguably marks this period of globalization by interpreting a set of arranged marriage discourses within its national and global contexts to expose the political, social, economic, and affective strategies being deployed through the polarized positions of individualism and communitarianism.

Acknowledgments

This book benefited from early advice from scholars generous enough to help me think through still incipient ideas. Roger Rouse read and talked to me about an early version of chapter 5; his incisive criticism and critical interlocution truly helped shape the direction the project took in the end. Zahid Choudhary was an extraordinarily thoughtful reader for the *Cultural Critique* article around which I built the book. Charu Charusheila, as well, put her intellectual acumen to work to influence my early thinking. Tanika Sarkar and Rajeswari Sunder Rajan were kind enough to engage my thoughts on the book proposal, even without knowing me. Only now, looking back at their early e-mails, do I see how important was their preliminary counsel.

As the work took shape, I relied on several people to read parts of the manuscript. My colleague Doug Coulson brought his expertise in law and the American discourse of race and immigration to bear on more than one of the chapters. Paul Eiss read with the training of a cultural anthropologist and the kindness of a friend. Andreea Ritivoi gave me the gift of her sharp mind and true love of the idea. I relied on Anita Mannur's help as I made inroads into fields new to me. Lisa Tetrault forced me to the point on more than one conclusion.

It is one of the ironies of academic publishing that a project is often most in debt to people whose names we don't know. I was lucky enough to have two anonymous readers who were supportive and exacting in the most productive way. The final version of the book grows out of their generative thinking and generous labor.

Richard Morrison contracted this book, as he did my first. I have always appreciated his unfailing enthusiasm and support for my academic scholarship, and professionally I am deeply indebted to it. Danielle Kasprzak took on the project with gracious enthusiasm after Richard left the University of Minnesota Press. I truly appreciated her patience as I took more time than either of us expected to complete the work. I'd like to thank Anne Carter for her editorial assistance and Ana Bichanich for managing the production. Holly Monteith was a keen-eyed and respectful copy editor.

My undergraduate and graduate students over the past years have probably been the most regular audience for the ideas in this book. They have always been unfailingly excited to talk about the issues of love, arranged marriage, and consent, and the discussions we have had in class certainly found their way into this book. I want to specifically thank a couple who consistently extended these conversations outside the classroom. Pavithra Tantrigoda has been an unfailing supporter, both by reading chapters and by asking about my progress, even as she worked on her own dissertation. Aqdas Aftab brought her interests in South Asian sexualities to bear on these ideas. Souri Somphanith edited draft chapters in her capacity as a research assistant during her master's program. Lauren Sealey Krishnamurti offered important research work midway in the project, and Elana Larson Palladino was there at the beginning, helping to gather together the bibliography. Former student Ross MacConnell continued to show support by doing last-minute reconnaissance research.

My colleagues in the Literary and Cultural Studies program and Department of English at Carnegie Mellon University offered professional and personal support during the writing of this book, which was also the period I gained tenure. The conversations I've had with Chris Warren, Kristina Straub, Jon Klancher, David Shumway, Kathy Newman, Jeff Williams, and Richard Purcell have sustained me during our years in Baker Hall. I want to single out Peggy Knapp for her unfailing enthusiasm for learning and her public support of my career. Similarly, during his time here, Terrance Hayes gave me the gift of publicly validating my work at a critical time.

From outside my university, Sangeeta Ray, Ali Behdad, Robert Young, and Caren Kaplan have made me feel like my scholarship matters to the field. My former dissertation director, R. Radhakrishnan, still guides my critical thinking in all ways. As I wrote, this group of supporters often functioned as imaginary readers, ones who would invariably ask me to push my ideas just a bit further.

Carnegie Mellon University has been nothing but generous with institutional support. I thank my current dean, Richard Scheines, for his ongoing support as well as former head Chris Neuwirth for giving me the financial means to pursue this project.

My husband has lived almost as intimately with this project as I have for the past years. He helped me manage the day-to-day labor of such a large project by sustaining me intellectually, emotionally, and logistically. I thank him for being a great partner. Finally, I thank my children, Bianca and Julian, for so often sharing their mama with that other living thing in our house: "the book."

Bibliography

Abu-Lughod, Lila. *Do Muslim Women Need Saving?* Cambridge, Mass.: Harvard University Press, 2013.
———. "Seductions of the 'Honor Crime.'" *Differences* 22, no. 1 (2011): 17–63.
Adiga, Aravind. *The White Tiger: A Novel.* New York: Free Press, 2008.
Ahmad, Aijaz. *On Communalism and Globalization: Offensives of the Far Right.* New Delhi: Three Essays Press, 2002.
Ahmed, Nazir, and Pola Manzila Uddin. *A Choice by Right: The Report of the Working Group on Forced Marriage.* London: Home Office Communications Directorate, 2000.
Ahmed, Saira, and Andrew Crofts. *Disgraced: Forced to Marry a Stranger, Betrayed by My Own Family, Sold My Body to Survive, This Is My Story.* London: Headline Review, 2008.
Ahmed, Sara. *The Cultural Politics of Emotion.* New York: Routledge, 2004.
Aldridge, Ruqayya. "Thursday Women (Open Space): By the Book." *The Guardian,* August 3, 1989.
Ali, Kamran Asdar. "'Pulp Fictions': Reading Pakistani Domesticity." *Social Text* 22, no. 1 (2004): 123–45.
Ali, Monica. *Brick Lane: A Novel.* New York: Scribner, 2003.
Ali, Sameem. *Belonging.* London: John Murray, 2008.
Allana, Gulam. *Pakistan Movement: Historic Documents.* Karachi: Paradise Subscription Agency, Dept. of International Relations, University of Karachi, 1967.
Anderson, John Ward, and Molly Moore. "Born Oppressed; Women in the Developing World Face Cradle-to-Grave Discrimination, Poverty." *Washington Post,* February 14, 1993.
Anitha, Sundari, and Aisha Gill. "Coercion, Consent and the Forced Marriage Debate in the UK." *Feminist Legal Studies* 17, no. 2 (2009): 165–84.
Appadurai, Arjun. *Modernity at Large: Cultural Dimensions of Globalization.* Minneapolis: University of Minnesota Press, 1996.
Aslam, Nadeem. *Maps for Lost Lovers.* London: Faber and Faber, 2004.
Aulakh, Raveena. "Speed Dating Meets Arranged Marriage; Sick of the Singles' Scene Here, Some South Asians Are Turning to Tradition to Help Them Find a Mate." *Toronto Star,* December 28, 2008.

Badami, Anita Rau. *Tamarind Mem*. New York: Penguin Books, 1996.
Bald, Vivek. *Bengali Harlem and the Lost Histories of South Asian America*. Cambridge, Mass.: Harvard University Press, 2015.
Ballard, Catherine. "Arranged Marriages in the British Context." *Journal of Ethnic and Migration Studies* 6, no. 3 (1978): 181–96.
Bangladesh National Women Lawyer's Association. *Forced Marriages: A Blot in Women's Freedom of Expression*. Dhaka: Bangladesh National Women Lawyers Association, 2001.
Barjatya, Sooraj R. *Hum Aapke Hain Koun...!* DVD. Directed by Sooraj R. Barjatya. Mumbai: Eros International, 2007.
Barron, Alexandra Lynn. "Fire's Queer Anti-Communalism." *Meridians* 8, no. 2 (2008): 64–93. https://muse.jhu.edu/article/242224.
BBC. "Every Good Marriage Begins with Tears." *Storyville*. BBC Four. http://www.bbc.co.uk/programmes/b007tjgr.
Beauvoir, Simone de. *The Second Sex*. New York: Modern Library, 1968.
Bentley, Paul. "Why an Arranged Marriage Is More Likely to Develop into Lasting Love." *Daily Mail*, March 5, 2011.
Berlant, Lauren. *The Female Complaint: The Unfinished Business of Sentimentality in American Culture*. Durham, N.C.: Duke University Press, 2008.
Bhansali, Sanjay Leela. *Devdas*. DVD. Directed by Sanjay Leela Bhansali. Mumbai: Eros Entertainment, 2009.
——. *Hum Dil De Chuke Sanam*. DVD. Directed by Sanjay Leela Bhansali. Venice, Calif.: Pathfinder Home Entertainment, 2005.
Bhargava, Gura. "Seeking Immigration through Matrimonial Alliance: A Study of Advertisements in an Ethnic Weekly." *Journal of Comparative Family Studies* 19, no. 2 (1988): 245–59.
Bhopal, Kalwant. *Gender, "Race," and Patriarchy: A Study of South Asian Women*. Aldershot, U.K.: Ashgate, 1997.
Black, Debra. "Ottawa to Take a Closer Look at Forced Marriage; Foreign Affairs Minister Pledges to 'Stand Up for These Girls' at UN Meeting." *Toronto Star*, September 26, 2013.
Boggan, Steve. "MPs Told: Don't Aid Forced Marriages." *Independent*, August 8, 1998.
——. "Women's Groups Demand Action on Forced Marriages." *Independent*, July 21, 1998.
Boggan, Steve, Fran Abrams, and Peter Popham. "Huge Rise in Forced Marriages." *Independent*, July 20, 1998.
Bolan, Kim. "Happy with the Arrangement: B.C. An Indo-Canadian Psychology Graduate Set Out to Study Whether Arranged Marriages Brought Happiness. The Results Surprised Him." *Vancouver Sun*, February 24, 2007.
——. "Women 'Victims' of Arranged Marriage: They Tell of Being Beaten, Robbed,

BIBLIOGRAPHY · 237

Abandoned by Men Using Marriage to Gain Entry to Canada." *Vancouver Sun,* November 18, 2006.

Borden, Robert. "Truly, Madly, Pradeeply." *Outsourced,* season 1, episode 7. Directed by Victor Nelli Jr. Aired November 4, 2010.

Bradby, Hannah. "Negotiating Marriage: Young Punjabi Women's Assessment of Their Individual and Family Interests." In *Ethnicity, Gender, and Social Change,* edited by Rohit Fenton Barot, 152–66. New York: Palgrave Macmillan, 1999.

Bradley, David. "Duress and Arranged Marriages." *Modern Law Review* 46, no. 4 (1983): 499–504.

Bradney, T. "Duress, Family Law, and the Coherent Legal System." *Modern Law Review* 57, no. 6 (1994): 963–72.

Brah, A. *Cartographies of Diaspora: Contesting Identities.* New York: Routledge, 1996.

Bredal, Anja. "Arranged Marriages as a Multicultural Battlefield." In *Youth, Otherness, and the Plural City: Modes of Belonging and Social Life,* edited by Yngve Georg Lithman, Ove Sernhede, and Mette Andersson, 67–89. Gothenburg, Sweden: Daidalos, 2005.

Briggs, J. Z. *Jack and Zena: A True Story of Love and Danger.* London: Orion, 1997.

Burke, Jason. "Special Investigation: The Wife Killers: Love, Honour, and Obey—or Die." *Observer,* October 8, 2000.

Butler, Judith. "Judith Butler on Consent." *Law/Culture* (blog), March 5, 2010. http://blogs.law.columbia.edu/lawcultureproject/2010/11/15/1581491391/.

Butler, Pamela, and Jigna Desai. "Manolos, Marriage, and Mantras Chick-Lit Criticism and Transnational Feminism." *Meridians* 8, no. 2 (2008): 1–31. http://www.jstor.org/stable/40338745.

Carroll, Lucy. "Law, Custom, and Statutory Social Reform: The Hindu Widows' Remarriage Act of 1856." In *Women in Colonial India: Essays on Survival, Work, and the State,* edited by J. Krishnamurty, 1–26. Delhi: Oxford University Press, 1989.

Cattopadhyaya, Saratcandra. *Devdas: A Novel.* New Delhi: Penguin Books, 2002.

Chadha, Gurinder, Guljit Bindra, Paul Mayeda Berges. *Bend It Like Beckham.* DVD. Directed by Gurinder Chadha. Beverly Hills, Calif.: 20th Century Fox Home Entertainment, 2003.

Chadha, Gurinder, and Meera Syal. *Bhaji on the Beach.* DVD. Directed by Gurinder Chadha. Culver City, Calif.: Columbia TriStar Home Video, 1995.

Chandra, Bipan. *Communalism in Modern India.* New Delhi: Vikas, 1984.

Chatterjee, Partha. *The Nation and Its Fragments: Colonial and Postcolonial Histories.* Delhi: Oxford University Press, 1995.

Chauhan, Anuja. *The Zoya Factor.* New Delhi: HarperCollins, 2008.

Cherian, Anne. *A Good Indian Wife: A Novel.* New York: W. W. Norton, 2008.

Chohan, Satinder. "Oh Yes You Do." *Guardian,* August 16, 1999.

Chopra, Aditya. *Dilwale Dulhane Le Jeyenge.* DVD. Directed by Aditya Chopra. Mumbai: Yash Raj Films, 1995.

———. *Rab Ne Bana Di Jodi*. DVD. Directed by Aditya Chopra. Mumbai: Yash Raj Films, 2009.

Comaroff, John L., and Jean Comaroff. *Christianity, Colonialism, and Consciousness in South Africa*. Vol. 1 of *Of Revelation and Revolution*. 1st ed. Chicago: University of Chicago Press, 1991.

Constable, Nicole. *Romance on a Global Stage: Pen Pals, Virtual Ethnography, and "Mail-Order" Marriages*. Berkeley: University of California Press, 2003.

Cott, Nancy F. *Public Vows: A History of Marriage and the Nation*. Cambridge, Mass.: Harvard University Press, 2000.

CP. "Indian Wives in Suicide Pact Escape Arranged Marriages." *Toronto Star*, August 19, 1986.

———. "Marriage Arranged by Sikhs." *Globe and Mail*, September 10, 1981.

Crenshaw, Kimberle. "Mapping the Margins: Intersectionality, Identity Politics, and Violence against Women of Color." *Stanford Law Review* 43, no. 6 (1991): 1241–99.

Cryer, Ann. "House of Commons Hansard Debates for 10 Feb 1999 (pt 7)." http://www.publications.parliament.uk.

Curry, Bill. "Fraud Squads Chase Down Marriages of Convenience; Ottawa Dispatches Secret Teams in Bid to Crack Down on Phony Foreign Weddings." *Globe and Mail*, May 21, 2008.

Das Gupta, Monisha. *Immigrants: Rights, Activism, and Transnational South Asian Politics in the United States*. Durham, N.C.: Duke University Press Books, 2006.

Daswani, Kavita. *For Matrimonial Purposes*. Reprint ed. New York: Plume, 2004.

———. *Salaam, Paris*. New York: Plume, 2006.

———. *The Village Bride of Beverly Hills*. New York: G. P. Putnam's Sons, 2004.

De, Shobhaa. *Spouse*. New Delhi: Penguin India, 2005.

Desai, Jigna. "Homo on the Range: Mobile and Global Sexualities." *Social Text* 20, no. 4 (2002): 65–89. https://muse.jhu.edu/article/38470.

Desai, Kiran. *The Inheritance of Loss: A Novel*. New York: Atlantic Monthly Press, 2005.

Dhaka Courier. "Must We Not Save the Families?" June 1, 2009. http://www.highbeam.com/doc/1P3-1736919751.html.

Dhawan, Sabrina. *Monsoon Wedding*. DVD. Directed by Mira Nair. Los Angeles, Calif.: Universal Studios, 2002.

Dhingra, Pawan. *Life behind the Lobby: Indian American Motel Owners and the American Dream*. Stanford, Calif.: Stanford University Press, 2012.

Dhooma, Rashida. "Arranged Marriages Going Strong in Canada: Many South Asians in Canada Are Using Personal Ads in Newspapers and on the Internet to Meet Their Potential Mates." *Vancouver Sun*, February 12, 1999.

Divakaruni, Chitra Banerjee. *Arranged Marriage: Stories*. New York: Anchor Books, 1995.

Duggan, Lisa. *The Twilight of Equality? Neoliberalism, Cultural Politics, and the Attack on Democracy.* New York: Penguin, 2003.

Dwyer, Rachel. *Bollywood's India: Hindi Cinema as a Guide to Contemporary India.* London: Reaktion Books, 2014.

Enright, Máiréad. "Choice, Culture, and the Politics of Belonging: The Emerging Law of Forced and Arranged Marriage." *Modern Law Review* 72, no. 3 (2009): 331–59.

Epstein, Robert, Mayuri Pandit, and Mansi Thakar. "How Love Emerges in Arranged Marriages: Two Cross-Cultural Studies." *Journal of Comparative Family Studies* 44, no. 3 (2013): 341–60. http://www.jstor.org/stable/23644606.

Esposito, John L., and Natana DeLong-Bas. *Women in Muslim Family Law.* Syracuse, N.Y.: Syracuse University Press, 2001.

Feldman, Shelley. "(Re)presenting Islam: Manipulating Gender, Shifting State Practices, and Class Frustrations in Bangladesh." In *Appropriating Gender: Women's Activism and Politicized Religion in South Asia,* edited by Patricia Jeffery and Amrita Basu, 33–52. New York: Routledge, 1998.

Felski, Rita. *Beyond Feminist Aesthetics: Feminist Literature and Social Change.* Cambridge, Mass.: Harvard University Press, 1989.

Forced Marriage (Civil Protection) Act, 2007, c. 20 (U.K.). http://www.legislation.gov.uk/ukpga/2007/20/contents.

Freed, Lisa, and John Leach, prods. "A Family's Honor." *48 Hours,* season 25, episode 19. Aired April 7, 2012. http://www.cbsnews.com/videos/a-familys-honor-50130559/.

Friedman, Marilyn. "Autonomy, Social Disruption, and Women." In *Relational Autonomy: Feminist Perspectives on Autonomy, Agency, and the Social Self,* edited by Catriona Mackenzie and Natalie Stoljar, 35–51. New York: Oxford University Press, 2000.

Gagoomal, Prashina J. "A 'Margin of Appreciation' for 'Marriages of Appreciation': Reconciling South Asian Adult Arranged Marriages with the Matrimonial Consent Requirement in International Human Rights Law." *Georgetown Law Journal* 97, no. 2 (2008): 589–620.

Gandhi, Mahatma. *My Soul's Agony.* Bombay: Bombay Provincial Board, Servants of Untouchables Society, 1933.

Gangoli, Geetanjali, and Khatidja Chantler. "Protecting Victims of Forced Marriage: Is Age a Protective Factor?" *Feminist Legal Studies* 17, no. 3 (2009): 267–88.

Gangoli, Geetanjali, and Melanie McCarry. "Criminalising Forced Marriage." *Criminal Justice Matters* 74, no. 1 (2008): 44–46.

Gay, Oonagh. "Forced Marriage." House of Commons Parliament Library Research Paper SN/HA/1003. January 21, 2015.

Geddes, John. "Canadian Anti-Muslim Sentiment Is Rising, Disturbing New Poll Reveals." *Macleans,* October 3, 2013. http://www.macleans.ca/politics/land-of-intolerance/.

Geertz, Clifford. *The Interpretation of Cultures: Selected Essays.* New York: Basic Books, 1973.
Ghosh, Durba. *Sex and the Family in Colonial India: The Making of Empire.* Cambridge: Cambridge University Press, 2006.
Giddens, Anthony. *The Transformation of Intimacy: Sexuality, Love, and Eroticism in Modern Societies.* Stanford, Calif.: Stanford University Press, 1993.
Gill, Aisha K., and Sundari Anitha. Introduction to *Forced Marriage: Introducing a Social Justice and Human Rights Perspective,* edited by Aisha K. Gill and Sundari Anitha, 1–22. London: Zed, 2011.
Goodale, Gloria. "First the Marriage, Then the Courtship." *Christian Science Monitor,* September 9, 2008. http://www.csmonitor.com/The-Culture/Family/2008/0909/p17s01-lifp.html.
Gopinath, Gayatri. *Impossible Desires: Queer Diasporas and South Asian Public Cultures.* Durham, N.C.: Duke University Press, 2005.
Gordon, Alison. "Our Rickshaw Ride from Marriage Medieval Style." *Mail on Sunday,* December 24, 2000.
Gottlieb, Lori. "The Arrangement." *New York Times,* August 31, 2008.
Gray, John. *Liberalism.* Minneapolis: University of Minnesota Press, 1986.
Grewal, Inderpal. *Transnational America: Feminisms, Diasporas, Neoliberalisms.* Durham, N.C.: Duke University Press, 2005.
———. "'Women's Rights as Human Rights': Feminist Practices, Global Feminism, and Human Rights Regimes in Transnationality." *Citizenship Studies* 3, no. 3 (1999): 337–54.
Grewal, Inderpal, and Caren Kaplan, eds. Introduction to *Scattered Hegemonies: Postmodernity and Transnational Feminist Practices.* Minneapolis: University of Minnesota Press, 1994.
Griffin, Keven. "Mixing East and West Often Best for Newcomers." *Vancouver Sun,* March 19, 1993.
Grylls, James. "Victory for Girl Forced to Marry; Judge's Ruling Gives Hope to Asian Child Brides." *Daily Mail,* October 2, 1992.
Guha, Ramchandra. "Ian McEwan Rules the Lists." May 24, 2007. http://www.india-forums.com/news/art-culture/3308.
Gulzar, Meghna. *Just Married: Marriage Was Only the Beginning.* DVD. Directed by Meghna Gulzar. Mumbai: Pritish Nandy Communications, 2007.
Gupta, Rahila. *From Homebreakers to Jailbreakers: Southall Black Sisters.* London: Zed Books, 2003.
Haag, Pamela. *Consent: Sexual Rights and the Transformation of American Liberalism.* Ithaca, N.Y.: Cornell University Press, 1999.
Hall, Catherine. "Of Gender and Empire: Reflections on the Nineteenth Century." In *Gender and Empire,* edited by Philippa Levine, 46–76. Oxford: Oxford University Press, 2004.

Hall, Macer. "22,000 Come Here to Wed, but Many Face Misery and Violence; Brides of Doom." *Daily Star,* September 22, 2004.

Hall, Stuart. "Cultural Identity and Diaspora." In *Colonial Discourse and Postcolonial Theory: A Reader,* edited by Patrick Williams and Laura Chrisman, 392–403. New York: Columbia University Press, 1994.

———, ed. *Representation: Cultural Representations and Signifying Practices.* London: Sage/Open University, 1997.

Harris, Gardiner. "Websites in India Put a Bit of Choice into Arranged Marriages." *New York Times,* April 24, 2015. http://www.nytimes.com/2015/04/26/world/asia/india-arranged-marriages-matrimonial-websites.html.

Hart, Jayasri. *Roots in the Sand.* DVD. Directed by Jayasri Hart. San Francisco: Center for Asian American Media, 1998.

Henderson, Stephen. "Rakhi Dhanoa and Ranjeet Purewal." *New York Times,* August 18, 2002. http://www.nytimes.com/2002/08/18/style/weddings-vows-rakhi-dhanoa-and-ranjeet-purewal.html.

Hess, Gary R. "The Forgotten Asian Americans: The East Indian Community in the United States." *Pacific Historical Review* 43, no. 4 (1974): 576–96.

HinduNet. "Marriage." http://www.hindunet.org/alt_hindu/1995_Feb_1/msg00052.html.

Hindu Widows' Remarriage Act, 1856 (Act No. XV).

Hirani v. Hirani, (1982) 4 F.L.R. 232.

Holzer, Kellie D. "Tying the Knot: A Conjoined Genealogy of Marital Fictions in Colonial India and Victorian England." PhD diss., University of Washington, 2007.

Home Office. "Forced Marriage Consultation." https://www.gov.uk/government/consultations/forced-marriage-consultation.

Hussein (otherwise Blitz) v. Hussein, [1938] 2 A.L.L. R 344.

Hutchinson, Clair. "Our Lost Generation." *Wales on Sunday,* February 12, 2012.

Ind, Jo. "Helping Muslim Couples Find Marital Harmony." *Birmingham Post,* September 3, 2008.

India Today. "Online Marriage Business May Touch Rs 1,500 Crore by 2017." December 18, 2013. http://indiatoday.intoday.in/story/online-marriage-business-may-touch-rs-1500-crore-by-2017-assocham/1/331691.html.

Indo-Canadian Women's Association. *International Arranged Marriages.* Edmonton, Alberta: Indo Canadian Women's Association, 2005.

Jaffrelot, Christophe, and Ingrid Therwath. "Western Hindutva: Hindu Nationalism in the United Kingdom and North America." In *Communalism and Globalization in South Asia and Its Diaspora,* edited by Deana Heath, 44–56. New York: Routledge, 2011.

Jain, Anita. *Marrying Anita: A Quest for Love in the New India.* 1st U.S. ed. New York: Bloomsbury, 2008.

Jaiswal, Nimisha. "Old Custom, New Couples: Gay Indians Are Having Arranged

Marriages." Public Radio International. April 1, 2016. https://pri.org/stories/2016-04-01/old-custom-new-couples-gay-indians-are-having-arranged-marriages.

Jamal, Amina. "Gender, Citizenship, and the Nation-State in Pakistan: Willful Daughters or Free Citizens?" *Signs* 31, no. 2 (2006): 283–304.

Janmohamed, Shelina Zahra. *Love in a Headscarf.* Boston: Beacon Press, 2010.

Johar, Karan, and Sheena Parikh. *Kabhi Khushi Kabhie Gham.* DVD. Directed by Karan Johar. Mumbai: Yash Raj Films, 2007.

Johnston, David. "A History of Consent in Western Thought." In *The Ethics of Consent: Theory and Practice,* edited by Franklin G. Miller and Alan Wertheimer, 25–54. Oxford: Oxford University Press, 2010.

Joshi, Gunjan, Rajpal Yadav, Ashok Khanna, Pankaj Saraswat, and Pankaj Saraswat. *Main, Meri Patni... Aur Woh!* DVD. Directed by Chandan Arora. Mumbai: UTV Motion Pictures, 2005.

Jury, Louise. "Judge Annuls Forced Marriage." *Guardian,* June 17, 1993.

Kakar, Sudhir. "Match Fixing." *India Today,* October 26, 2007. http://indiatoday.intoday.in/story/Match+fixing/1/1660.html.

Kaur, Raminder, and Ajay J. Sinha, eds. *Bollyworld: Popular Indian Cinema through a Transnational Lens.* New Delhi: Sage, 2005.

Kennedy, Miranda. "Husband, by Arrangement." *Guardian,* March 19, 2011.

Kernochan, Sarah. *Learning to Drive.* DVD. Directed by Isabel Coixet. Los Angeles, Calif.: Broad Green Pictures, 2015.

Khandelwal, Madhulika S. *Becoming American, Being Indian: An Immigrant Community in New York City.* Ithaca, N.Y.: Cornell University Press, 2002.

Khan-Din, Ayub. *East Is East.* DVD. Directed by Damien O'Donnell. Burbank, Calif.: Miramax Home Entertainment, 2000.

Kiley, Sam. "Forced Marriages May End in Divorce." *Times* (London), March 16, 1988.

Kleinig, John. "The Nature of Consent." In *The Ethics of Consent: Theory and Practice,* edited by Franklin G. Miller and Alan Wertheimer, 3–22. Oxford: Oxford University Press, 2010.

Koshy, Susan. Introduction to *Transnational South Asians: The Making of a Neo-Diaspora,* edited by Susan Koshy and R. Radhakrishnan, 1–39. New Delhi: Oxford University Press, 2008.

Krishnamachari, Nars, dir. *Arranged Marriage: Can Love Be Arranged?* Roughcut Films, 2011.

Kumar, Sunaina. "The Rise of Ladki-Lit." *Indian Express,* October 7, 2006. http://archive.indianexpress.com/news/the-rise-of-ladkilit/14234/.

Kureishi, Hanif. *The Buddha of Suburbia.* New York: Viking, 1990.

Lahiri, Jhumpa. *The Namesake.* Boston: Houghton Mifflin, 2003.

———. "Sexy." In *Interpreter of Maladies: Stories,* 83–110. Boston: Houghton Mifflin, 1999.

Lakshmi, Rama. "India's Cheeky 'Chick Lit' Finds an Audience." *Washington Post,*

November 23, 2007. http://www.washingtonpost.com/wp-dyn/content/article/2007/11/22/AR2007112201415.html.
Lee, Ji Hyun. "Modern Lessons from Arranged Marriages." *New York Times*, January 18, 2013. http://www.nytimes.com/2013/01/20/fashion/weddings/parental-involvement-can-help-in-choosing-marriage-partners-experts-say.html.
Leonard, Karen. *The South Asian Americans*. Westport, Conn.: Greenwood, 1997.
Lewis, Tamzin. "Arranged Marriage and the Young Scots Mother Who Was Brutally Murdered." *Mail on Sunday*, March 9, 2003.
Lowe, Lisa. *Immigrant Acts: On Asian American Cultural Politics*. Durham, N.C.: Duke University Press, 1996.
Luhmann, Niklas. *Love as Passion: The Codification of Intimacy*. Cambridge, Mass.: Harvard University Press, 1986.
Mackenzie, Catriona, and Natalie Stoljar. "Introduction: Autonomy Refigured." In *Relational Autonomy: Feminist Perspectives on Autonomy, Agency, and the Social Self*, 3–31. New York: Oxford University Press, 2000.
Mackrael, Kim. "Experts Question Need for Polygamy Bill; Immigration Lawyers Say Proposed Law, Which Also Covers Early and Forced Marriages, Targets Only a Specific Subset of the Population." *Globe and Mail*, November 6, 2014.
Mahmood v. Mahmood, [1993] S.L.T. 589.
Mahmood, Saba. "Feminism, Democracy, and Empire: Islam and the War on Terror." In *Women's Studies on the Edge*, edited by Joan Wallach Scott, 81–114. Durham, N.C.: Duke University Press, 2008.
———. *Politics of Piety: The Islamic Revival and the Feminist Subject*. With a new preface by the author. Princeton, N.J.: Princeton University Press, 2011.
Mahmud v. Mahmud, [1994] S.L.T. 599.
Maira, Sunaina. *Desis in the House: Indian American Youth Culture in New York City*. Philadelphia: Temple University Press, 2002.
Majumdar, Rochona. *Marriage and Modernity: Family Values in Colonial Bengal*. Durham, N.C.: Duke University Press, 2009.
Mani, Bakirathi. *Aspiring to Home: South Asians in America*. Stanford, Calif.: Stanford University Press, 2012.
Mani, Lata. *Contentious Traditions: The Debate on Sati in Colonial India*. Berkeley: University of California Press, 1998.
Marriage Act, 1949, 12, 13 & 14 Geo. 6, c. 76 (U.K.). http://www.legislation.gov.uk/ukpga/Geo6/12-13-14/76/contents.
Matrimonial Causes Act, 1973, c. 18 (U.K.).
May, Simon. *Love: A History*. New Haven, Conn.: Yale University Press, 2013.
McKay, Hollie. "Because Mom Said So: Are Arranged Marriages the Next Big Trend?" *Fox News*, June 29, 2007.
Mehta, Deepa. *Fire*. DVD. Directed by Deepa Mehta. New York: New Yorker Video, 2000.

Miller, Katherine. "Mobility and Identity Construction in Bharati Mukherjee's Desirable Daughters 'The Tree Wife and Her Rootless Namesake.'" *Studies in Canadian Literature/Études En Littérature Canadienne* 29, no. 1 (2004): 63–73.

Mishra, Vijay. *Bollywood Cinema: Temples of Desire*. New York: Routledge, 2002.

Mody, Perveez. *The Intimate State: Love-Marriage and the Law in Delhi*. Critical Asian Studies. New Delhi: Routledge, 2008.

Mohammad-Arif, Aminah. "Religion, Diaspora, and Globalization: The Vishwa Hindu Parishad and the Jama'at-i Islami in the United States." In *Communalism and Globalization in South Asia and Its Diaspora*, edited by Deana Heath and Chandana Mathur, 165–78. New York: Routledge, 2011.

Moretti, Franco. *The Way of the World: The Bildungsroman in European Culture*. London: Verso, 1987.

Morgan, Robin. Introduction to *Sisterhood Is Global: The International Women's Movement Anthology*, edited by Robin Morgan, 1–37. Garden City, N.Y.: Anchor Press/Doubleday, 1984.

Mukerji, Dhan Gopal. *Caste and Outcast*. Edited by Gordon Chang, Akhil Gupta, and Purnima Mankekar. 1923; reprint, Stanford, Calif.: Stanford University Press, 2002.

Mukherjee, Bharati. *Desirable Daughters: A Novel*. New York: Hachette Books, 2003.

———. *Wife*. Boston: Houghton Mifflin, 1975.

Myers, Jane E., Jayamala Madathil, and Lynne R. Tingle. "Marriage Satisfaction and Wellness in India and the United States: A Preliminary Comparison of Arranged Marriages and Marriages of Choice." *Journal of Counseling and Development* 83, no. 2 (2005): 183–90.

Nair, Mira. *So Far from India*. Directed by Nira Mair. New York: Filmakers Library, 1982.

Nair, Suresh, and Ritesh Shah. *Namastey London*. DVD. Directed by Vipul Amrutlal Shah. Mumbai: Eros Entertainment, 2007.

O'Neil, Peter. "Marriage Fraud 'a Threat'; India a Key Problem Spot as Phoney Relationships Exploit Immigration." *Gazette* (Montreal), April 8, 2015.

Ong, Aihwa. *Flexible Citizenship: The Cultural Logics of Transnationality*. Durham, N.C.: Duke University Press, 1999.

Pais, Arthur J. "The Rediff Interview/Kavita Daswani." *Rediff: India Abroad*, August 10, 2004. http://www.rediff.com/.

Palmer, Howard. "Mosaic versus Melting Pot? Immigration and Ethnicity in Canada and the United States." *International Journal: Canada's Journal of Global Policy Analysis* 31, no. 3 (1976): 488–528.

Palriwala, Rajni, and Patricia Uberoi, eds. *Marriage, Migration, and Gender*. New Delhi: Sage, 2008.

Pandey, Harrish. "Harrish Iyer: Indian Matrimonial Ad Seeks 'Groom' for Gay

Activist." BBC News. May 20, 2015. http://www.bbc.com/news/world-asia-india-32810434.
Parekh, Bhikhu C. *Rethinking Multiculturalism: Cultural Diversity and Political Theory.* Cambridge, Mass.: Harvard University Press, 2000.
Pearl, David. "Arranged Marriages." *Cambridge Law Journal* 29, no. 2 (1971): 206–7.
Phillips, Anne, and Moira Dustin. "U.K. Initiatives on Forced Marriage: Regulation, Dialogue, and Exit." *Political Studies* 52, no. 3 (2004): 531–51.
Powers, Lucas. "Conservatives Pledge Funds, Tip Line to Combat 'Barbaric Cultural Practices.'" CBC News. October 2, 2015. http://www.cbc.ca/news/politics/canada-election-2015-barbaric-cultural-practices-law-1.3254118.
Pradhan, Monica. *The Hindi-Bindi Club.* New York: Bantam Books, 2007.
Prashad, Vijay. *The Karma of Brown Folk.* Minneapolis: University of Minnesota Press, 2000.
Pratt, Mary Louise. *Imperial Eyes: Travel Writing and Transculturation.* New York: Routledge, 2008.
Proudman, Charlotte Rachael. "The Criminalisation of Forced Marriage." *Fam Law,* April 2012, 460–65.
Punjabi Graphics. "Arranged Marriage: Exciting in More Ways Than One." http://www.punjabigraphics.com/arranged-marriage-exciting-in-more-ways-than-one-hearts-picture/.
Puri, Jyoti. *Woman, Body, Desire in Post-colonial India: Narratives of Gender and Sexuality.* New York: Routledge, 1999.
Purkayastha, Bandana. *Negotiating Ethnicity: Second-Generation South Asian Americans Traverse a Transnational World.* New Brunswick, N.J.: Rutgers University Press, 2005.
Quora. "How Does It Feel to Have Sex with Your Spouse on Your Wedding Night When He/She Is a Stranger?" https://www.quora.com/How-does-it-feel-to-have-sex-with-your-spouse-on-your-wedding-night-when-he-she-is-a-stranger.
Radhakrishnan, Smitha. *Appropriately Indian: Gender and Culture in a New Transnational Class.* Durham, N.C.: Duke University Press, 2011.
Rai, Bali. *(Un)arranged Marriage.* London: Corgi Childrens, 2001.
Ramdya, Kavita. *Bollywood Weddings: Dating, Engagement, and Marriage in Hindu America.* New York: Lexington Books, 2010.
Rattansi, Ali. *Multiculturalism: A Very Short Introduction.* New York: Oxford University Press, 2011.
Raveena. "Wedlock Seen as 'Cure' for Gays; 'They Think They're Doing What's Best for the Child'; Rescue in Punjab Shows Disturbing Tradition Is Alive in Canada." *Toronto Star,* November 14, 2009.
Regan, Pamela C., Saloni Lakhanpal, and Carlos Anguiano. "Relationship Outcomes in Indian-American Love-Based and Arranged Marriages." *Psychological Reports* 110, no. 3 (2012): 915–24.

Riley, Ferzanna. *Unbroken Spirit: How a Young Muslim Refused to Be Enslaved by Her Culture.* London: Hodder and Stoughton, 2007.
Rouse, Roger. "Mexican Migration and the Social Space of Postmodernism." *Diaspora: A Journal of Transnational Studies* 1, no. 1 (1991): 8–23.
Roy, Bimal. *Devdas.* Drama, Musical, Romance, N-A.
Roy, Sandip. "What It's Like to Be Gay in Modern India." *Telegraph,* January 27, 2015. http://www.telegraph.co.uk/men/relationships/11365516/What-its-like-to-be-gay-in-modern-India.html.
Rushdie, Salman. *Imaginary Homelands: Essays and Criticism, 1981–1991.* New York: Granta Books, 1991.
Salzman, Marian, and Ira Matathia. *Next Now: Trends for the Future.* 1st ed. New York: Palgrave Macmillan, 2006.
Sanghera, Jasvinder. *Daughters of Shame.* London: Hodder Paperbacks, 2009.
———. *Shame.* London: Hodder Paperbacks, 2007.
———. *Shame Travels: A Family Lost, a Family Found.* London: Hodder and Stoughton, 2011.
Sardana, Sharat, Richard Pinto, Sanjeev Bhaskar, and Meera Syal. "Gay Son." *Goodness Gracious Me,* season 1, episode 1. Directed by Gareth Carrivick. Aired January 12, 1998.
Sarkar, Tanika. *Hindu Wife, Hindu Nation: Community, Religion, and Cultural Nationalism.* New Delhi: Permanent Black, 2001.
Satthianadhan, Krupabai. *Kamala: The Story of a Hindu Child-Wife.* New York: Oxford University Press, 1998.
SAWNET. "Bookshelf." http://sawnet.org/books/.
Schaefer, Stefan C., and Yuta Silverman. *Arranged.* DVD. Directed by Diane Crespo and Stefan C. Shaefer. United States.
Sedgwick, Eve Kosofsky. *Tendencies.* Durham, N.C.: Duke University Press Books, 1993.
Seth, Reva. *First Comes Marriage: Modern Relationship Advice from the Wisdom of Arranged Marriages.* New York: Touchstone, 2008.
Seth, Vikram. *A Suitable Boy: A Novel.* New York: HarperCollins, 1993.
Shah, Nayan. *Stranger Intimacy: Contesting Race, Sexuality, and the Law in the North American West.* Oakland: University of California Press, 2012.
Shakespeare, William. *The Tragedy of Romeo and Juliet.* New Folger Library Shakespeare. New York: Pocket Books, 1992.
Shan, Sharan-Jeet. *In My Own Name: An Autobiography.* London: Women's Press, 1987.
Shankar, Shalini. *Desi Land: Teen Culture, Class, and Success in Silicon Valley.* Durham, N.C.: Duke University Press, 2008.
Sharpe, Jenny. "Gender, Nation, and Globalization in *Monsoon Wedding* and *Dilwale Dulhania Le Jayenge.*" *Meridians* 6, no. 1 (2005): 58–81.

Shopna, Mohsena Reza. "A New Year Gift: Shobhaa De's 'Marriage Manual.'" *United News of Bangladesh,* January 15, 2010.

Shukla, Sandhya. *India Abroad: Diasporic Cultures of Postwar America and England.* Princeton, N.J.: Princeton University Press, 2003.

Shumway, David. *Modern Love: Romance, Intimacy, and the Marriage Crisis.* New York: New York University Press, 2003.

Siddiqi, Dina M. "Of Consent and Contradiction: Forced Marriages in Bangladesh." In *"Honour": Crimes, Paradigms, and Violence against Women,* edited by Lynn Welchman and Sara Hossain, 283–307. London: Zed Books, 2005.

Sidhwa, Bapsi. *The Pakistani Bride.* Minneapolis, Minn.: Milkweed Editions, 2008.

Singh v. Kaur, [1981] Court of Appeal (Civil Division).

Singh v. Singh, [1971] 2 All E.R. 828.

Singh, Sonia. *Goddess for Hire.* New York: William Morrow, 2004.

Sivanandan, A. "It's Anti-racism That Was Failed, Not Multiculturalism That Failed." Institute of Race Relations. October 12, 2005. http://www.irr.org.uk/news/its-anti-racism-that-was-failed-not-multiculturalism-that-failed/.

SK, Re (2004) EWHC 3202 (Fam) (U.K.).

Smith, Paul. *Discerning the Subject.* Minneapolis: University of Minnesota Press, 1988.

Sohrab v. Khan, [2002] S.C.L.R. 663.

Sollors, Werner. *Beyond Ethnicity: Consent and Descent in American Culture.* New York: Oxford University Press, 1986.

Sommer, Doris. *Foundational Fictions: The National Romances of Latin America.* Berkeley: University of California Press, 1991.

Soofi, Mayank Austen. "Pakistan Diary—Reading Chick Lit in Karachi." *Delhi Walla,* March 27. http://www.thedelhiwalla.com/2010/03/27/pakistan-diary-%e2%80%93-reading-chick-lit-in-karachi/.

Southall Black Sisters. "Forced Marriage Campaign." http://www.southallblacksisters.org.uk/.

Spivak, Gayatri Chakravorty. "Can the Subaltern Speak?" In *Marxism and the Interpretation of Culture,* edited by Cary Nelson, 271–313. Urbana: University of Illinois Press, 1988.

Sreenivas, Mytheli. *Wives, Widows, and Concubines: The Conjugal Family Ideal in Colonial India.* Bloomington: Indiana University Press, 2008.

Star, Debra Black. "Ottawa to Take a Closer Look at Forced Marriage; Foreign Affairs Minister Pledges to 'Stand Up for These Girls' at UN Meeting." *Toronto Star,* September 26, 2013.

Stone, Lawrence. *The Family, Sex, and Marriage in England 1500–1800.* New York: Harper and Row, 1977.

Sunder Rajan, Rajeswari. *Real and Imagined Women: Gender, Culture, and Postcolonialism.* New York: Routledge, 1993.

———. *The Scandal of the State: Women, Law, Citizenship in Postcolonial India.* Durham, N.C.: Duke University Press, 2003.

Szechter (otherwise Karsov) v. Szechter, [1971] P. 286; [1971] 1 W.L.R. 171.

Tasker, Yvonne, and Diane Negra, eds. *Interrogating Postfeminism: Gender and the Politics of Popular Culture.* Durham, N.C.: Duke University Press, 2007.

Thaindian News. "'The Secret,' 'Brisingr' Top Bestselling Lists." http://www.thaindian.com/newsportal/uncategorized/the-secret-brisingr-top-bestselling-lists_10099830.html.

Thomas, Anjali. "What's Love Got to Do with It?" *Times of India,* March 12, 2010. http://timesofindia.indiatimes.com/life-style/relationships/man-woman/Whats-love-got-to-do-with-it/articleshow/5516432.cms.

Toronto Star. "Arranged Marriages: Cherishing Tradition Love May Follow Naturally in Unions That Emphasize Similar Backgrounds, Values." August 29, 1989.

Toronto Star. "Immigrants Angered by Request for Letters." December 17, 1990.

Toronto Star. "Indian Wives in Suicide Pact Escape Arranged Marriages." August 19, 1986.

Troper, Harold. "Canada's Immigration Policy since 1945." *International Journal* 48, no. 2 (1993): 255–81.

Udas, Sumnima. "Arranged Marriage Is Not Forced Marriage." CNN Freedom Project. http://thecnnfreedomproject.blogs.cnn.com/2012/05/30/arranged-marriage-is-not-forced-marriage/.

UNICEF. "Improving Children's Lives, Transforming the Future—25 Years of Child Rights in South Asia." http://www.unicef.org/publications/index_75712.html.

United Nations Human Rights Office of the High Commissioner. "Convention on Consent to Marriage, Minimum Age for Marriage." http://www.ohchr.org/EN/ProfessionalInterest/Pages/MinimumAgeForMarriage.aspx.

U.S. Department of Homeland Security. "Fiancé(e) Visas." U.S. Citizenship and Immigration Services. https://www.uscis.gov/family/family-us-citizens/fiancee-visa/fiancee-visas.

Verma, Lalmani. "ABVP: 'We Didn't Coin Love Jihad, Used by Perpetrators First.'" *Indian Express,* September 22, 2014.

Volpp, Leti. "Blaming Culture for Bad Behavior." *Yale Journal of Law and the Humanities* 12 (2000): 89–116.

Waheed, Rekha. *The A–Z Guide to Arranged Marriage.* London: Monsoon Press, 2005.

Waites, Matthew. *The Age of Consent: Young People, Sexuality, and Citizenship.* New York: Palgrave Macmillan, 2005.

Welchman, Lynn. *"Honour" Crimes, Paradigms, and Violence against Women.* New York: Zed Books, 2005.

Wertheimer, Alan. *Coercion.* Princeton, N.J.: Princeton University Press, 1987.

Wilson, Amrit. "The Forced Marriage Debate and the British State." *Race and Class* 49, no. 1 (2007): 25–38.

Wray, Helena. *Regulating Marriage Migration into the UK: A Stranger in the Home.* Burlington, Vt.: Ashgate, 2011.

Yefet, Karin. "What's the Constitution Got to Do With It? Regulating Marriage in Pakistan." *Duke Journal of Gender Law and Policy* 16, no. 2 (2009): 347–78. http://scholarship.law.duke.edu/djglp/vol16/iss2/6.

Yuval-Davis, Nira. *The Politics of Belonging: Intersectional Contestations.* London: Sage, 2011.

Zaigham, Inayatullah. "Letter: Arranged Marriages." *Independent,* July 29, 1989.

Zama, Farahad. "First Comes Marriage." *New York Times,* June 7, 2009. http://www.nytimes.com/2009/06/07/fashion/07love.html.

Zaman, Sadia. "Growing Pains: Like Hundreds of South Asians, Farah Grew Up Thinking That White Was 'Normal.'" *Toronto Star,* October 15, 1992.

Index

Abu-Lughod, Lila, 108, 122, 131, 134
Adiga, Aravind, 201
African American–Indian marriages, 145
agency, 5–7, 12, 37–42, 212–13; Ali on, 91–96; Anitha on, 41–42, 74, 84, 85; collective, 38, 44, 73–74, 83–84; culturalism and, 66, 219, 225; definitions of, 37, 41; Divakaruni on, 167; family influence on, 37–41, 71–74, 77, 82–84; Foucault on, 41–42; Grewal on, 203, 209; Kureishi on, 87–88; Mackenzie on, 42, 55–56; Saba Mahmood on, 41, 211; Mehta on, 161–62; modes of, 91–96; Mukherjee on, 164–66; relational autonomy and, 42; in Shah's *Namastey London*, 226; structural inequalities and, 84–86; transnational mobility and, 23–24. *See also* individualism
Ahmad, Aijaz, 12, 66, 104
Ahmed, Nazir, 33, 71–72, 105–7, 115–20, 123–26, 223
Ahmed, Saira, 2, 40, 123–24
Ahmed, Sara, 12
Ali, Monica, 68, 133–34, 222. *See also* *Brick Lane*
Ali, Sameem, 123
Ambedkar, B. R., 48
Amin, Idi, 174

Anderson, John Ward, 154, 156
Anitha, Sundari, 68, 118; on agency in consent, 41–42, 74, 84, 85; on identity-conferring community, 96
annulment, 2, 65, 74–84, 227–28. *See also* divorce
Appadurai, Arjun, 18, 19, 197
Arora, Chandan, 182, 190
arranged marriage, 12–14, 154–57; annulment of, 2, 65, 74–84, 227–28; Bollywood films about, 63, 64, 182, 187–90; "choice" of, 203, 209, 218; colonial notions of, 45; construction of community and, 52–61; cultural revival of, 181–83; defining of, 6–15; domestic, 17; forced marriage versus, 3, 11–14, 69–72, 117–18; immigration fraud by, 13, 110–14, 117, 172–80; intercaste, 48–49, 59–60; for LGBT people, 56–57, 158–61; multiculturalism and, 17–18, 61, 62, 67, 78–79
Arranged Marriage (Divakaruni), 20, 23, 143, 159–60, 167–69, 181
Aslam, Nadeem, 68, 222, 229. *See also* *Maps for Lost Lovers*
astrology, 7, 210
Asylum and Immigration (Treatment of Claimants) Act of 2004 (UK), 121

Aulakh, Raveena, 177
Austen, Jane, 39, 40
Australia, 217
Awami League, 50–51

Badami, Anita Rau, 160, 173, 222
Bald, Vivek, 144, 145
Ballard, Catherine, 69
Barjatya, Sooraj R., 187–88, 208
Barron, Alexander, 161
beauty pageants, 65
Beauvoir, Simone de, 42
Begum, Tasleem, 109
belonging, 39, 42, 53–56, 216; affective elements of, 99, 182, 199, 213; communitarianism and, 60, 142, 169; diversity and, 61–62, 83, 137, 223; Enright on, 61, 106–8; gender and, 58, 88–91, 154, 158, 162, 222; immigrant children and, 116; politics of, 44, 91, 101–3, 110, 114, 224–25; transnational, 140–41, 178, 199
Berlant, Lauren, 209; on "intimate public," 182, 198–200, 202, 204, 210–13
Bhansali, Sanjay Leela: *Devdas*, 57–58, 182, 185–86; *Hum Dil De Chuke Sanam*, 63, 182, 188–89
Bharatiya Janata Party, 61
Bhopal, Kalwant, 105
bildungsroman, 169–72, 216; feminist, 21, 125, 143–44, 158–69, 228–29
Bolan, Kim, 178
Bollywood films, 8, 207, 216; about arranged marriage, 63, 64, 182, 187–90; Divakaruni on, 167; Mehta on, 160, 161; Shankar on, 64
Bradby, Hannah, 97
Bradley, David, 78, 87
Bradney, A., 77

Brah, Avtar, 43, 55
Brahminism, 48, 80
Bredal, Anja, 70
Brick Lane (Ali), 20, 22, 26, 133, 181; Aslam and, 133–34; class in, 9; coercion in, 74; modes of agency in, 91–96; obligation in, 208; Sanghera and, 130
Briggs, J. Z., 2, 24, 123–28, 130, 132
Buddha of Suburbia (Kureishi), 23–27, 86–89
Butler, Judith, 63
Butler, Pamela, 193, 200, 206–7, 209

Cable Act of 1922 (U.S.), 146
California Alien Land Law, 146
Caron, Nancy, 13
caste, 6, 37, 211; marriages between, 48–49, 59–60; Mukerji on, 149–50, 162–63; Parekh on, 106
Chambers, Simon, 68, 87, 223; *Every Good Marriage Begins with Tears*, 2, 10, 23–24, 55, 94–100, 131
Chanda, Gurinder, 39
chastity, 22, 57–58, 92, 119
Chatterjee, Partha, 210
Chattopadhyay, Sarat Chandra, 58, 186
Chauhan, Anaju, 194–96
"chick-lit," 192–93. *See also* "ladki-lit"
child marriage, 13, 227; annulment of, 79; colonial laws on, 46, 81; among lower castes, 48; transnational, 82, 155. *See also* consent: age of; forced marriage
Child Marriage Restraint Act of 1929 (India), 81
Chopra, Aditya, 63, 182, 188, 190
coercion, 13–14, 71–84; continuum of, 75; psychological, 11, 67, 77. *See also* consent
Coixet, Isabel, 141

Comaroff, Jean, 85
Comaroff, John L., 85
communalism, 61–62, 70; Ahmad on, 104; communitarianism versus, 55, 60; individualism versus, 15, 143; multiculturalism and, 218
communitarianism, 31–32, 37–38, 42; communalism versus, 55, 60; definition of, 221–22; family role in, 142; globalization and, 226, 229; individualism versus, 31–32, 42, 229; in *Meet the Patels*, 218
community: construction of, 52–61, 150–54; identity-conferring, 42, 85, 96, 219
companionate marriage, 3, 8, 185; in Austen's novels, 39, 40
consent, 13–15, 67–73, 220; age of, 16, 46, 73–82, 221; Ali on, 92; Bradley on, 78; "constrained," 74; Cott on, 82–83, 148–49; culture of, 67–75, 83–84, 100; definitions of, 73; Hobbes on, 82; in human rights law, 38, 72–73, 83; Kleinig on, 38–39; "reality" of, 77; "reluctant," 83; structural inequalities in, 84–86; UN convention on, 38, 72–73. *See also* coercion
Constable, Nicole, 10
Continuous Journey Act (Canada), 174
Cott, Nancy, 38; on arranged marriage, 14–15, 147–49; on consent, 82–83, 148–49; on public character of marriage, 16
Crespo, Diane, 62
critical discourse analysis, 5, 21, 37, 215–16, 229
Crofts, Andrew, 2, 40, 123–24
Cryer, Ann, 114, 115, 121, 123, 124
culturalism, 12, 28, 103–10; agency and, 66, 219, 225; definition of, 220; globalization and, 66, 222. *See also* multiculturalism
"cultural streamlining," 63, 204–5
cultural studies, 25–30, 106, 220, 226–27
culture, 105, 203; as choice, 163, 166, 190, 194, 200–202, 216–17; of consent, 67–75, 83–84, 100; definitions of, 104, 106; Geertz on, 66, 139; Stuart Hall on 66, 106, 139

Das Gupta, Monisha, 137
Daswani, Kavita, 196; *For Matrimonial Purposes*, 194; *Salaam, Paris*, 193, 194, 196–97; *The Village Bride of Beverly Hills*, 9, 194, 197, 201, 205, 208, 210
dating, 55, 60, 99, 152, 170; arranged marriage and, 182, 183, 195, 196, 218; courtship and, 14; in "ladki-lit," 194, 207, 210; websites for, 8, 11, 19, 142, 183, 203
Denmark, 217
Desai, Jigna, 160, 193, 200, 206–7, 209
Desai, Kiran, 201
Desi Land (Shankar), 8, 54, 55, 59, 64
Desis in the House (Maira), 2, 54, 64, 145, 152, 172
Dhingra, Pawan, 30, 144
Divakaruni, Chitra Banerjee, 162–64, 222; *Arranged Marriage*, 20, 23, 143, 159–60, 167–69, 181
diversity, 61–62, 103–7, 126, 147; experience of displacement and, 54. *See also* multiculturalism
divorce, 47, 50, 113; in arranged marriages, 7, 189; in interfaith marriages, 217; in self-made marriages, 70, 189. *See also* annulment

domestic violence, 74, 109, 118, 154, 179. *See also* violence
dowries, 6, 7, 19, 21, 82, 204, 208
Dustin, Moira, 68, 120–22, 130–31

East India Company, 44, 46
East Is East (Khan-Din), 32, 40, 56, 59, 88–91
East Is East (O'Donnell), 26, 59, 68, 88–91
Enright, Máiréad, 61, 68, 106–8
"escape memoirs," 71, 102, 123, 131–32, 137
ethnicity, 104, 107; belonging to, 53–55; gender and, 164; mixed marriages and, 145; "reactive," 87. *See also* identity
Every Good Marriage Begins with Tears (Chambers), 2, 10, 23–24, 55, 94–100, 131
exclusion, 66; family, 76; of immigrants, 146–48, 174; of LGBT people, 40, 56; politics of, 91; racist, 84–85, 89
"exit strategy," 102, 130–31, 143, 169, 179–80

Faiz, Faiz Ahmed, 136
family, 6–10, 16, 54, 67; in colonial India, 44–48; communitarianism and, 142; individual agency and, 37–41, 71–74, 77, 82–84; joint, 14–15, 52–53, 205–9; Muslim laws on, 51; networks of, 18–20, 25
Felski, Rita, 144, 158–59
feminist bildungsroman, 21, 125, 143–44, 158–69
Fire (Mehta), 154–62, 167, 181, 208
forced marriage, 12–14, 113–22, 179–80; arranged marriage versus, 3, 11–14, 67–72, 117–18; culture of consent and, 71–75, 175; definitions of, 71, 118; immigration fraud by, 13, 113–15; memoirs of, 122–32; rape and, 21, 64, 227; self-made versus, 15, 37, 200; structural inequalities in, 84–86; transnational mobility and, 17–19; as un-American, 144–50; violence in, 102, 108–9, 154; Working Group on, 33, 71–72, 105–7, 115–20, 123–26, 223
Forced Marriage (Civil Protection) Act of 2007 (UK), 71, 118, 123
Foucault, Michel, 4, 41–42
Friedman, Marilyn, 41

Gagoomal, Prashina, 68, 83
Gandhi, Mohandas, 48–49
Geertz, Clifford, 66, 139
gender, 45–46, 59, 92, 115; belonging and, 58, 88–91, 154, 158, 162, 222; displacement and, 54; family networks and, 19–20; postfeminism and, 203; structural inequalities of, 84–86. *See also* heteronormativity
gender roles, 9, 164, 189, 204; in Ali, 93, 95; in Divakaruni, 23–24, 167; hierarchies in, 20; modernity and, 162; in Mukherjee, 165–66; transnational mobility and, 25
genealogies, 43–52
ghazal poems, 184
Giddens, Anthony, 39–40, 185, 190
Gill, Aisha, 68, 118; on agency in consent, 41–42, 74, 84, 85; on identity-conferring community, 96
Gindha, Anita, 109
globalization, 6, 15, 155–57, 212–13; communitarianism and, 226, 229; cultural relativism and, 219;

dynamics of, 69; individualism and, 63, 226; transnationalism and, 18, 194. *See also* neoliberalism
Goodness Gracious Me (TV show), 57
Gordon, Alison, 72
Gottlieb, Lori, 195–96
Gray, John, 38
Grewal, Inderpal, 52, 163–66, 193, 200; on agency, 203, 209; on love marriage, 210
Gulzar, Meghna, 182, 188, 207

Haag, Pamela, 113, 148, 221
Hall, Catherine, 45, 47
Hall, Stuart, 4, 66, 106, 139
Hart-Cellar Act of 1965 (U.S.), 146
heteronormativity, 26, 154, 160–61, 181, 193, 221, 222; chastity and, 57–58; LGBT people and, 40, 56–57, 79–80, 158–61; patriarchy and, 88–91. *See also* gender
Hindi-Bindi Club (Pradhan), 6–7, 62–65, 194–95, 201–2; recipes in, 205; on romantic love, 185; wedding rituals in, 210
Hindu Code bill, 49–50
Hinduism, 80, 106; authenticity and, 54–55; colonial marriage reforms and, 46–49; interfaith marriages and, 61; nationalism and, 60–61
Hindu Marriage Act of 1955 (India), 49
Hindu Widows' Remarriage Act of 1856 (India), 48
Hindu Wife (Sarkar), 47, 80, 204
Hirani v. Hirani (1982), 77, 79
HIV disease, 153
Hobbes, Thomas, 82
Holzer, Kellie, 28
homosexuality. *See* LGBT people
"honor killings," 12, 69–70, 101–2, 108–9, 117; in Aslam's novel, 133, 135. *See also* violence
human rights, 38, 72–73, 83, 114, 116–17
Hussein (otherwise Blitz) v. Hussein (1938), 74, 75

identity, 85, 107, 174–75, 211; communitarian, 60, 143; Stuart Hall on, 66, 106, 139; Khan-Din on, 88–91; neoliberal, 15. *See also* ethnicity
identity-conferring community, 42, 85, 96, 219
Immigrant Act of 1917 (U.S.), 146, 148
Immigrant Act of 1952 (Canada), 174
immigration, 17, 83, 220, 221; British laws on, 69, 72, 111–15, 119–20; Canadian laws on, 172–80, 221; multiculturalism and, 101–10, 114–15; U.S. fiancé(e) visas for, 27, 65, 139; U.S. laws on, 140, 144–46, 148, 150
Immigration and Asylum Act of 1999 (UK), 121
immigration fraud, 13, 27, 110–15, 172–80, 221; Primary Purpose Rule and, 69, 72, 111–12
Indian Majority Act (1875), 81
individualism, 38–39, 89–90; communalism versus, 15, 143; communitarianism versus, 31–32, 42, 229; globalization and, 63, 226; marriage reforms based on, 80–81; multiculturalism and, 95. *See also* agency
In My Own Name (Shan), 69, 72, 124
Internet. *See* websites
intersectionality, 41, 52, 110, 155
intimacy, 16–17, 63–64, 160–62, 184; discourse of, 8, 9, 208; immigration

policies and, 27; personal freedom and, 40–41, 154–55
"intimate public," 182, 198–200, 202, 204, 210–13
Intimate State (Mody), 45, 49, 52–53, 81
Islamophobia, 12, 61, 81, 107–8, 121–22, 133. *See also* Muslims

Jack and Zena (Briggs), 2, 24, 123–28, 130, 132
Jaffrelot, Christophe, 60–61
Jain, Anita, viii–ix, 196; *Marrying Anita*, 2, 185, 194–97, 201, 202
Jama'at-i-Islami, 51
Janmohamed, Shelina, 193, 195, 210
Jews, 80; arranged marriage among, 62, 148, 153
Johar, Karan, 188
Johnson, David, 82
July 7 attacks (London), 17
Just Married (Gulzar), 182, 188, 207

Kakar, Sudhir, 6, 206
Kala, Advaita, 207
Karma Nirvana, 132
Karthika, V. K., 200–201
Kennedy, Miranda, 183
Khandelwal, Madhulika, 151
Khan-Din, Ayub, 68, 222–23; *East Is East*, 32, 40, 56, 59, 88–91
kidnapping, 74, 108
Kleinig, John, 38–39, 73
Koshy, Susan, 30, 165, 172
Kureishi, Hanif, 68; *The Buddha of Suburbia*, 23–27, 86–89

"ladki-lit" (women's popular fiction), 1, 192–97; Bollywood films and, 207; dating in, 194, 207, 210;

"intimate public" of, 198–200, 210, 212–13; neoliberalism and, 200–204; politics of, 209–13
Lahiri, Jhumpa, 154, 162–64, 229; *The Namesake*, 1, 10, 20–23, 26, 53–55, 144, 169–72; "Sexy," 22
Leonard, Karen, 54, 144, 145
LGBT people, 40, 56–57, 158–61; child marriage and, 79–80. *See also* heteronormativity
Love in a Headscarf (Janmohamed), 193, 195, 210
"Love Jihad" controversy, 61
love marriage, 200; "arranged," 15, 164, 207, 226; Bhansali on, 186; divorce rate in, 7; Grewal on, 210; Pradhan on, 6–7; Puri on, 186–87. *See also* self-made marriage
Lowe, Lisa, 54
Luce Cellar Act of 1946 (U.S.), 146
Luhmann, Niklas, 39

Mackenzie, Catriona, 42, 55–56
Mahmood, Saba, 41, 211, 212, 219
Mahmood v. Mahmood (1993), 78, 81, 83
Mahmud v. Mahmud (1994), 77, 81
Maine, Henry, 80
Maira, Sunaina, 2, 54, 64, 145, 152, 172
Majumdar, Rochona, 14, 45, 49–50, 206
Mani, Bakirathi, 64–65, 173
Mani, Lata, 46
Maps for Lost Lovers (Aslam), 23, 27, 102–3, 132–39, 181; class in 9; on Islamic communalism, 61; Sanghera and, 130; on "Wilderness of Solitude," 27, 136
marriage, 7, 72–73; colonial reforms of, 44–49, 80–81; consanguineous,

6, 16, 221; consummation of, 40, 63, 74–75, 80, 87–88, 189; of convenience, 17, 176; endogamous, 60–61, 145, 147, 152, 183, 223; exogamous, 145; Hindu beliefs about, 189–90; intercaste, 48–49, 59–60; intercultural, 215; interfaith, 61; interracial, 145; matrilocal, 24–25; mobility with, 19–23; newspaper ads for, 10, 56; public character of, 16; remarriage and, 46–48, 50, 74; same-sex, 16, 56–57; state regulation of, 220–21; "transacted," 155; virilocal, 14, 82; websites for, 10–11, 60, 152–53, 183, 203. *See also specific types of marriage*

Marriage Act of 1949 (UK), 38, 73, 74

Married at First Sight (TV show), 183, 217

Marrying Anita (Jain), 2, 185, 194–97, 201, 202

Matrimonial Causes Act of 1973 (UK), 73, 76

May, Simon, 40, 167

McCarran-Walter Act of 1952 (U.S.), 146

McCarthy, John, 124–27

McCrum, Mark, 124, 127

McEwan, Lord, 65

Meet the Patels (film), 2, 218, 222, 224

Mehta, Deepa, 143, 222; *Fire,* 159–62, 167, 181, 208

Mexican-Indian marriages, 145

Mittal, Anupam, 152

modernity: bildungsroman and, 158; joint family and, 43–46; rhetoric of, 37; romance and, 207, 219; traditional family and, 206–7, 209; transnational, 151, 194

Mody, Perveez, 184; *Intimate State,* 45, 49, 52–53, 81

Monsoon Wedding (Nair), 8, 141, 157, 182, 188–92, 207

Moore, Molly, 154, 156

Moretti, Franco, 158

Morgan, Robin, 154–55

Mukerji, Dhan Gopal, 149–50, 162–63

Mukherjee, Bharati, 143, 162–64, 168–69, 222; *Wife,* 10, 20, 164–69, 181

multiculturalism, 12, 103–10, 114, 125, 137–38; arranged marriage and, 17–18, 61–62, 67, 71, 78–79; assimilation versus, 70–71, 108, 115–17, 221; communalism and, 218; diversity and, 103–4; immigration and, 101–10, 114–15; individualism and, 95; neoliberalism and, 63–66, 114–15, 173–74, 180, 222. *See also* culturalism; diversity

Muslims, 80, 178, 193; arranged marriages of, 1–2, 60, 134; forced marriages among, 69, 71–72, 117–19, 123, 224, 227; interfaith marriages among, 61; Islamophobia and, 12, 81, 107–8, 121–22, 133; Shari'a of, 47, 50–51; women's rights and, 17–18, 50, 62

Nair, Mira, 143, 154, 162; *Monsoon Wedding,* 8, 141, 157, 182, 188–92, 207; *So Far from India,* 2, 155–57

Namastey London (Shah), 63–64, 182, 188, 207, 225–26

Native Americans, 147

Naz, Rukhsana, 108–9

Negra, Diane, 203

Nehru, Jawaharlal, 49

neoliberalism, 15, 190–91; culture as

choice in, 163, 166, 190, 200–202, 216–17; definitions of, 193; multiculturalism and, 63–66, 114–15, 173–74, 180, 222. *See also* globalization
Norway, 70

O'Donnell, Damien, 26, 59, 68, 88–91
Ong, Aihwa, 193
online dating. *See* websites
Ormrod, Roger, 76, 77
Outsourced (TV show), 1, 65

Palriwala, Rajni, 20, 21, 23–25
Parekh, Bhikhu, 104, 106
Patel, Geeta, 2, 218, 222, 224
Patel, Ravi, 2, 218, 222, 224
Pearl, David, 76
Phillips, Anne, 68, 120–22, 130–31
pluralism: cultural, 103, 104, 137. *See also* multiculturalism
polygamy, 13, 145, 179
postcolonialism, 32, 155–57, 181; marriage reforms and, 43, 45, 49–52; post-1965 generation, 150–54
Powell, Enoch, 89
Pradhan, Monica, 196. See also *Hindi-Bindi Club*
Primary Purpose Rule of 1993 (UK), 69, 72, 111–12. *See also* immigration fraud
prostitution, 16–17, 133, 155, 221; movement against, 147–48; sex trafficking for, 21–23
protectionist discourse, 15, 84, 102, 104, 125, 131
Proudman, Charlotte Rachael, 68
psychotherapy, 8, 35, 144, 190, 208
Puri, Jyoti, 9, 183–84, 186–87, 199
Purkayastha, Bandana, 54, 59–60, 152

racism, 148, 162, 220; exclusion from, 84–85, 89; in Kureishi, 26, 87; multiculturalism and, 104; socioeconomic forces of, 27
Radhakrishnan, Smitha, 63, 204–5
Rai, Bali, 59
rape, 74, 155; wedding night as, 21, 27, 40, 64
Rashtriya Swayamsevak Sangh, 61
Regan, Pamela C., 3
remarriage, 46–48, 50, 74
Riley, Ferzanna, 123
romantic love, 14, 123, 147, 166–67; discourse of, 184–87; Giddens on, 39–40, 185, 190; individual will and, 39; modernity and, 207, 219. *See also* Bollywood films
Romeo and Juliet (Shakespeare), 39
Roy, Bimal, 58, 186
Roy, Sandip, 56, 57
Rushdie, Salman: *Imaginary Homelands*, 151, 162

Salaam, Paris (Daswani), 193, 194, 196–97
Salzman, Marian, 183
Sanghera, Jasvinder, 123–24, 127–30, 132, 222
Sarkar, Tanika, 47, 80, 204
sati, 46, 47. *See also* suicide
sayamvara (choice), 149–50
Scarman, Lord, 104
Schaefer, Stefan C., 62
self-made marriage, 7, 145; arranged versus, 15, 37, 200; in Austen's novels, 39, 40; in Bollywood films, 188; consent in, 83–84; divorce in, 70, 189; individual freedom and, 21–22, 147, 179; intercultural, 215. *See also* love marriage

September 11 attacks (New York), 17
Seth, Vikram, 1, 58
sex trafficking, 21–23, 155
sexual harassment, 155
sex work, 16–17, 133, 147–48, 155, 221
Shah, Nayan, 144, 146
Shah, Vipul Amrutlal, 63–64, 182, 188, 207, 225–26
Shakespeare, William, 39
Shan, Sharan-Jeet, 69, 72, 124
Shankar, Shalini, 8, 54, 55, 59, 64
Shari'a, 47, 50, 51
Shariat Application Act (1937), 50
Sharpe, Jenny, 210
Shumway, David, 188, 198–99
Siddiqi, Dina, 51, 92
Sidhwa, Bapsi, 22, 159
Sikhs, 128; forced marriage among, 69, 76, 123, 224; marriage ceremony of, 189; separatist movement of, 178; in Vancouver, 174–75
Simon, Jocylen, 76
Singh, Sonia, 210
Singh v. Kaur (1981), 76, 81
Singh v. Singh (1971), 73–76, 87–88
Sivanandan, A., 104
Sohrab v. Khan (2002), 65, 78, 87
Sollors, Werner, 147
Sommer, Doris, 126
Southall Black Sisters (SBS), 119–20
Special Marriage Act (1954), 49
Spivak, Gayatri, 46
Sreenivas, Mytheli, 44
Stoljar, Natalie, 42, 55–56
Stone, Lawrence, 185
Straw, Jack, 112
suicide, 11–12, 77, 175; sati and, 46, 47
Sunder Rajan, Rajeswari, 43, 50
Szechter (otherwise Karsov) v. Szechter (1971), 75

Tasker, Yvonne, 203
Thatcher, Margaret, 104
Therwath, Ingrid, 60–61
Thind, Bhagat Singh, 146
transnationalism, 16–25, 226; definition of, 18; identity and, 64–65; imagined communities and, 55
transnational mobility, 194, 202, 209; agency and, 23–24; forced marriage and, 17–19

Uberoi, Patricia, 20, 21, 23, 206, 208
Uddin, Pola Manzila, 33, 71–72, 105–7, 115–20, 123–26, 223
Uganda, 174
UNICEF, 82
United Nations Convention on Consent to Marriage, 38, 72–73
United States v. Bhagat Singh Thind (1923), 146

Vidyasagar, Pandit, 48
Village Bride of Beverly Hills (Daswani), 9, 194, 197, 201, 205, 208, 210
violence, viii; domestic, 74, 109, 118, 154, 179; in forced marriage, 102, 108–9, 154; of rape, 21, 27, 40, 64, 74, 155. *See also* "honor killings"
virginity, 22, 57–58, 119
Vishwa Hindu Parishad (World Hindu Council), 61
Volpp, Leti, 109, 119, 123–24

Waheed, Rekha, 193
Waites, Matthew, 79
websites: dating, 8, 11, 19, 142, 183, 203; matrimonial, 10–11, 60, 152–53, 183, 203; Q & A, 64

Wertheimer, Alan, 73
Wife (Mukherjee), 10, 20, 164–69, 181
Wilson, Amrit, 84–85, 121–22
Working Group on Forced Marriage, 12, 33, 71–72, 105, 107, 115–20, 123–26, 223
World Hindu Council (Vishwa Hindu Parishad), 61
Wray, Helena, 113

Yuval-Davis, Nira, 103; on "politics of belonging," 44, 91, 101–3, 110, 114, 224–25

Zama, Farahad, 7
Zero Tolerance for Barbaric Cultural Practices Act (Canada), 13, 65, 179, 223
Zia-ul Haq, Muhammad, 50

MARIAN AGUIAR is associate professor in the Literary and Cultural Studies Program in the Department of English at Carnegie Mellon University and the author of *Tracking Modernity: India's Railway and the Culture of Mobility* (Minnesota, 2011).